Taking the Group Seriously

The International Library of Group Analysis
Edited by Malcolm Pines, Institute of Group Analysis, London

The aim of this series is to represent innovative work in group psychotherapy, particularly but not exclusively group analysis. Group analysis, taught and practised widely in Europe, has developed from the work of S.H. Foulkes.

INTERNATIONAL LIBRARY OF GROUP ANALYSIS 5

Taking the Group Seriously
Towards a Post-Foulkesian
Group Analytic Theory

Farhad Dalal

Foreword by Malcolm Pines

Jessica Kingsley Publishers
London and Philadelphia

First published in the United Kingdom in 1998 by
Jessica Kingsley Publishers Ltd
116 Pentonville Road
London N1 9JB, England
and
325 Chestnut Street
Philadelphia, PA 19106, USA

www.jkp.com

Text Copyright © 1998 Farhad Dalal
Foreword Copyright © 1998 Malcolm Pines

Library of Congress Cataloging in Publication Data
A CIP catalogue record for this book is available from the
Library of Congress

British Library Cataloguing in Publication Data
Dalal, Farhad N.
Taking the Group Seriously : towards a post-Foulkesian group analytic theory. -
(International library of group analysis ; 5)
1.Group psychoanalysis
I.Title
616.8'9152

ISBN 1 85302 642 5

Printed and Bound in Great Britain by
Athenaeum Press, Gateshead, Tyne and Wear

Contents

Acknowledgements

I would like to thank the friends who have supported and helped with this venture, Parizad Bathai, Lesley Caldwell, Julian Lousada, Susannah Radstone and Amal Treacher. Thanks are also owed to my colleagues at the Group Analytic Network, Gill Barratt, Sheila Ernst, Mike Kelly and Anne Morgan. Especial thanks to my teachers at the Institute of Group Analysis: Malcom Pines for the generosity of his support as well as for his kindly encouragement and comments on the work; Dennis Brown who continues to teach me about the group; also Liesel Hearst and Harold Behr who spent considerable time gestating my group analytic development. Particular thanks to Barry Richards and Phil Cohen at the University of East London for their sensitive tutoring, as well as for the enabling way with which they shared their knowledge. And last but not least, my wife Pauline Henderson Dalal, whose fortunate habit of testing the argument has contributed much to whatever clarity the reader might find.

For Nadir, Dilber, Veera and Navaz – my first group

Foreword

Farhad Dalal has written a tough, exciting book. He makes a radical, critical and appreciative scrutiny at the corpus of group analytical theory found in the writings of S.H. Foulkes and of his close collaborator James Anthony. Inevitably he finds the illogicalities and inconsistencies that appear in any theoretical system when exposed to this close scrutiny, but he does so appreciatively. He recognises the originality and the importance of Foulkes' vision and intends to make us aware of its reach, to see where Foulkes falls short in his intention to create a socially-based theory of the person distinct from, yet related to, psychoanalysis, which together with dynamic neurology, Gestalt psychology and the historical sociology of Norbert Elias were his basic allegiances.

Dalal writes with admirable clarity; he looks closely at Freud's developmental, structural and social theories, then similarly at Foulkes'. His exposition of Norbert Elias is original; no previous psychotherapeutic text has given such attention to the radical and impressive corpus of Elias' writings. Elias is difficult to read, particularly for psychotherapists as his thinking is sociological, philosophical and historical. His ideas have gained ground in sociology but not yet in psychotherapy, either group or individual. Dalal has rendered an essential service enabling us to appreciate the grandeur of Elias' vision.

Group analysts have always known that our theory represents an interweaving of Foulkes' psychoanalysis and Elias' sociology. Now for the first time, apart from articles that have appeared in *Group Analysis*, we can read a detailed authoritative exposition of Elias' opus. Students, by which I mean teachers and learners both, have the opportunity to examine the theoretical basis of group analysis.

Farhad Dalal tackles difficult subjects with enthusiasm and a deft touch: structuralism, Matte-Blanco, modern socio-biology, communication and discourse theory. He writes clearly and authoritatively. His final chapter, 'Elements of a post-Foulkesian group analytic theory', is a notable essay in integration and anticipation.

It is gratifying to be the editor of a series of group analytic books that can now give evidence to the new generation of scholars and practitioners who devote considerable powers of criticism and exposition to group analytic theory. Morris Nitsun's *Anti-Group* book has received wide attention – I do not doubt that Farhad Dalal's work will be widely read, discussed and appreciated.

Malcolm Pines

Introduction

A patient announced in a psychotherapy group that he now realized how controlled he had been all his life by other people's wishes and desires. From now on, he proudly said, he was going to try to follow his own desires and if others did not like it – well, they could go hang, that was their problem.

This attempt at health is a rather peculiar proposition, as it implies that the patient can live without other people, as some kind of pure individual. The point of view the patient is expressing is a form of the not unusual belief that to know one's true self, one has to look within; and being with others is of necessity a contamination of this truth. The patient's problem, as he himself defined it, was that in the presence of the Other he disappeared. His solution to the problem was to make the Other disappear instead. It is clear that the cure is no better than the disease. This is an expression of an age-old dilemma – which is often put in terms of a conflict between individual interests and group interests. It is thought that the individual inevitably loses something by being in a group – at the very least attention is diluted.

It is exactly at this point that the psychoanalyst and group analyst S. H. Foulkes (1898–1976) made his contribution, by questioning the very basis of the division between individual and group. This questioning formed the basis of his group analytic theory. Foulkes' theory problematizes the patient's solution by providing a new model of the relationship between individual and group. His theory is potentially a fusion between psychoanalysis and sociology. This is reflected in the fact that Foulkes has two theoretical masters, the psychoanalyst Sigmund Freud, and the sociologist Norbert Elias. Group analytic theory as expounded by Foulkes is an attempt to bolt these two disciplines together, which he has done to some degree. However, in the process he has left a trail of inconsistencies and contradictions, which to my mind have never been spelled out, and has led to many confusions, leaving the theoretical field of group analysis in some disarray.

The most critical of these inconsistencies is the fact that Freud and Elias derive the individual from opposite directions. Freud moves from biology to the individual to the social; his theory is then made more complex by the fact that the social then curls back and re-enters the individual. Meanwhile, Elias begins with the social, which precipitates not only the individual, but also the structures of experience, both internal and external. The social, according to Elias, does not lie outside the individual to determine her/him from without; the individual also contributes to and constructs the social. These two viewpoints, as they stand, contradict each other. However, the structure of both theories is similar in that neither is simplistically linear. Each theory is recursive, that is, circular and systemic – the snake eating its tail. So in Freud, society is born out of instinctual conflict and the resulting sublimation, but then society enters the individual as the superego, from whence it moderates the individual's engagement with the social. Meanwhile, Elias uses the notion of 'constraint' to describe the situation where individuals are limited to what they may do, be and think by social forces, but says that they also contribute to the construction of these cultural and social forces.

Despite these structural similarities, the fact remains that the metaphysical assumptions of each theory stand in contradiction to each other. To my mind, Foulkes tries to slide past this difficulty by using the Gestalt notion of 'figure-and-ground'(Kahl 1971; Hunt 1993). He implies that sometimes it is the individual that is in the foreground, and thus Freudian psychoanalytic principles operate, and at other times it is the group that is in the foreground, when it is assumed that group dynamic formulations are more appropriate. This strategy is a theoretical sleight of hand.

One of the most exciting ideas launched by Foulkes (taken from Elias) is that there is no such thing as an individual that exists apart from and outside the social. This idea eventually leads to a subversion of a number of dichotomies, that of individual and group, of external and internal, and of nature and nurture. But now, we have a problem. Having said this exciting thing, we then have to ask: so what difference does it make to one's practice as a group analyst, what difference does it make to how one views group phenomena? If one looks at Foulkes' clinical writings, then the answer is very little difference. In the *practice of group analysis* almost all of Foulkes interpretations are couched in individualistic terms, and often in Freudian language. Even group specific concepts like scapegoating are given an individualistic basis.

It is this that gives this book its title. It seems to me that although Foulkes tried to take the group seriously, for a variety of reasons, he was unable to do so. To my mind, to take the group seriously means to evolve a new language, a new way of thinking, and a new way of *experiencing* oneself and the group. This is a large task indeed; it was in fact one of Foulkes' intentions: 'All concepts used in discussing group behaviour should be concepts specifically derived from the study of groups. The application of ready-made concepts from individual psychotherapy only serve to blur the sharpness of our observation and distort it' (Foulkes and Anthony 1957, p.250). Unfortunately, this intention is in direct conflict with his insistence that first and foremost he is a Freudian.

It seems to me that in the contemporary clinical practice of Foulkesian group analysis, group events are primarily understood in the light of the mother–infant paradigm, which has its basis in individual psychoanalysis. What I mean by this is that group events (why patients behave as they do) are understood through the transference by reference to past history, and the history that is used is the *history of asocial individuals*. Whilst this in itself is important and useful, it does throw into relief the absence of a group analytic paradigm, one which might take account of the *history of social groups*.

These are some of the preoccupations that have given rise to the idea of this book. One of the tasks of this work is to put in place the philosophical and metaphysical foundations of a possible group analytic paradigm. Thus, this work seeks to *begin* the process of rethinking group analysis, to move past Foulkes' confusions, into a post-Foulkesian territory, a territory from which one can *begin* to take the group seriously.

The book is continually preoccupied with a number of dichotomies which form an undercurrent below the main discussions. Internal and external world, nature and nurture, the infinite and the finite, the individual and society, the eternal and the transient – these are some of the dichotomies that will persistently make their presence felt, and test the arguments being presented. To be more precise, implicit in the ideas and proposals examined, we will find these dichotomies in particular arrangements – which is prioritized over which, what are the consequences of each, and so on. The examination of these arrangements will help lay bare the hidden agenda in theory – what Foucault calls discourse, and Elias calls ideology.

As Foulkes gives so much weight to his Freudian antecedents, the book will begin with an abbreviated, critical overview of Freud. In particular we will take note of how Freud orders the dichotomies, and see what bearing these have on his understanding of the relation of group to individual. Partly this will be done in order to understand Foulkes' position and confusion better.

The second part of the book engages critically with Foulkes' theory as expounded in his writings, testing it for *self consistency* against the aims and objectives as set out by Foulkes himself. One of the things that becomes clear through this exploration is that Foulkes is constantly torn between Freud and Elias, and this gives birth to two different sorts of theories. The theoretical elements that take the group seriously I have called 'radical' and designated them to an idea of a Radical Foulkes. The elements of his theory that he is unable to free from his Freudian antecedents, I have designated to an Orthodox Foulkes. This separation helps unravel many of the confusions and contradictions in his work.

Before taking up the ideas of Elias, the third section gives two brief overviews. First, the roles allocated to the external and internal in some psychoanalytic theories is described, and second, an overview of structuralism and post-structuralism is given. These prepare the ground for considering Elias' contribution.

The next part of the book sets about describing the ideas of Elias. Interestingly, Elias is almost completely absent from group analytic discourse. On the Qualifying Course at the Institute of Group Analysis, London (the main training for group analysts in Britain and perhaps Europe), he is not explicitly studied. There are some who are trying to change this, Dr Malcolm Pines and Dr Earl Hopper to name two. The absence of Elias conspires to keep group analysis in an individualistic frame. So partly the task of this section is informative and educative, to raise the profile of Eliasian ideas. When this is done, it is discovered that many, if not most, of the ideas of Radical Foulkes have their basis in Elias. However, what is also discovered is that Foulkes has had to water some of them down, in order to try and remain within a Freudian frame.

The fact that Elias has been so neglected in group analytic discourse is a phenomenon to be investigated in itself. To my mind this has occurred partly for reasons that are central to Elias' preoccupations: the social current that has increasingly divorced the individual from society, and prioritized the individual over the group. Inevitably, this social current has organized and structured the internal politics of the world of psychotherapy. The first of these is that for a variety of reasons group psychotherapy is often thought of as a poor second cousin of individual psychotherapy. And second, in the hierarchy of status and power relations (both notions that are central in Elias) between different schools of psychotherapy, psychoanalysis is clearly at the top of the tree. So whilst group analysis might lose some ground by virtue of being 'group' instead of 'individual', it gains status by virtue of it being an 'analysis', and thus in the vicinity of the rulers of the roost. I think that the discipline of group analysis has avoided looking too closely at its linkages with sociology, because to do so would threaten the status it has through virtue of it being a group *analysis* and not a group psychotherapy or a group sociology.

So another outcome of this work is to question the positioning of group analysis in relation to psychoanalysis, and individual psychotherapy in relation to group psychotherapy. In effect, the book is also a theoretical challenge to the assumptive world of individual psychoanalysis and humanistic psychotherapy.

The fifth part takes up insights from biology, evolutionary theory, and game theory. One of the things that is emerging in the general *Zeitgeist* is a new way of reading the findings of biology and genetics. Until recently, through ideas like the 'selfish gene' and so forth, biology has been taken to be the champion of individualism. But now biologists like Dawkins and others use descriptions at the genetic level that prioritize the notion of the group over and above the individual organism. This climate change will be described in some detail to lend weight to the general argument of the book.

The final part of the book is where the task of building a post-Foulkesian group analysis will be begun, and this will have several elements. Some other theoreticians will be introduced, but in less detail. One of these is Matte-Blanco (1988). To my mind his theory of thinking lends itself well to the development of a post-Foulkesian group analysis. So in this section his ideas will be described, and parallels and overlaps with Freud, Foulkes and Elias will be delineated. The other theoreticians to be brought in here are Fairbairn and Winnicott. It seems to me that each has a helpful contribution to make to the notion of taking the group seriously. For example, Fairbairn makes relatedness critical to the developmental process, and Winnicott describes the genesis of the individual, the first I AM moment, as the first group. The discussions in this and previous sections will suggest new ways of thinking about several central concepts, for example group processes, identity, the unconscious and the superego. The domains of 'race' and racism are used as a test ground for the ideas being developed, and this in turn will shed new light on notions of similarity and difference.

Anticipating some of the content that is to follow, an inevitable consequence of the formation of a group is that other things are excluded. Thus this book leaves out many things, for example attachment theory and self psychology – lines have to be drawn somewhere. Additionally, in the following pages reference is made to generalized groupings like 'the psychoanalysts' or 'the Kleinians' and so forth. This inevitably misrepresents the positions some of those pooled together. The inevitability of misrepresentation is also part of the subject matter of the book, the problem of homogeneity and heterogeneity. Another way of putting it is that in order to say something, something else needs to be left unsaid.

CHAPTER I

Freud

Introduction

The nature–nurture debate is the only game worth playing in town. Plotkin (1997) says this in a volume on biology. To my mind this is true also of the townships psychoanalysis and group analysis, where despite the increasing sophistication of the language and technique, the various schools and streams differentiate themselves on the basis of the degrees of emphases they give to elements that are thought to be innate or learned.

The psychoanalyst and group analyst Earl Hopper (in a 1996 personal communication) put the problem in the form of a succinct question: does a particular theory emphasize projection or introjection during infant development? The answering of the question leads us to see that the emphasis on projection prioritizes the internal world, 'nature' and instinct; whilst the emphasis on introjection prioritizes the external world, 'nurture' and culture. These are of course broad generalizations that cover a multitude of variations. Further, no theory worth its salt has purely emphasized one polarity. They all allow some interaction between inside and outside, but they differ in the degree and kind of interaction they allow.

As is well known, this difference in emphasis has a long and lively history and can be encapsulated by the positions taken by Plato and Aristotle. We can think of them as two templates: Plato standing for the emphasis on the internal world and Aristotle for the emphasis on the external world.

Socrates taught that knowledge was inborn and could be accessed through reasoning. Plato went further with his Theory of Forms by saying that this 'true' inborn, conceptual knowledge was *more* real than knowledge gained from perceptions. He argued that this was so because the former, the idea of chair, was eternal and unchanging, whilst the latter, a particular chair, was mutable and so illusory.

Aristotle on the other hand placed a greater emphasis on sense perceptions and the external world, teaching a doctrine of empiricism. Where Plato emphasized deduction, Aristotle added induction. Whilst Plato elevated the general, the universal over the particular, Aristotle turned it around and 'came close to saying that universals have no existence except in the thinking mind' (Hunt 1993, p.30).

But why begin a book on groups with this 'old saw', the nature–nurture dichotomy? The answer in part is because of the bearing it has on another dichotomy, more directly related to the topic of the book – the individual–group dichotomy. It is the way of dichotomies that they are often inappropriately laid one on top of the other – thus it is tempting to somehow equate the notion of nurture with that of the group, and nature with that of the individual. And indeed in many metapsychologies, this is precisely the case, where the assumption is that the true nature of the human being is to be found within the individual. The outcome is that the individual is given ontological priority over the group. It is said that individuals come first, and they then join together to form groups. The argument continues that when they do form groups, then something of their true nature gets contaminated and corrupted by the presence of the group. Not only do these sorts of ideas pervade the fields of individual psychoanalysis and coun-selling, they also pervade the field of group analysis. For example, a group-analyst saying to participants in a workshop: 'Look *inside* you to find your true self'. It would appear then, that in folk psychology at least, Plato has clearly won the day. And as we will discover, this is also true of many areas of psychoanalysis and group analysis.

With the use of the word 'inside', the reader might have noted that another dichotomy has been surreptitiously introduced and mapped onto the others: internal–external. To be sure, the dichotomy was already implicitly there in Hopper's question, and we can see that things are already getting confusing and complicated. Thus, as we proceed, we will have to be ever vigilant to disentangle the overlappings and conflations between the various dichotomies. So for example, in a common sense way of thinking, 'nature' is implicitly linked with 'true', and both of these are located 'inside'. How often is the phrase 'true nurture' ever heard? We will have to tread cautiously, and sometimes pedantically, because the weights and meaning given to the polarities of each dichotomy will be of critical significance to the project of this book – to take the group seriously.

Some assumptions are so deeply embedded that they appear to be self evident, and one has to be ever vigilant even to notice their presence. For example, in a book on groups it seems pertinent to ask – what after all *is* a group? The usual sort of answer is that it is a collection of individuals. Implicit in the forms of the question and the answer is the assumption that the individual is more basic than the group, and further whilst the nature of the group is up for discussion, the nature of the individual is not – it is sort of 'understood' what the individual is.

One can see then that behind this question is a more fundamental one – are groups formed by a collection of individuals joining together, or are individuals precipitated somehow out of groups? This then is the question that is central to the book, and the answers found will not be straightforward ones.

At the heart of group analysis is its progenitor, S. H. Foulkes, and he himself was firmly grounded in Freudian psychoanalysis. So before we get on to studying Foulkesian group analysis proper, we should begin with its psychoanalytic antecedent – the theories of Freud. Whilst the overview will of necessity be vastly abbreviated, the emphasis of the overview will be to examine the roles allocated to internals and externals, and nature and nurture. And interestingly, in Freud we will find all the old philosophical saws, teeth still as sharp as ever, struggling one against the other.

Freud: culturalist or nativist?

Sigmund Freud is regarded by some as a radical with revolutionary potential, and by others as a doyen of conservatism. How is this possible?

In part, these contradictory views are possible because of the range and complexity of Freud's thoughts: he constructed not one theory but several, and further, as Freudian scholars like Laplanche and Pontalis (1973) have pointed out, many of his theoretical constructs are ambiguous, as they have been given contradictory definitions in different places. So, in much the same way that one can use selected quotes from the Bible to argue either for a merciful or vengeful God, one can use the complexity and depth of Freud's writings to construct, within certain limits, quite different 'Freudian individuals'. For example, although both Klein and Lacan claim to base their theories on Freud, they have each emerged with radically different models of the human mind.

There are two prongs to the Freudian schema. First, the individual is a compromise that is said to be structured through a conflict between the demands of nature and nurture, that is, biology and society. But second, things are complicated by the fact that the psychological structure of the individual and *society itself* are seen to be the developmental outcome of a conflict between two biological instincts (initially love and hunger, and later, life and death) that are said to reside within all individuals.

Thus the Freudian schema is not a straightforward linear model of cause and effect, but a complicated dialectic between the inside and the outside. Progressive ideologues who use Freud to view humanity through a radical lens begin their explication with the first formulation, of how individuals are structured through an engagement with the outside. Meanwhile critics of Freud, those who see his formulation as biologistic, focus on his emphasis on instinct, and that which is thought to be innate. For example, Terry Eagleton (1983) emphasizes the culturalist Freud with this quote: 'The motive for human society is in the last resort an economic one'. Next to this we can put some of Freud's words that can be used to substantiate the nativist line: 'What we describe as a person's "character" is built up to a considerable extent from the material of sexual excitations and is composed of instincts...' (1905, p.238). In order to unpack this ambiguity we will look briefly at the philosophical basis of Freud's theories.

Freud: idealist[1] or materialist?

Freud is often located in the philosophical stream of idealism because of two reasons: first, the priority he gives to the internal world over the external, and second, the fact that he derives culture as an epiphenomenon of internal dynamics. Whilst this is a true representation of his theory, to my mind it does not make him an idealist. This is because, although he derives things from the inside, it is not from the mind (as it is with the idealists), but from the body. *In fact he derives the mind from the body.* In this sense he is a materialist or even at times a mechanist. It seems to me that he is tussling to find the answer to the biggest question of all: what is life itself? What force makes something autonomous and self activating? One can imagine that as a medical doctor he looks at a live person and a cadaver and asks: what makes the difference between them? He eschews religious answers like 'the breath of God' and answers: chemistry. 'What distinguishes the instincts one from another and endows them with specific qualities is their relation to *their somatic sources* and to their aims...excitations of two kinds arise from the somatic organs, *based upon differences of a chemical nature.*' (1905, p.168). These 'excitations' are the well-known instincts or drives (depending on how one translates the German *trieb*). He stated this view early in his career and it remained one of the invariants in his evolving theoretical edifice. For example in the 'Project for a scientific psychology' he says something similar by describing soma as the 'mainspring of the psychical mechanism'. He also says 'in the interior of the system there arises the impulsion which sustains all psychical activity' (1895, pp.316–317).

In this sense Freud's theory is an attack on idealism. It seems to me that what Freud offered at the turn of the century is an undermining of the ancient view of man as something poised between the animal and the divine, by saying that that which we call divine is in fact a fantasy and is derived from the animal. It is true, however, that having derived the psychological from the material, he then derives everything else from the psychological. If one limits oneself to this, the latter part of his schema, then it is true to call him an idealist.

It seems to me that there is a constant tension in Freud between the two philosophical positions of idealism and materialism. It is demonstrated in the struggle he had throughout his career with the role of external reality: how

---

[1]   The philosophical stream of idealism gives priority to mental processes over and above physical ones. Conversely, materialism gives priority to matter over and above ideas or mental processes.

significant was it? What impact did it have on development? And so on. In his early theorizing, external reality was given a structuring role in the creation of neurosis. This was encapsulated in both the wish theory of the psyche and the seduction theory. To explain: the early Freudian psyche was driven by wishes. Greenberg (1991) makes the point that the structure of 'a wish' inevitably has an object embedded within it. That is, one has to wish *for something*. In other words, the external, the object, exists prior to the wish – which is an internal event. The 'seduction theory' said that the genesis of neurosis occurred with the *actual* seductions and molestations of small children by adults. Later, with the instinct theory, Freud abandoned this position and derived all neurosis endogenously. And later again (1917) he allowed external reality a role, but in a limited and ambiguous fashion.

As the different theories unfold through the book, we will find this same preoccupation between the internal and external emerging time and time again, albeit it in different forms and shapes. But despite the diversity and range of Freud's thought, it is possible to some extent (with Greenberg and Mitchell) to pick certain themes that stay more or less consistent through his long career, and use these to sketch out the roles given to internal and external realities in the developing structure of the Freudian infant.

The Freudian infant

Although Freud oscillates between the internal and the external, in the end he prioritizes internal reality over external reality. Ultimately, the external is allocated two conflicting roles, both of which are related to the instincts: (1) as the thing that satisfies instinct (external objects), and (2) as that which inhibits the satisfaction of instinct (internalizations).

The nature of instincts

At the beginning of life, the Freudian infant is objectless. It is a closed energetic system, driven from within, by two distinct 'wellsprings' of energy – the instincts. It is salient that although the aim of both is to seek discharge, they are in *conflict* with each other, and so each disrupts the straightforward functioning of the other. As has already been described above, the instincts themselves derive their energy ultimately from the chemical substrate of the body. This is the beginning and the source of everything that follows – individuals and the societies they live in.

For the early Freud, the two instinctual wellsprings were the self preservative instincts and the sexual instincts. The self preservative instincts operate more or less according to the Reality Principle and the sexual instincts according to the Pleasure Principle. In 1920, he subsumed the above two instincts under the new rubric, the Life Instinct, and set it against the Death Instinct.[2] The ultimate 'desire' of an organism is to discharge its tensions and energies (the Pleasure Principle), and the ultimate reduction is zero, death. He calls this the Nirvana Principle, the cessation of life itself.

To elaborate with a hydraulic analogy: it is easier for water to flow downhill, to a lower energy state, than for it to flow uphill. In that sense the downhill movement is more 'natural' and inevitable. It is the constant work one has to do to get the water uphill that is difficult and interminable. This is the task of the life instinct, but it is being constantly threatened and undermined by the forces pulling downwards – gravity, decay, death. The myth of Sisyphus comes to mind. In this sense it can be seen that in the Freudian schema, *existence itself* is a precarious developmental achievement that is under constant threat of being undone.

Aggression

The only way an organism can survive this onslaught from within, that is, this impetus to die, is to put it outside of itself in some way, and this it achieves through projection. Freud says that each of us projects out parts of the death instinct onto external objects in order to protect the self, to stop us from dying. This projection outwards of the death instinct he calls the Aggressive Instinct. 'The aim of the aggressive instinct is the destruction of the object' (Laplanche and Pontalis 1973, p.16).

So once again, the individual is compromised; in order for the self not to be destroyed, it has to destroy, or at least injure, something else. Additionally, the external object is now experienced by the self as hostile and dangerous, containing as it does the death instinct. There is no way out of this conundrum; the death instinct has to go somewhere. One can see that the argument leads us to say that it is death and destruction that are 'natural' and inevitable, and that all we can do is moderate this drive to some degree with the life instinct operating under the auspices of the Reality Principle. But the cost when this occurs is neurosis for the individual.

The development of psychological structures

The id

In the beginning there is only id and the psyche is completely unconscious. The id is the reservoir of instinctual energy. This is a state of undifferentiation, where energy is 'free' and can readily flow from one thing to another. The instincts are

2   The Pleasure Principle is modified at this point and is no longer derived from the straightforward reduction of tension, but more from a rhythmic fluctuation in the energies.

the *initiators* of mental activity, that is, they start the mind functioning in order for it to facilitate the achievement of their aim – discharge. In this sense, consciousness is merely the instincts' means to their end.[3] This is what Freud meant when he said that instinct made a demand upon the mind for work – the *demand* starts the mind working (1915a, p.122). Initially, as the instinctual charge (needs) builds up the infant tries to satisfy them autoerotically, that is, it hallucinates its satisfactions. Freud then says that as the hallucination does not really satisfy the infant, it is forced into an engagement with the external world. At this point, the infant's solipsistic world is punctured, never to be repaired again; the infant has broken out of its psychological shell. Now, in order for the id to engage with the external world, it needs a new structure – the ego.

However, before moving on to that, a crucial point needs to be stressed, which is that the external objects that the infant actually engages with are made incidental and almost arbitrary. Freud says '…What is *most variable* about an instinct and is not originally connected with it, but becomes assigned to it only in consequence of being peculiarly fitted to make satisfaction possible…' (1915a, p.122; emphasis added). He also says some years later, 'repeated situations of satisfaction have *created* an object out of the mother' (1926, p.170).

This of itself is an extraordinarily interesting idea – that the *notion* of mother is sculpted out of the progressive layerings of satisfied *internal* desire, one on top of the other. This implies that relationships are made because they fulfil a function – the discharge of tension – and not because of anything implicitly valuable in the notion of the relationship itself. Moreover, it seems that the psychological emotion, 'satisfaction', is also but a means to the end – an epiphenomenon that encourages the discharge of instincts. An analogy would be the pleasure of orgasm; this can be construed as the carrot that encourages one to engage in the act of coitus, but behind the scenes the (true) biological aim is something else – replication.

The ego

As Laplanche and Pontalis (1973) point out, there is a lot of ambiguity about the genesis of the ego. There are several suggestions: first as 'an agency of adaptation which differentiates itself from the id on contact with external reality. Alternatively it is described as the product of identifications culminating in the formation, within the personality, of a love object cathected by the id' (Laplanche and Pontalis 1973, p.130). There is a third suggestion by Freud, which is that the ego is first derived from the body. Once stated the idea is never developed. 'The

---

3   This is not dissimilar to the idea proposed by the sociobiologists, that the human being is merely the gene's way of replicating itself (see Part 5: Biology).

ego is first and foremost a bodily ego; it is not merely a surface entity, but is itself the projection of a surface.' 'The ego is ultimately derived from bodily sensations, chiefly from those springing from the surface of the body...' (1923, p.26).

In 1911 the more significant idea is that of the ego as an agency of adaptation, and as such the first 'object' that is cathected by the id. Freud says: '[there is] an original libidinal cathexis of the ego, from which some is later given off to objects, but which fundamentally persists and is related to the object-cathexes much as the body of an amoeba is related to the *pseudopodia* which it puts out.' (1914, p.75; emphasis added). This 'original libidinal cathexis' is called 'primary narcissism'. The ego is the first object for the id, but it has been created out of itself. It is endogenously derived. Later, the same energy is used to cathect external objects. However, Freud's metaphor of the 'pseudopodia' is a telling one: it implies that the external cathexis is the pseudo connection – not the 'real' one.

So the ego is there partly to manipulate the world so that the instincts may be satisfactorily discharged. It is also there to moderate the excessive demands of the id.

Identification

It was in 1917 in 'Mourning and melancholia' that Freud first described a mechanism through which the external world entered and modified the internal world. The 'contents' of the ego consist of identifications with lost objects – a sort of internal graveyard populated by ghosts of departed objects. He describes the idea as follows: when some external object is lost, then the libido that was attached to that object is withdrawn into the ego 'to establish an *identification* of the ego with the abandoned object. Thus the shadow of the object fell upon the ego...' (1917, p.249). Some five years later, Freud saw this as a normal part of development – he said famously: 'the character of the ego is a precipitate of abandoned object cathexes and...it contains the history of those object-choices' (1923, p.29).

To my mind Laplanche and Pontalis overstate it when they say that, 'In Freud's work...the concept [of identification] comes to have central importance [as]...the operation whereby the human subject is constituted' (1973, p.206). This is because identification, as Freud describes it, is actually a turning away from the outside world back into a solipsistic universe; he calls identification a *regression* from object choice (1921). As Freud says elsewhere, the ego says to the id: 'Look, you can love me too – I am so like the object' (1923, p.30). So whilst it is possible to read this mechanism as a description of impressions left by 'experiences' on the ego, to my mind this is not quite what Freud was emphasizing.

The tension between the inside and outside continues in the story of the third psychic structure – the superego.

The superego

This structure is the outcome of the Oedipal drama – as Freud put it: the superego is heir to the Oedipal complex. The Oedipal drama is driven by powerful instinctual forces, and consists of the battle to deflect and incarcerate them. With the genesis of the superego the individual is positioned in the world and becomes a social being – up to a point that is.

As Freud describes it, the drama takes place between the ages of three and five. Briefly, the child powerfully desires the parent of the opposite gender to itself, and wishes to annihilate its competitor, the parent of the same gender. It is the subjugation of these powerful impulses of desire and death that constitute the Oedipal complex. In the successful resolution of the complex, the child renounces these impulses, in the sense of making them unconscious. But in order to keep them unconscious, a new repressive structure is constituted out of the ego – the superego. Freud says that in the first instance the contents of the superego consist of identifications with parental authority figures, and that later other social and cultural rules are added. Additionally, the contents of the superego consist of word-presentations as opposed to thing-presentations in the id. He makes the following crucial point in discussing the contents of the superego:

> …a child's super-ego is in fact constructed on the model *not of its parents but its parents' superego*; the contents which fill it are the same and it becomes the vehicle of tradition and of all the time-resisting judgements of value which have propagated themselves in this manner from generation to generation… Mankind never lives entirely in the present. The past, the tradition of the race and of the people, lives on in the ideologies of the superego, and yields only slowly to the influences of the present and to new changes; and so long as it operates through the super-ego it plays a powerful part in human life, independently of economic conditions. (1933, p.67; emphasis added)[4]

So one can see that the mechanism for the genesis of the superego is similar to that of the ego with one difference. Whilst the ego partly consists of identifications with *lost* objects, the superego consists of identifications with *renounced* objects.

Oedipus

Here too, in the Oedipal drama, one can trace Freud's struggle with internal and external forces. In 1910 the *actual* external parents are given weight: '[the child] usually follows some indication from its parents, whose affection bears the clearest characteristics of a sexual activity… As a rule a father prefers his daughter and a mother her son; the child reacts to this by wishing, if he is a son to take his

---

4   We will come back to this passage several times in the course of the book, its importance lying in the fact that it describes a version of the internalization of the social.

father's place [and vice versa]' (1910, p.47). But later he reiterates the priority of endogenous forces: 'the original severity of the superego does not...represent the severity which one has experienced from...[the object], or which one attributes to it; it represents rather one's own aggressiveness towards it' (1930, pp.129–130). Elsewhere he says that the basis of the aggression in the superego is to be found in the child's aggressiveness towards his parents for which he was unable to effect a discharge...' (1933, p.109). Greenberg and Mitchell impress the point further when they add: 'Freud states that its [Oedipus complex] establishment and dissolution are "determined and laid down by heredity"' (1983, p.73). In other words, regardless of the actual interpersonal transactions that take place, the Oedipal phase will pass 'when the next *pre-ordained* phase of development sets in' (Freud 1924, p.174; emphasis added). As for the result of the phase itself, he holds that 'in both sexes the relative strength of the masculine and feminine sexual dispositions is what determines whether the outcome of the Oedipus situation shall be an identification with the father or with the mother' (1923, p.33). It would seem then, that although in earlier times Freud allowed the external some role, in the end Freud supposed that the external did not penetrate sufficiently to modify the deep biological programming within the individual; thus what is said to drive the developmental themes are innate 'dispositions' and 'pre-ordained phases'.

Phylogeny

There is one other mechanism through which Freud allows the external world to enter the psyche. And this is through phylogenetic inheritance, that is from the mythic times of prehistory. Let Freud speak more fully:

> Reflection at once shows us that no external vicissitudes can be experienced or undergone by the id, except by way of the ego, which is the representative of the external world to the id. Nevertheless it is not possible to speak of direct inheritance in the ego. It is here that the gulf between an actual individual and the concept of the species becomes evident. Moreover...[one should remember] that the ego is a specially differentiated part of the id. The experiences of the ego seem at first to be lost for inheritance; *but when they have been repeated often enough and with sufficient strength in many individuals in successive generations, they transform themselves, so to say, into experiences of the id, the impressions of which are preserved by heredity.* Thus in the id, which is capable of being inherited, are harboured residues of the existences of countless egos; and, when the ego forms its superego out of the id, it may perhaps only be reviving shapes of former egos and be bringing them to resurrection. (1923, p.38; emphasis added)

This metapsychological passage is in contradiction to the usual way Freud talks about the id – as something purely chemical and biological, as something asocial.

The passage is an anomaly, and important precisely because of that. Here, Freud reveals that at times he thinks like a Lamarckian – saying in effect that things learned through experience end up being biologically inherited. The importance of the point cannot be overemphasized – because here, Freud allows the id to be acculturated, albeit primitively.

A thing to note here (and it recurs in many other places) is the point that whenever the mature Freud allows the external world an impact on the deep structure of the psyche, it is always from beyond any region that may be accessed – prehistory, that is, a metaphysical region that can only be speculated about.[5]

We can see then that the contents of each of the layers of the tripartite Freudian psyche are derived from different domains. The id is the container of *biological* and phylological history as embodied in the instincts: 'a seething cauldron' as it has been called. This system is in conflict with the superego. The superego is the repository of *social* rules and prohibitions – also *derived from previous generations*. And the ego, the mediator and moderator, the container of contemporary but lost experiences, is a referee but not really a player in the internal drama; the ego is only a player in the sense of manipulating the external in the aim of the internal. So the human being is the arena in which two ancient awesome armies confront each other, with the ego, powerless to diminish their energies, engaged in a damage limitation exercise.

Whilst Freud allocates the external a role, in the end, it is always subordinate to the internal: '[Internal perceptions] are more primordial, more elementary, than perceptions arising externally...[they have] greater economic significance' (Freud 1923, p.22). It is evident then that in the orthodox Freudian schema, what can be achieved through 'nurture' in the face of 'nature' is severely limited. There is no happy ending with Freud, no going off into the sunset to live happily ever after. Life is a struggle – right to the end.

In and between groups

Freud problematizes all relationships as developmental achievements that are tenuously maintained in the face of forces that tend to disrupt and destroy them.

Freud's model is similar to Rousseau's in that both thought that man existed in a 'natural' state before the advent of civilization. But whilst Rousseau idealized

---

5   In a sense this criticism of Freud is unfair because no system of thought can ever be completely self referential, evolving itself out of itself, or to put it another way, generating itself out of nothing. All systems and philosophies always allude to something outside and beyond them, one can call it the God Factor. This was demonstrated dramatically through mathematics by Godel's (1962) Incompleteness Theorem which has a bearing on *all* axiomatic systems. In everyday language this states that any logically consistent system *has* to be incomplete, and its converse, that any complete system *will have* logical inconsistencies. In Freud's case his psychology is premised on something outside psychology – the instincts, which are derived from biology and chemistry, and they in turn are said to be material representations of internalized experiences in prehistory.

that state – the noble savage, man living in harmony with nature – Freud thought otherwise. Freud thought that prehistory was no happy ideal time, quite the reverse. During this time he thought the instinctual drives had no 'civilized' prohibitions and so ran rampant with no bounds – 'nature, red in tooth and claw'. However, according to Freud, even at that time humanity was riven, divided and set against itself. He said: '…in the primal family only the head of it enjoyed this instinctual freedom; the rest lived in slavish suppression. In that primal period of civilisation, the contrast between a minority who enjoyed the advantages of civilisation and a majority who were robbed of those advantages was, therefore, carried to an extreme' (1930, p.115). In another place he added:

> …the class structure of society goes back to the struggles which, from the beginning of history, took place between human hordes only slightly differing from each other. Social distinctions…were originally distinctions between clans or races. Victory was decided by psychological factors, such as the amount of constitutional aggressiveness, but also by the firmness of the organisation within the horde, and by material factors, such as the possession of superior weapons. (1933, p.177)

The importance of this passage lies in the fact that it clearly demonstrates Freud's view, that contemporary social differences are to be derived from, and understood in the light of, imagined prehistoric social differences. Moreover, in a Darwinian mode, he suggests that the ones that were victorious were so because they were constitutionally better equipped to win. In other words contemporary socio-economic differences are a 'natural' consequence of a law of nature. He elaborates further:

> The undoubted fact that different individuals, races and nations behave differently under the same economic conditions is alone enough to show that economic motives are not the sole dominating factors…not only were [psycho-logical factors] concerned in developing the economic conditions, but even under the domination of those conditions men can only bring their original instinctual impulses into play… (1933, p.178)

To use Barthes' idea, history has been naturalized. A consequence of this, as always, is that one can only accept things for what they are, because that is how they ought to be.

Freud attends to the mechanisms of inter and intra group dynamics, looking at how groups form, and also what happens between groups. The mechanism for the formation of a group he describes as follows: 'a psychological group is a collection of individuals who have introduced the same person into their super-ego and, on the basis of this common element, have identified themselves with one another in their ego' (1933, p.67). But now the group is said to have a problem which is a logical and inevitable consequence of the death instinct – the management of aggression.

Freud[6] described two separate theories, but never explicitly distinguished between them. In one theory difference is *used* to manage hatred, and in the other theory difference is said to *cause* hatred. In fact one is a theory of difference, and the other is a theory of aggression and hatred. The two are usually conflated.

Freud's first theory is his theory of aggression and is grounded in the instincts. This theory describes how difference is *used* in the service of aggression and hatred. He says: 'Every emotional relationship...contains a sediment of feelings of aversion and hostility, which only escapes perception as a result of repression...' (Freud 1921, p.101). Having repressed the hostility, which is instinctual, the second step follows, which is projection. 'The advantage which a comparatively small cultural group offers of allowing this instinct an outlet in the form of hostility against intruders is not to be despised. It is always possible to bind together a considerable number of people in love, so long as there are other people left over to receive the manifestations of their aggressiveness' (1930, p.114).

One can see then that in this theory, the Other is *used* as a container in which to deposit hatred, but the hatred itself is instinctual and primary. Thus the external difference is subordinate to, and is used by, the internal instincts. The difference itself is of little consequence to the aggression – apart from signifying 'not-me' – the target is innocent. This theory of aggression has prioritized the internal over the external.

The second theory of aggression, named 'the narcissism of minor differences' is one where the external is prioritized over the internal. Here, the difference is said to *cause* the hatred.

Here Freud argued that it was when differences were minor that they were at their most virulent.

> Every time two families become connected by a marriage, each of them thinks itself superior to...the other. Of two neighbouring towns each is the others most jealous rival... Closely related races keep one another at arms length; the South German cannot endure the North German, the Englishman casts every kind of aspersion upon the Scot, the Spaniard despises the Portuguese. (1921, p.101)

According to him, these minor differences affronted the self preservative instinct. The self preservative instinct was said to experience something different from itself as a criticism of itself. Thus it attacked and felt hostile to the thing that was different.

Next, the argument goes, if minor differences cause such strong feelings, then major differences must cause even stronger feelings: '...when men come together in larger units... We are no longer astonished that greater differences should lead to an almost insuperable repugnance, such as the Gallic people feel for the

6   This section appeared previously in a paper entitled 'The colour question in psychoanalysis' *Journal of Social Work Practice* (Dalal 1997b).

German, the Aryan for the Semite, and the white races for the coloured' (1921, p.101).

Now, there is a fundamental flaw in the argument, as he sets it out. He begins by saying that hostility is *inversely proportional* to difference, that is, that the smaller the difference the greater the hostility. But he then goes on to reverse this and argue the opposite, saying that if minor differences cause such ructions, we are not to be surprised that bigger differences cause even more ructions. Now, hostility is made *directly proportional* to difference. Freud has begun with a theory of Minor Differences, and ended in a theory of Major Differences.

Freud clearly cannot have it both ways, as the two theories of difference are mutually exclusive. This can be clearly seen if we represent them in a pseudo-algebra.

The theory of Minor Differences, where hostility is said to be *inversely* proportional to difference, would look like this:

$$\text{Amount of Hostility} \quad \alpha \quad \frac{1}{\text{Amount of Difference}}$$

And the theory of Major Differences, where hostility is said to be *directly* proportional to difference, would look like this:

$$\text{Amount of Hostility} \quad \alpha \quad \frac{\text{Amount of Difference}}{1}$$

Despite the anomaly, the main thrust of this second theory of aggression remains – that external difference causes internal hatred.

The Freudian view of groups

On the whole, groups do not come off very well in Freud's ruminations. Groups might best be described as a necessity – but an unfortunate necessity. Freud built his theory of groups mainly on the descriptions of Le Bon. Le Bon, a physician and sociologist, wrote an influential book at the end of the nineteenth century, *The Crowd* (1986). Le Bon was 'an enemy of the populace' and assembled his reflections on his opinion of the activities of French revolutionary crowds (Turner and Giles 1981, p.7). In the group, the individual was said to regress to a primitive state. The word 'primitive' is being used in three senses. First, psychologically primitive in the sense of primary process thinking – thus likened to insanity;

developmentally primitive in the sense of early in life – thus likened to children; and third, evolutionarily primitive in the sense of peoples – thus likened to non-Europeans. This word, 'primitive', is the locus around which Le Bon and Freud build the equivalence between the mental states of groups, primitive peoples and children.[7] On this matter Freud says: 'how well justified is the identification of the group mind with the mind of primitive people' (1921, p.79). The group is a place of extremes, where primary thinking thought processes predominate: 'The feelings of a group are always very simple and very exaggerated. So that a group knows neither doubt nor uncertainty. … In groups the most contradictory ideas can exist side by side…without any conflict arising from the logical contradiction' (1921, pp.78–79). Groups might be moral at times, but not out of any natural tendency, only 'under the influence of suggestion' (1921, p.79). In groups, the instincts are said to run rampant, thus 'when individuals come together in a group all their individual inhibitions fall away and all the cruel, brutal and destructive instincts, which lie dormant in individuals as relics of a primitive epoch, are stirred up to find free gratification' (1921, p.79).

Explanation for the fact that groups do in fact work together at times, is given by the theory of libido and attachment. Freud describes how the individual identifies with the other members of the group. However, even this identification is problematic and has its basis in envy. He argues as follows: the older child feels murderous towards the younger sibling. However, he or she cannot proceed to enact their feelings because the outcome would be self destructive – the parents would turn against them. Thus the child identifies with the younger sibling. This is a reaction formation in which the hated object is loved instead. Next, Freud says, 'If one cannot be the favourite oneself, at all events no one else shall be favourite' (1921, p.120). This then leads to a wish for equality and justice. But it is a wish of deprivation. If I cannot have all the cake (which is what I would really like) then I will make sure that we all have exactly the same amount of cake. 'Social justice means that we deny ourselves many things so that others may have to do without them as well' (1921, p.121). Things are not looking too hopeful for groups, and they get worse: 'Groups have never thirsted after truth. They demand illusions, and cannot do without them' (1921, p.80). A group fears autonomy, it wants 'to be ruled and oppressed and to fear its masters' (1921, p.78).

Feelings of empathy that might exist in a group are explained by the notion of 'contagion' which is redolent with meanings of contamination, disease and the like. Thus any mutuality that might arise in a group is a kind of disease and is to be resisted. Another way that Freud allows mutuality to arise in the group is through

---

7   The linkages between these three regions form the basis of the theory of recapitulation, which is
     described more fully a little later in the book. Also, see Dalal (1988) for Jung's use of 'primitive'.

an identification that is based on the fact that all the members of a group are said to have internalized the imago of the leader.

To my mind, this next passage is a fair summary of Freud's view of groups:

> the weakness of intellectual ability, the lack of emotional restraint, the incapacity for moderation and delay, the inclination to exceed every limit in the expression of emotion and to work it off completely in the form of action – these and similar features...show an unmistakable picture of a regression of mental activity to an earlier stage such as we are not surprised to find among savages or children. (1921, p.117)

No wonder then that groups are not well thought of. It is important to note that Freud was not inventing the speculations about groups and what they were or were not supposed to be capable of. Rather, Freud used the then generally understood view of groups, and tried to give them explanation from within the theory of psychoanalysis. So in a sense what Freud has done is to institutionalize this generic view of groups in the discipline of psychoanalysis. To a large degree, even today, many a person, many a psychoanalyst, still holds this view of groups.

Summary

We have seen that Freud's theory is not a simplistic one, of the internal straightforwardly imposing itself on the external. There is a complex interplay between the two, each modifying the other. However, having said that, the bottom line in Freud is that he gives ontological priority to the internal over the external, to the biological over the social, and to the individual over the group. The engagement with the external is a later developmental event than the engagement with the internal, which is where the beginning of things takes place. The critical element that stops Freud's theory being a linear one is the fact that once the external exists, it curves back to enter the psyche, to modify the internal. Thus a complex feedback loop is created, making development an intricate recursive and iterative process. It should not be forgotten that the beauty and grandeur of Freud's theory, encompassing as it does all cultural and psychological life, is built out of the conflict of two instincts. And these in turn have their basis in the chemistry of the body. Whatever else it is, Freud's theory is extraordinarily elegant, deriving and weaving operas and torture chambers out of the interplay between just two chemical states.

Having set the scene, as it were, we will now move on to Foulkes, to see what he has made out of this inheritance.

CHAPTER 2

Foulkes

Introduction

Foulkes is a mixed bag – exciting thinking, which is at the same time disappointing, as ultimately, he does not carry out his challenges through to a satisfactory end.

Foulkes announces several radical challenges to traditional ways of thinking about the individual. It is not overstating it to say that he attempts a major redefinition of the nature of what constitutes an individual, by placing the group and not the individual at the centre of theory. He also announces several new theoretical constructs that are born out of the repositioning of the individual and the group. These constructs try to be group specific, and it is part of the disappointment that he is unable to hold to the task, and so they do not fulfil their radical potential.

As a writer, around certain key ideas, he is repetitious to an extraordinary degree. Not only does he repeat certain ideas over and over again, he uses exactly the same phrases, and sometimes entire passages (without acknowledgement) verbatim. One can speculate that these are the places where he is unable to push through to something new theoretically, and so is doomed, like some troubled ghost in a story, to return to the same place time and time again. To be sure, this is overstating it somewhat, as an entire school of analytic thought and practice has grown out of his ideas, and even in their incomplete form they form a substantial challenge to traditional psychoanalytic theory and practice.

It seems to me that Foulkes implicitly has in mind the orthodox psychoanalytic community at all times, and is acutely aware of the position of his group analytic theory in relation to them. He is very aware that his ideas are a direct challenge to the psychoanalytic orthodoxy. Sometimes he confronts the issues head on and stands his ground, and at other times he tries to have his cake and eat it too. He pulls his punches. He does this I imagine in order not to alienate the psychoanalysts, and he does this at times by watering down the thrust of his theory, by reassuringly saying in many places that despite what he says about the group, the individual is still central.[1] In other places he seeks to lend his views a legitimacy by alluding to his Freudian antecedents, in effect his pedigree. He was first of all a trained Freudian psychoanalyst.

True, many of his psychological ideas are completely Freudian, but he cannot take up all of Freud, because that would undermine the radical basis of his conceptualizations. And he cannot fully take up his own conceptualizations, because they would differentiate him too much from Freud and the psychoanalytic community. At times, this leaves him in a halfway land. In doing this, Foulkes is no different from many other psychoanalytic theoreticians, all of whom try to add, change or remove parts of Freud's theory, whilst proclaiming themselves 'really' Freudian.

One way of unravelling the difficulties is to think in terms of there being two Foulkes, a radical one and a more orthodox one. The two Foulkes set out two sorts of theories. One could say that the orthodox Foulkes sets out a linear theory, a 'weak' challenge to the traditional psychoanalytic framework. Meanwhile radical Foulkes sets out a systemic and multidimensional theory, which constitutes a 'strong' challenge to psychoanalysis. Further, despite his protestations, radical Foulkes is not Freudian at all, but anti-Freudian. This is because radical Foulkes does away with instinct and inheritance completely, and instead replaces them with the external and transmission.

A difficulty is that it does not appear that Foulkes himself distinguishes between these two theories, which results in him constantly contradicting himself. However, as one reads through his four books, it is possible to see his view change from an individual psychoanalytic viewpoint to one that is increasingly radical, systemic, and group oriented.

The basis of Foulkes' radical ideas

Before we can proceed to Foulkesian psychology, we have to begin in the domain of philosophy and metapsychology, as this is the basis of his redefinition of the individual. His thinking here is informed in part by social psychology – in particular that of Norbert Elias, in part by the psycho-social ideas from the Frankfurt school, and also by the school of Gestalt psychology, regarding notions of wholes and parts.

He begins with the idea that the Renaissance gave birth to a false ideation – the abstractions and dichotomies of mind/body, inside/outside, nature/nurture, group/individual. He argues:

1   For example: 'group-analytic psychotherapy...it is a form of psycho-analytical psychotherapy, and its frame of reference is the group as a whole. *Like all psychotherapy it puts the individual into the centre of its attention*' (Foulkes 1964, p.39). And 'group psychotherapy...does not treat the group for the group's sake, to improve its working efficiency, in the way...a team might be treated. The group is treated for the sake of its individual members, and for no other reason. All psychotherapy is, in the last resort, treatment of the individual' (Foulkes and Anthony 1957, p.37).

…each individual – itself an artificial, though plausible, abstraction – is basically and centrally determined, inevitably, by the world in which he lives, by the community, the group, of which he forms part…the old juxtaposition of an inside and outside world, constitution and environment, individual and society, phantasy and reality, body and mind and so on, are untenable. (Foulkes 1948, p.10)

Herein lies part of Foulkes' importance, his insistence on the interconnected nature of existence itself. Foulkes says that it might be a useful logical device to abstract one element out of a whole, in order to comment upon it; however it is important to remember that these abstractions have no real meaning or existence on their own. To give a simple example, take a circle: it has an inside, an outside, and a boundary separating the two (see Figure 2.1).

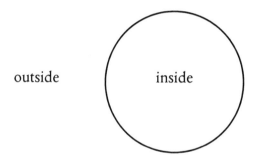

Figure 2.1

The three categories, inside, outside and boundary, are interrelated and none of them can exist in isolation from the others. The 'inside' needs both the 'outside' and the boundary line to give existence to itself, similarly for the other two entities. Remove one, and the other two cease to exist. Remove the inside and the circle collapses till there is nothing. Remove the outside and the circle expands until there is everything, and thus nothing.

Foulkes argues that once these dichotomies have been constructed, one element is inevitably, but wrongly, prioritized over the other. Mind over body, individual over group, internal over external, nature over nurture. He equates this view with what he calls the classical psychoanalytic view: 'the psychoanalytical point of view should also be seen as a deliberate abstraction, the individual being deliberately abstracted and considered isolated from his context' (Foulkes 1973a, p.227). In contrast to this he argues for a holistic view: 'Psychology is thus neither "individual" nor "group" except by abstraction' (Foulkes 1973a, p.230); 'There can be no question of a problem of group versus individual. These are two aspects, two sides of the same coin' (Foulkes and Anthony 1957, p.26). However, in other places he cannot hold the holistic tension and collapses on one or other side of the dichotomies, usually on the side of the group, the social, the external. These will emerge in the course of the chapter.

It should also be said here that the psychoanalysis that Foulkes refers to is very much his version of psychoanalysis, a parody that he uses at times to make his points against. Freud does not by any stretch of the imagination consider 'the individual…isolated from his context'.

Group and individual: external and internal

Foulkes inverts the normal relationships between internal and external realities, and also that of group and individual: 'What stands in need of explanation is not the existence of groups but the existence of individuals. The phenomenon of an individual standing in relative isolation from the group is something which only began to develop in historical times' (Foulkes and Anthony 1957, p.235). He argues that whilst the prioritization of the individual might be a useful device for the psychoanalytic dyad, it is not a true description of reality:

> we must reverse our traditional assumption, shared also by psychoanalysis, that the individual is the ultimate unity, and that we have to explain the group from inside the individual. The opposite is the case. The group, the community, is the ultimate primary unit of consideration, and *the so-called inner processes in the individual are internalizations of the forces operating in the group to which he belongs*. (Foulkes 1971, p.212; emphasis added)

This is an important passage and so needs spelling out. He is saying that the 'so-called inner processes' are not inner processes *per se*. But that they are internalized group dynamics.

The radical nature of this idea becomes more evident if we contrast it with Melanie Klein's ideas. Klein says that the neonate is born with certain mechanisms and forces within it – which it then projects onto the external world. Thus according to her, in the early days, the external world is very much a reflection of the internal world. As development proceeds, the experience of the external world progressively moderates and modifies the internal world, until the two are more congruent. Her direction is from inside to the outside. Foulkes is saying the opposite. He is saying that the neonate is born into certain mechanisms and forces, which it then introjects. His direction is from outside to the inside. The Kleinian infant uses elements of its internal world to structure its external world, whilst the Foulkesian infant uses elements of its external world to structure its internal world.[2]

---

2   Aside: Foulkes is very close to Fairbairn here – yet for some reason he appears to dislike him and the whole notion of internalized object relations. It is not clear to me why he is so insistent about this false distinction.

Effectively, Foulkes is making the group more fundamental than the individual. He says:

> The basic situation – historically also the oldest – is the group or community situation, which should be the matrix from which to define the position of the isolated individual or the two-personal transference relationship, and not, as so often happens, the other way round, when an attempt is made to 'explain' group dynamics in terms of transference'. (Foulkes 1957, p.112)

Another one of the more dramatic re-castings that he attempts is that of the relationship between individual and society. He says two things: first, the individual is embedded in the social, and second, the individual is permeated by the social.

> The Psychology of the Individual is comparable to microscopical anatomy and pathology, the Microcosm of the Individual repeating and reflecting the microscopical changes of the Society, of which he forms a part. The individual is not only dependent on the material conditions, for instance economic, climatic, of his surrounding world and on the community, the group, in which he lives, whose claims are transmitted to him through the parents or parental figures, but is literally permeated by them. He is part of a social network, a little nodal point, as it were, in this network, and can only artificially be considered in isolation, like a fish out of water. (Foulkes 1948, pp.14–15)

In making this statement, he is in a sense ahead of his time, as he anticipates some of the thoughts emerging from modern biology and genetics – that the human being is not a unity in any sense of the word, but is a collection of entities, a group.[3] So even at the level of a single cell, we find within it a group. Dawkins calls the cell 'an enclosed garden of bacteria' (1995, p.53). Foulkes says '...the individual is pre-conditioned to the core by his community, even before he is born, and his personality and character are imprinted vitally by the group in which he is raised' (Foulkes 1966, p.152).

There are several major consequences that follow out of these ideas. First, the nature of psychological illness has to be redefined. Second, 'culture' is made more important than 'biology'. Third, the external is prioritized over the internal.[4] For Foulkes, things always begin on the outside. This radical group of ideas forms the kernel of group analysis, and sets him fundamentally apart from the body of orthodox psychoanalysis, although many of his thoughts echo those of Winnicott, Fairbairn, and of course Freud. The theory against which he sets

---

3   These ideas will be explored more fully in Chapter 5.

4   So already here, Foulkes has given up on the holistic view, where everything is equivalent. This in fact is his true belief, that the external is prioritized over the internal, that nurture makes more impact than nature, and so forth. The one place where he does manage to retain his holistic view more successfully is on the mind/body dichotomy, but then this does not play a significant role in his theory.

himself up most clearly is that of Klein. In particular her emphasis on the internal world and projection. But despite this, some of his ideas echo hers. But more of that later.

Now, having suggested that the individual is 'embedded in the social', what does he mean by that?

Frames and contexts

Foulkes is very aware of context. We could put it in this way: *things need to be framed in order for them to be made visible*. 'In order to see something whole we have, I believe, to see it in relation to a greater whole, so that we can step outside of that which we want to see' (Foulkes 1973a, p.230). He repeats the point in many different guises: things are never isolated, they are always part of a greater thing. Foulkes goes on to spell out that not only is this true on the level of the individual in relation to the group, but *that it is also true of the group itself.* He is saying, although he does not put it in this language, that all the things we see are to some extent constructions and reifications. For example, '"traffic" is also an abstraction for something that does exist and yet does not exist. There is no such thing as traffic, there are only moving cars, lorries, obstacles of all sorts and people who wish to move from one point to another' (Foulkes 1975a, p.253). In keeping with this idea, he says 'there is no such thing as "a group" in the abstract' (Foulkes 1971, p.210). His thinking here is very modern, 'post-modern' even, and is a bold step as it potentially subverts the very object of his study, the group.

Strangely, this notion of abstraction, that there is no such thing as 'traffic' or 'group', appears to ally him with the former Conservative prime minister of Great Britain, Margaret Thatcher, when she famously said 'I don't believe in society. There is no such thing, only individual people, and there are families' (1987). However, I think that they are saying something very different from each other.

The dilemma is born out of the fact that we cannot help but conglomerate things like 'cars' into complexities like 'traffic'. The dilemma is that on the one hand the notion of 'traffic' only exists in our minds (a reification), and on the other hand the 'invented' complexity 'traffic' also appears to have a life of its own. Moreover, the complexity affects the behaviour of the individual particles that constitute it – cars.

This is where Foulkes would part company with Thatcher. He is saying that the group does in fact exist, but only in relation to other things – not in a vacuum. 'Human beings always live in groups. Groups in turn cannot be understood, *except in their relation to other groups* and in the context of the conditions in which they exist. We cannot isolate biological, social, cultural and economic factors, except by special abstraction' (Foulkes 1975a, p.252).

Thatcher is not only saying that individuals *per se* exist in a vacuum, but also that effectively everything exists in a vacuum and nothing is connected to anything else. If society is a set of unconnected individuals, then no one is responsible for anyone else. The powerful thing about the notion of the group is that responsibility becomes a shared issue. Here is one of the places where Foulkes is political. On this issue he says, as though replying to Thatcher:

> Ultimately it would mean that the whole community must take a far greater responsibility for outbreaks of disturbing psychopathology generally. There is therefore a very specific defensive interest at play in denying the fact of the interdependence which is here claimed; the cry 'but each is an individual' and 'surely the mind is a matter for the individual' means, in this sense, 'each for himself, I am not to blame for what happens to the other person, whether he is obviously near to me, or whether I am involved in concealed ways, or even quite unconsciously.' (Foulkes 1973a, p.225)

This idea is critical in Foulkes: disturbance, even though it may manifest in an individual, is in fact always a disturbance in the larger group. This is Foulkes' notion of '*location*'. Thus even though one may see a symptom in one place, one constantly has to ask: what and where is the real disturbance that is causing this symptom? Intimately linked to the notion of location are two other important Foulkesian concepts – community and communication. In order to understand them we have to look at a larger theme, his view of the nature of human society, in effect his developmental model.

But just before we do that it will be as well to summarize the main elements of Foulkes' thinking described in this section:

1. The 'part' is always connected to the 'whole'.

2. The 'whole' determines what takes place in the 'part'.

3. The 'whole' is always an artifact, an abstraction that is carved out of a greater complexity.

Foulkes' developmental model

Foulkes never explicitly described an infantile developmental theory. One can speculate that this startling omission (for an analytic theory) takes place for two possible reasons: first, because he takes Freudian infantile development as read and understood, therefore it does not need to be repeated. Second, he says that the purpose of group analysis is not to seek out the genetic cause of a disturbance in the past, but to seek it out in the contemporary network. 'Psycho-analysis is essentially a search for genetic origins... Group-analysis is not so much concerned with the question of how people have become what they are than with the question: What changes them or prevents them changing?' (Foulkes 1964, pp.141–144). Can we take this idea seriously? He actually appears to be saying that infantile development is not that pertinent to the project of group analysis.

Everything that *needs* to be found *can* be found in the here-and-now group experience. This element is reminiscent of an existential stance.

The developmental theory that Foulkes says that he follows is that of Freud. But when one gathers up what he implies in his works, in bits and pieces, then we discover that the radical Foulkes' developmental theory is quite different from that of Freud. The orthodox Foulkes too differs somewhat from Freud, but less so. What Foulkes does make explicit is in the region of metapsychology rather than psychology, and that is where we must begin.

The social

He begins: 'we take as our starting point the practice and theory of psychoanalysis' (Foulkes and Anthony 1957, p.16). He then delineates his version of the psychoanalytic model (a parody, as we have noted earlier):

> [psychoanalysis] is based on the individual in Cartesian isolation; one body, one brain, one mind. The world is built up from bodily needs and sensations, although an outside reality, impersonal and objective, is recognized. Social relations are secondary, the primary relationship or even unity with the mother is understood to start with only as a relationship between two erotogenic zones: the mouth and nipple. (Foulkes 1964, p.124).

This is where he strikes his first hammer blow – he asserts that social relations are not secondary after-events, but that they permeate everything and that they critically inform all psychological states and structures. In contrast to Freud, who emphasized the instinctual nature of human beings, Foulkes emphasizes the social nature of human beings. But in order to make the point, Foulkes misrepresents the complexity of Freud. Further, with this idea Foulkes comes closer to Fairbairn than anyone else, but either he does not see it, or he fails to mention it.

We will take up two aspects of the social separately. The first concerns the notion of a social 'instinct' which belongs with the orthodox Foulkes, and the second the notion of social relations which belongs with radical Foulkes.

The 'social instinct'

For Foulkes, the primary impetus is to belong. 'Man is primarily a social being, a particle of a group' (Foulkes and Anthony 1957, p.234). 'In the most asocial and antisocial individuals, one can discern the wish [to belong], which is tantamount to saying that, fundamentally, man is a group animal' (Foulkes and Anthony 1957, p.157).

However, orthodox Foulkes derives this primary urge to belong in a rather peculiar way – he derives it from a version of phylogenetic inheritance. He has a view that groups are more fundamental than individuals *because* groups arose in antiquity. He equates this with primitive states of mind. It is a version of 'recapitulation' – of ontogeny recapitulating phylogeny – and in this formulation he is truly Freudian: 'The more elementary and primitive the level of human existence that we observe, the less personal individuality and independence from the group do we meet' (Foulkes and Anthony 1957, p.234).

It is possible to discern an important error in logic here. Foulkes has historicized what might well be a cognitive or even a subjective experiential truth. This possible 'truth' is that what we *first* experience is the greater whole, which we *then* fragment into parts.[5] Foulkes has historicized a contemporary experience by equating the notion of 'fundamental' with 'earlier in time'. The error is to take a contemporary sequence of events in an individual, be it developmental or cognitive, and then to say that it happens in this order now, *because* it must have happened like so in the history of the species. This is another version of the psychological fallacy which says that 'deeper' inevitably means 'earlier'. The slippage in logic continues with a series of associations that are conflated: from 'fundamental' to 'earlier' to 'primitive' to 'primitive humans'.

Thus Foulkes and Anthony are saying that groups evolved during a primitive time of human evolution, and to be in that state today is *to be* less individuated and more primitive. This is a strangely anti-group formulation which is further compounded a little later: 'The assumption of a 'social instinct' inside this individual could be looked upon as an example of Freud's concept of the 'conservative' nature of instincts, in the sense that their 'aim' is to restore a previous state of affairs' (Foulkes and Anthony 1957, p.234). They are saying that the 'social instinct' is part of the phylogenetic inheritance, and that it is an attempt to get back to a lost era. They have, in a sense, pathologized the impulse to belong and participate, by describing it as a throwback to a primitive time. It seems to me that they have missed an opportunity to make something substantial of the social – and have instead reduced it to something prehistoric. They have rendered the notion of belongingness no real services here.

Let us look at this next passage closely:

> When a number of isolated individuals are brought together…we observe bewilderment, suspicion, fear…and…an overwhelmingly strong impulse…to make contact and to re-establish the old and deeply rooted modes of group behaviour. We think indeed that as the group takes hold and the formerly isolated individuals have felt again the compelling currents of ancient tribal feeling, it permeates them to the very core and that all their subsequent interactions are inescapably embedded in this common matrix. (Foulkes and Anthony 1957, p.235)

---

5   '[T]he whole is more elementary than the parts…what we experience in the first place is the *group as a whole*.' (Foulkes 1966, p.154)

It is rather a strange notion that sets about evacuating meaning from the present, and projecting it into the past. The passage implies that people do not group in the present because of contemporary needs and desires, but to fulfil a desire from a lost prehistoric time – the time of ancient tribal feelings. This is pure Le Bon, to be in a group is to be in a primitive frame of mind.

Interestingly, ten years earlier Foulkes had chastised 'Psycho-Analysis' for doing the very same thing, for jumping to hypothetical assumptions of prehistoric life:

> ...what forms the content and object of our mental life...is of necessity being constantly modified by these 'external' circumstances. This statement might surprise Psycho-Analysts for the moment,...until they understand that Psycho-Analysis alone holds the key position for a scientific understanding of this process... namely, in showing how the restrictions which society demands are communicated to the growing child until they become second nature, and why and in what way the prohibitions accumulated in history become transferred to each new generation... All this, it should be noted, can be shown to take place in historical times, *and there is no need to jump at once to hypothetical assumptions of prehistoric life.*' (Foulkes 1948, pp.13–14; emphasis added)

It seems curious that in order to give explanation for the existence of the need to belong to a group he feels the need to revert to these self same hypothetical assumptions. In summary, orthodox Foulkes says that there is an impulse to belong but this is a throwback to a more primitive time.

Social relations

Radical Foulkes argues that the usual way of viewing 'social relations' as something 'outside' is a fallacy, because the very dichotomy inside/outside is a fallacy.

> As group analysts we do not share the psychoanalytical juxtaposition of an 'internal' psychological reality and an 'external' physical or social reality which, for psychoanalysis, makes good sense. What is inside is outside, the "social" is not external but very much internal too and penetrates the innermost being of the individual personality. (Foulkes 1973a, pp.226–7)

This critical statement means that one now has to find a way to theorize the internalization of culture. But here, even as we *begin* to speak about this, saying things like 'the internalization of culture' – language itself starts to fail. To elaborate: implicit in the word 'internalization' is the idea that culture starts on the 'outside' and goes inside; but this is the very thing that is being argued against. The strong version of Foulkes' theory leads to something much more difficult to describe – where culture is neither outside nor inside – it is everywhere; to use his favourite word – it permeates.

Unfortunately, Foulkes does not take this thought any further. Having said that culture permeates, he does not go on to tussle with *the way* in which it permeates – he just says that it does. This is a serious omission in his theory. This is one of the statements that he repeats many times in his four volumes, almost word for word. One can speculate that he did not proceed further than this, because he could not. If nothing is added to the assertion that culture permeates, if no elaboration is given, then the assertion is reduced to sentiment rather than scientific argument. The task he has avoided is an extremely difficult one, because one has to theorize anew not only *how* culture permeates, but also *what culture actually is*. This is because the version of 'culture' that is familiar to us is one that is born out of the false[6] dichotomy, nature and nurture. As things stand, the only way we *can* currently think and speak about culture, is as something on the outside that then goes inside. We literally have to find a new way and new language for thinking about it.

The problem is compounded by the fact that Foulkes uses the three terms, 'culture', 'social' and 'external', interchangeably.[7] Moreover, his use of the words 'culture' and 'social', are curiously asocial. *Much like Fairbairn, he uses 'culture' and 'social' to mean 'external'.* To elaborate: 'social relations' means, at the very least, relations between people; and this means, at the very least, that one has to take into account the social positioning of people relative to each other, social hierarchies, power relations between people and groups, and so forth. Given the significance Foulkes tries to attribute to the arena of the social, the absence of a theorization of social relations from his own work is striking. I have found just one passage in which weight is given to social *relations* themselves:

> Infantile sexuality, incest barriers, are all based on the species and its cultural development... The culture and values of a community are inescapably transferred to the growing infant by its individual father and mother as determined by their *particular nation, class, religion, and region*. They are transmitted verbally or non-verbally, instinctively, and emotionally twenty four hours a day and night. Even the objects, movements, gestures, and accents are determined in this way by these representatives of the cultural group. On top of this, but all permeating, is the particular individual father and mother. (Foulkes and Anthony 1957, p.27; emphasis added)

For me, this is Foulkes potentially at his most exciting. He is breaking new ground here, beginning to move away from universalistic psychologies of development. He is saying that the thing that is internalized is *the social relation*, and not just an external object. However, the full implication of this statement leads into very

6   According to Foulkes that is.

7   For example in this sentence: '...an "external" physical or social reality' (Foulkes 1973a, pp.226–227; emphasis added).

dangerous territory: it implies that the form and content of the internal object relational world will be partly dependent on *where* one is positioned in the socio-cultural context, and will also be dependent on *which* socio-cultural context one is born into. This would literally mean that *the structure of the psyche* varies from peoples to peoples. The structure of the psyche is particularized, and made contingent on positioning within the socio-political context. This is to take the logic of his statement to an extreme, and has led us from a place of saying 'we are all the same' to saying 'we are all inexorably different'. Left like this it appears to give authority and justification for apartheid. This problematic idea will be examined in more detail in the last section of the book.

In his earlier group analytic writings, Foulkes seeks to remain within the psychoanalytic orthodoxy by saying that in emphasizing the social, he is not contradicting the crucial role of the instincts: 'Conceiving the social nature of man as basic does not deny or reduce the importance of the sexual instinct in the sense of psychoanalysis, nor of the aggressive instinct. The infant–mother relationship is the first social relationship in the same sense as it is the first sexual and love relationship' (Foulkes 1964, p.109). But some years later radical Foulkes does in fact challenge the basis of the instincts: 'the so-called inner processes in the individual are internalizations of the forces operating in the group to which he belongs' (Foulkes 1971, p.212). More of that later.

Modifying the Freudian developmental frame

A major consequence of the elevation and prioritization of culture is not only a modification in the genesis of the ego and superego, but also, in the most radical version of his theory, a modification of id, the bastion of biology itself.

Foulkes begins with Freud. However, he only takes up half of Freud. It will be remembered that Freud described two sorts of conflict. The first Freudian conflict is between the instincts themselves – endogenous, and not dependent on experience. The second Freudian conflict is that between desire and reality, formulated in his theory of the two principles – pleasure and reality. Despite Foulkes' underlining of his Freudian lineage, he only ever takes up the latter conflict, and neglects the former. It is a curious fact that Foulkes does not directly refer to instinctual conflict, even to disagree with it. It cannot be that Foulkes does not know about it, he was a fully trained psychoanalyst after all. There might be two possible reasons for this. First, it does not suit his argument, in which experience is made to count for everything. Second, and more important, if he elaborates on this difference with Freud too much, then it will expose the radical nature of his stance, thus jeopardizing his standing in the psychoanalytic community. Effectively, Foulkes has collapsed this complexity into a version of the nature–nurture dichotomy. However, it will be possible to find some theoretical justification for this collapse, as we proceed.

To begin with Freud's developmental model. His infant enters the world all id. A little later the ego is precipitated, to facilitate the instincts to fulfil their aim (discharge). And lastly, the superego is born out of the resolution of the Oedipus Complex, when the child is between three and five years old. According to Freud, the resolution of the Oedipus Complex is when the social enters the psyche, relatively late, and enters only as far as the superego and ego. The id is untouched by the social.

For Foulkes' idea to work, the cultural element has to be there much earlier, thus the ego and superego, as containers of elements of the social, have also to exist much earlier. This aligns him closely with Klein's (1933) notion of the early development of the ego and superego. Interestingly, he does not mention her here,[8] and instead uses Spitz. 'I completely agree with Rene Spitz (1958)...Spitz has clearly shown that ego and superego formation is underway in the earliest periods of life' (Foulkes 1973b, p.247).

Now, Foulkes elaborates two quite different theories, and, as before, there is one theory of radical potential, and another one that is more in line with psychoanalytic orthodoxy. And, as before, he neglects to differentiate between them. Let me begin with the more orthodox version.

The id – unbreached

Although Foulkes parts somewhat with Freud on the issue of the timing of the genesis of the ego and superego, in this theoretical version he still remains within a broad Freudian framework, the framework being the conflict between society and biology replicated and located in internal psychological structures. For example, Foulkes says: 'Freud has unearthed the human *conflict* which arises exactly between the dual biological and cultural inheritance of man...reflected by the conflict between the Id, and the Ego and Superego...' (Foulkes 1964, p.156).

In the main, this is the theory that Foulkes holds to, where, like Freud, he allows the social in as far as the superego and ego. Here are three examples: 'our ego and superego are socially conditioned institutions' (Foulkes 1941, p.84). 'the family group and its influence is precipitated in the innermost core of the human mind, incorporated into the child's growing ego and superego, forming their very nucleus' (Foulkes 1948, pp.15–16); 'we see therefore that cultural factors enter even into the study of constitution itself, that ego and superego are socially conditioned and quite certainly, that pathogenesis and cure depend essentially on the group.' (Foulkes 1964, p.148).

---

8   Again, this is a curious omission. To speculate: the split in the psychoanalytic community in London was in the main between the Kleinians and the Freudians. As a declared Freudian Foulkes could not allow himself to be seen to align himself so explicitly with Klein here – presumably it would have been seen as consorting with the enemy.

So there is nothing new here, nothing group analytic. Here he remains with Freud, and repeats him.

The breaching of the id

In his later writings we discover that Foulkes, when discussing the penetration of the psyche by the social, in statements like the ones above, occasionally and without announcing it in any way casually throws the id in with the ego and superego: 'what in later development can be usefully abstracted as superego, ego and id arise from a common matrix, beginning at birth or perhaps even prenatally' (Foulkes 1973b, p.236). This sleight of hand has enormous implications, it makes this part of the theory anti-Freud.

In doing this, Foulkes goes much further than anyone else. He says that *the id itself is acculturated*, thus allowing the forces of nurture to breach the id, the final stronghold of nature within the psyche. Other examples: 'the superego and the ego develop *pari passu*[9] with the id inside the family context...' (Foulkes 1974, p.276); 'Libidinal development, its culmination in the infantile Oedipus complex in the classical sense, the various defence mechanisms which fit in with various phases – all this remains undisputed, though *I think that even the libidinal phases and reactions to bodily functions are culturally conditioned*' (Foulkes 1974, p.275; emphasis added).

To spell this out some more: Foulkes appears to be implying that what looks to the eye like an endogenous conflict in the id, between two biological instincts and outside the domain of experience, is in fact a conflict between the Reality and Pleasure Principles. The following quote certainly seems to suggest something like this:

> the superego and the ego develop *pari passu* with the id inside the family context...early development produces many of the phenomena that are stressed by Melanie Klein, but I see this development as being brought about by the interaction of the whole family on these primitive levels. The basic human problems with which psychoanalysis is so much concerned I therefore see as being more transmitted than inherited, although the two are never watertight and apart. (Foulkes 1974, p.276)

To recapitulate, Foulkes has done two dramatic things in this radical version of his theory: first, he has surreptitiously transmuted Freud's inter-instinctual conflict into that of the nature–nurture conflict. And second, he has allowed culture to breach the final bastion of biology, the id – the roots of the psyche: 'This social influence is not added to the individual in a superficial or secondary way, but thrusts down to his roots' (Foulkes 1964, p.50).

9   Latin: 'in step with'.

This importance of this point needs further spelling out. When Foulkes says 'what in later development can be usefully abstracted as superego, ego and *id* arise from a common matrix, *beginning at birth or perhaps even prenatally*' (Foulkes 1973b, p.236; emphasis added), he is saying that the id itself is born out of experience and not inherited biology. 'What happens in every case is rather in the nature of a living *transmission* of the whole previous cultural and biological experience. I am inclined to see human development more in the light of transmission than in terms of direct, inherited, archaic repetition' (Foulkes 1973b, p.238).

As we have previously seen, there is a precedence for this idea in Freud. Remember, Freud speculated that over long periods of time, it was possible that the experiences of the ego somehow became part of the id. However, this idea and passage were never institutionalized by Freud into his schema, where the central idea remains — that the id is said to be outside and beyond the influence of experience. It is not clear whether Foulkes knew of this passage, and if he did, why he did not use it to lend weight to his argument. This speculative passage is perhaps an embarrassment to some Freudian scholars — and so little or no reference to it is ever made.

Returning to Foulkes, his two theories of the id give rise to two theories of the social unconscious, again one more challenging than the other.

The social unconscious

In his early writings Foulkes puts it like this:

> Psycho-Analysis has hitherto tried to trace the sources of the all important super-ego formation in the human species mainly in two directions: firstly, the phylogenetic, as a precipitation of pre-history (Oedipus Complex); secondly the psychogenetic, as an outcome of the history of the individual... In addition to these two modes of approach we seem to get gradual access to material which opens the way for a third, and perhaps not less important one, namely the sociogenetic (historical)...they are all linked up with each other and in a state of interaction... (Foulkes 1948, p.14)

With this idea Foulkes continues his subversion of 'inheritance' and 'biology'. It seems to me then that out of the trinity of biology, contemporary experience, and culture/history, Foulkes is led to give primacy to the last of the three — culture/history. He will be led to say that this is the thing that permeates the other two, that this is the thing that informs everything else. One can see then that he is not really for holism at all; he is for the weight of history over and above everything else. *In this sense he is a kind of Marxist.*

So what is the social unconscious supposed to be?

He begins by distinguishing the 'social unconscious' from the 'Freudian unconscious'. The location of the Freudian unconscious is said to be the id. He says:

> ...the group-analytic situation, while dealing intensively with the unconscious in the Freudian sense, [also] brings into operation and perspective a totally different *area of which the individual is equally unaware*...the individual is as much compelled and modelled by these colossal forces as by his own *id* and defends himself as strongly against their recognition without being aware of it... *One might speak of a social or interpersonal unconscious.* (Foulkes 1964, p.52; emphasis added)

He goes on to make an interesting distinction between the two types of unconscious; he says that the social unconscious *is* unconscious but *not repressed*, whilst the Freudian unconscious is both repressed and unconscious. Here he speaks about the social unconscious:

> we know that these events are covered by infantile amnesia and are in that sense dynamically unconscious...the core of the ego and superego thus formed – formed in my view from the very beginning – are also in their essential parts equally unconscious, *although not repressed.* They are unconscious because the values imbued, the whole relationship to the world...the way of expressing oneself, of breathing, of sleeping, of waking, of being amused, of speaking, the individual's total behaviour has been decisively shaped by the original family group. The individual is unconscious of this in that he is normally convinced that his way...is the natural and right one. (Foulkes 1973a, p.231)

But having said this, he does not make as much of this point as he might. Why is the social unconscious not repressed? Presumably it is because it is not 'difficult material', in other words it is not loaded up with affect. He is saying that it is unconscious in the sense of not being *aware* of it, but not because of pushing it away. The content of the social unconscious as he describes it consists of things like behaviour, ways of thinking, attitudes and so forth. These ideas give rise to two possible versions of the social unconscious, one 'weaker' and the other 'stronger' ('weaker' in the sense of being more palatable to traditional psycho-analytic theory, and 'stronger' in the sense of being more challenging of the same). Foulkes never spells out the two versions, which results in him erroneously using the term in both ways.

The 'weaker' version of the social unconscious is that it is unconscious in the sense of being *automatic*, rather than unconscious *per se*. Much in the same way one is not aware of the minutiae of walking or driving; the *automatic* elements of these processes are outside the realm of normal consciousness. These are things learnt, and so may be unlearnt, or different things learnt.

The 'stronger' version of the social unconscious says that it is unconscious in the sense that it is part of the weft and weave of the psyche itself, it forms the very *structure* of the psyche. To my mind this is the more enthralling and critical of the two ideas. This surely is the import of what he means when he says that the social permeates the psyche. To a greater or lesser extent most Anglo-Saxon psychoanalytic theories have a view in which the *structure* of the psyche is given more by biology, whilst the *content* of the psyche is given more by experience. Some theories even say that much of the content of the psyche is determined by biology and inheritance. In this, the 'strong' version of the social unconscious, Foulkes is saying that both *the structure and the content* of the psyche are profoundly informed by experience rather than inheritance: 'what in later development can be usefully abstracted as superego, ego and *id* arise from a common matrix, beginning at birth or perhaps even prenatally' (Foulkes 1973b, p.236). This is a radically different idea from the one which has the social sitting on top of the biological given, nature, or the social contained in a receptacle made by nature. In this radical version, the social unconscious constitutes the very 'bones' of the psyche, it forms the container as well as the contained. It seems to me that with this idea, Foulkes comes close to Lacan (1977), for whom the unconscious is structured by and like language – that is, by something external.

Between the internal and the external

A question that this book always has in mind is how much weight any theory gives to biology versus experience. Interrelated with this dichotomy are two others, inheritance versus transmission, and nature versus nurture. Each psycho-analytic and group analytic theory gives rise to a different configuration of the three dichotomies. Each of them has to tussle with the question of what the connection is between the inside and the outside. What is the connecting link, phenomenon, or bridge? How is it made? And so forth.

For Foulkes, in the contest between inheritance and transmission, transmission wins every time. He is in a sense a psychological Lamarckian rather than a psychological Darwinian. It has to be so within the logic of his theory. Given this fact, he has to find new explanations for early developmental phenomena. To elaborate: as we have seen, Foulkes says in some places that the dichotomies are fictions. In other places he does not really hold to this position – he is led to prioritize nurture over nature, transmission over inheritance, and experience over biology. In order to contextualize Foulkes' ideas, it might be helpful to recapitulate answers given by the other theories.

Let us begin at one end of the scale in which the supposition is that everything comes from inheritance. We then have to ask: what can be inherited? If the answer is only something biological, in which the infant knows nothing about the world, then we have a version of Freudian theory, with the infant coming into the world as instinct incarnate, all id. If one allows something about the world also to be inherited, then we arrive at a version of Kleinian theory, in which the instincts have a notion of their object embedded into them, the thing in the world that will satisfy them – such as a template of the breast. As is well known this is reminiscent of Kant's (1990) ideas.

Fairbairn's thought is that the infant comes into the world almost completely focused on it, ready to relate, as it were. His neonate has no inside. His infant inherits a desire to relate to the external world. Winnicott's answers to the questions are more complicated. His bridge between inside and outside is formed in the moment of the 'creative act' – the magical moment in which the presented-from-the-outside meets the imagined-from-the-inside.

We move to the other end of the scale, to Foulkes' supposition that experience counts for almost everything. He now has a problem. If experience is everything, what is going on in the infant before it has experience? How is he to explain the genesis of the powerful feelings that a new infant clearly has? Theories of inheritance have no difficulty to answer this, because they say that the infant comes into the world with the means to feel, and also, to some extent, what to feel (hate, envy, anxiety, love etc.). Foulkes gives two unrelated answers to the question.

First he says that the structures might begin before birth, 'that what in later development can be usefully abstracted as superego, ego and id arise from a common matrix, beginning at birth or perhaps *even prenatally*' (Foulkes 1973b, p.236; emphasis added). But to keep in line with his other ideas, this would mean that the social would somehow have to migrate across the womb and enter the neonate. He avoids engaging in the subject of how such an extraordinary thing might occur, which surely he is beholden to do.

Second, he adopts a Chomskian idea that what is inherited is 'potential': 'What is inherited is probably more in the nature of, say, *the capacity* to learn to speak or write; without preformed potential, experience alone could never produce these abilities' (Foulkes 1973b, p.238; emphasis added). Having given some ground to the notion of inheritance here, for Foulkes everything else comes from experience.

Recasting the life and death instincts

The explanation that both Klein and Freud gave for the infant's capacity to feel things very powerfully was that the infant came into the world with a tendency to organize experience into pure good and pure bad. This tendency was attributed eventually to the notion of the endogenous instincts of death and life.

Given Foulkes' emphasis on transmission and experience, he is led to derive the life and death instincts themselves out of experience.

He begins by arguing that:

> Complicated emotions can be felt even by the small child as they are actually represented and transmitted, however unconsciously, by the parents, brothers, sisters and so on. These norms and values are engraved in the individual; they form his ego and his superego from the beginning and are of incredible strength. (Foulkes 1974, p.276)

He then goes on to say that these powerful experiences polarize within the individual – and that these give the *appearance* of instincts:

The processes by which, since prehistoric times, human beings assimilate images produce condensations that can be both anxiety-ridden and highly destructive. *Polarizations can arise* between the absolutely pure, absolutely loved, on the one hand, and the absolutely hated, dangerous forces on the other. These may become attached to particular persons. (Foulkes 1990, p.282; emphasis added)

He is arguing that what look like the life and death instincts do not exist *a priori*, but are in fact born out of a set of assimilated (that is, taken in) images, that are *then* divided.[10]

He takes the point further and argues that *all* so-called internal objects have their basis in external objects:

It is justifiable to assume that this [the polarization] has an inner counterpart, that there is something not necessarily externalized corresponding to these processes inside our own minds. I think however, that these configurations – seen as 'inner objects' – are in themselves personifications and projections into our own minds. As a rule however they are not experienced as being inside our own minds, and they become conscious only when brought to life by being projected on other persons. (Foulkes 1990, p.282)

This is a critical passage, written late in his life, in which he confirms he thinks *that all psychological phenomena start on the outside: 'the so-called inner processes* in the individual are internalizations of the forces operating in the group to which he belongs' (Foulkes 1971, p.212; emphasis added). He had already nailed his colours to the mast many years before in his very first book:

We must…evaluate the analytical situation, including all its 'unconscious' components, as determined by the patient's total life situation, and not, contrawise, see 'life' and 'reality' merely as projection, screen and reflector of his 'unconscious phantasies', which they are indeed, at the same time. The truth is that the two [reality of projection] can never be separated. (Foulkes 1948, p.15)

On the surface it appears that Foulkes' notion of history permeating the psyche is very similar to Freud's version of the superego. It will be remembered that Freud had said:

…a child's super-ego is in fact constructed on the model not of its parents but its parents' superego; the contents which fill it are the same and it becomes the vehicle of tradition and of all the time-resisting judgements of value which have propagated themselves in this manner from generation to generation… (Freud 1933, p.67)

Compare this to Foulkes:

10   One has to ask here of Foulkes, why do the polarizations arise in the first place – why should the experiences be organized in this way? If he jettisons the death and life instincts, then what other explanation does he offer? He himself gives no answer, but in the last part of the book some new formulations will be proposed.

The original family is indeed the primary network in which the personality of the future individual is decisively formed... *It has, as it were, a vertical axis pointing to the past, to the parents, to the parent's own childhood, to the parent's relationship to their own parents, all of which enter into the innermost core of the forming child.* (Foulkes 1973a, p.231; emphasis added)

In effect the radical Foulkes has extended Freud. Foulkes has used the same mechanism that Freud allocates for the entry of the social into the superego, for the *contents* of *all* the psychic structures, as well as the *substance* of the structures themselves. But in doing this, Foulkes has extended Freud so far, that he has ended up reversing him. Now, Foulkes may no longer refer to his Freudian antecedents; in reframing the instincts in this way Foulkes has completely removed the basis of Freudian theory. To my mind it is not overstating it to say that this part of Foulkes' theory is anti-Freudian.

To recapitulate: the Foulkesian social unconscious has two components, the weight of tradition and history, as well as contemporary reality in the shape of the particular external mother and father. He has moved a long way from Klein with these ideas. It will be remembered that for her the instincts critically inform experience. Her direction being from inside to the outside, it matters less for her what the actual parents are like. One is *driven* to experience them in particularly extreme ways because of the instincts. Foulkes is saying the reverse. For him experience actually creates internal structures. His direction is from the outside to the inside. For Foulkes experience creates the instincts, or to be more precise, creates the things that *look like endogenous instincts* to Klein. For Foulkes the instincts are internalized coagulations of types of experience. The individual is 'pressed into shape' not by internal forces, but external ones:

When we look seriously at the group as the essential frame of reference in psychology, we understand that the individual is inevitably a fragment shaped dynamically by the group in which he first grew up...a piece of a jigsaw puzzle... When you take this individual fragment out of its context, it is shaped and formed, or deformed, according to the place it had and the experiences it received in this group. The first group is normally the family. This family, willy-nilly, reflects the culture to which it belongs and in turn transmits the cultural norms and values. (Foulkes 1974, p.275)

Some group specific ideas

The arguments in the chapter so far have been focused around the individual – how the individual is embedded and formed by the social, the group. We will now change levels, and view Foulkesian theory from the vantage point of the group itself. There are three critical ideas in Foulkes concerning the structure and nature of groups: those of community, of communication, and of location.

The notion of 'community'

Foulkes uses the term 'community' to describe several different sorts of things. First and foremost, 'community' is a description of the context in which human life takes place. The notion of community is used to describe social grouping on many scales: family, tribe, nation, humankind, among others. However, his use of the term is problematic. Up to now we have seen that Foulkes has been arguing that groups are abstractions, that they are contingent, that they can only be commented on and experienced in relation to other groups and so on. Effectively, he has been speaking about groups as a post-structuralist. It is an irony that with his notion of community, he begins to slip back into a logical positivist mode of thinking, by essentializing some groupings and elevating them above others:

> there are such fundamental social groups as the **family, the clan, or even an entire nation.** In such groups the members are vitally interdependent; as a class they are best called *communities*…human life is never found outside such groups. These fundamental groups, *root groups*, and especially the family group, are in one sense the true objects of treatment, for the mental health of the individual is dependent on his community. (Foulkes and Anthony 1957, p.31; bold added, italics original)

By saying that some social configurations are fundamental, he is saying two things. First, that they are 'natural' phenomena, thus they form inevitably, as night follows day. Additionally, the list of fundamental or root groups that he supplies in the above passage look very much like so-called 'blood' groups – family, clan, nation. We can see that Foulkes has stumbled here. *Despite his great stress on the social, he ends up giving his fundamental groupings – root groups – a biological basis.*

The second thing that follows out of the idea of fundamental groups is the implication that the other sorts of groupings that occur will be less fundamental, therefore less important. He alludes to these sorts of groups as 'spontaneous' groups: 'In our culture all sorts of groups arise *spontaneously*, each with a more or less clear purpose…gangs…neighbourhood groups, children's play groups, factory groups…[these are studied through] the work of the Tavistock Institute of Human Relations' (Foulkes and Anthony 1957, p.32). So, despite himself, he finds himself once more trapped in the nature–nurture dichotomy. Root groups are seen as born of nature, whilst spontaneous groups are born of nurture.[11] He implies that spontaneous groups, being artificial, have to have a sense of purpose, a reason to exist. Root groups, being natural, just become, they need no more reason to be than, say, a tree. These spontaneous groups are broken down into three further categories: *activity groups*, such as religious groups; *therapeutic groups*,

---

11   Foulkes has also slipped in a small attack on the other major theoretician of groups, W. D. Bion, and his territory, the Tavistock Clinic. By implication Foulkes studies 'real' groups, whilst the Tavistock studies 'spontaneous' or lesser groups.

that is, groups with a therapeutic purpose, such as music groups; *psychotherapeutic groups*, that is, treatment groups (Foulkes and Anthony 1957, pp.35–36).

If one is to naturalize anything, I would say that the thing that is natural to human beings is a tendency to group. This echoes Foulkes' sentiment that the human being is a social animal. I would disagree with Foulkes when he says that certain groups are more fundamental than others. To my mind, all groupings are contingent, and make more or less sense depending on the context in which they occur. Some groupings, like the family, appear everywhere, but this does not make them fundamental on the basis of 'blood'. It is not biology that makes family important, but the emotional and material functions that it serves. Also this debate begs the question of what a family actually is – which biological configuration will be called 'the' family? Foulkes elevates the family above all other groupings. This makes sense if one thinks of the family (as Foulkes sometimes does) as the element that mediates the transmission of the social to the individual child. The importance of the family, then, is due to its function, proximity and positioning, and not in any way due to its supposed essential nature. To my mind Foulkes has fallen into the essentialist fallacy by the *type* of importance he has designated to the family group.

The notion of 'communication'

Another way that Foulkes uses the term community is in a more poetic sense, and by this means he slides into another one of his basic ideas, that of communication: 'One of the assumptions we implicitly make is the basic and not the secondary character of the social nature of man, the existence of a constant stream of communication, verbal and non-verbal, conscious and unconscious, *indeed a community of experience*' (Foulkes 1964, p.125).

The passage above implies that the thing that holds together a community, the glue, as it were, is communication. The notion of communication follows out of Foulkes' central thesis – that the social nature of man is basic. 'Social' means things going on between people, and 'things going on' equals communication. He says that communication is 'making common'. 'Making common' is made identical to 'community'. Foulkes and Anthony say 'the close linguistic affinity between the words 'communication' and 'community' is an unconscious recognition of this fact' (1957, p.247).

The importance of the notion of communication in Foulkes' work cannot be overstated. Almost everything can be put in terms of communication. Foulkes even goes so far as to derive mind itself from the need to communicate. Freud, it will be remembered, suggested that the mind came about to help the instincts discharge. Meanwhile Foulkes suggests that it is the impulse or desire to communicate that gives rise to the mind. In other words, in Foulkesian theory, the first reason for the emergence of the mind is to function as a transmitter and receiver of communication – a radio station. 'I think that the real nature of mind lies in each individual's need for communication and reception' (Foulkes 1974, p.278).

He makes a similar suggestion for the existence of language, that it too exists because of a *need* to communicate: 'The fundamental instrument of communication is language and language is itself born from *the need to communicate*, from the very force which impels the members of a group to interact' (Foulkes and Anthony 1957, pp.244–245; emphasis added).

As the need to communicate is a consequence of the social nature of man, language and thus the mind are reframed as group phenomena.

> Language could not be acquired by any individual without his capacity to acquire it in his brain… Language is one of the main and most significant mental phenomena that can only be maintained and be meaningful as a group phenomenon…individuals…communicate without knowing it, so that one could say that it is in the first place these unconscious processes that go on between them which permeate each individual. (Foulkes 1974, p.278)

This leads to the innovative idea – that 'mind' which, up to now, has been firmly embedded inside a person, is reframed as an interpersonal phenomenon. 'I do not think that the mind is basically inside the person as an individual… *The mind that is usually called intrapsychic is a property of the group*, and the processes that take place are due to the dynamic interactions in this communicational matrix' (Foulkes 1974, pp.277–278; emphasis added).

The picture is being dramatically redrawn – and we are being inexorably led to a view of groups as a communicational network, in which the individuals are nodal points, with communicational lines criss-crossing through them. We have come a long way from a picture that gives primacy to the individual, and an individual that is constituted mainly by biology and internal dynamics. The individual is now, in a sense, relegated to a function. The main thing is communication – the individuals are but the means of achieving that. In the old picture, the important thing is the material *within* each individual. What is made important now is the function of the individual in the intercommunicational network. This is a fundamental shift in the philosophical vision of the nature and purpose of the human being.

Two models of communication

Foulkes has two types of description of communication, one complex and the other reductive. To my mind the first description is the more powerful one of the two, and draws its language from electromagnetic field theory:

> the group-analytic view would claim that all these interactional processes play in a *unified mental field* of which the individuals composing it are a part… The point I wish to stress is that *this network is a psychic system as a whole network*, and not a

superimposed social interaction system in which the individual minds interact with each other. (Foulkes 1973a, p.226; emphasis added)

Communication comes to stand for *everything* that happens between people: 'In talking of communication we are thinking of all these processes, conscious and unconscious, intentional and unintentional, understood and not understood, which operate between people in a group' (Foulkes and Anthony 1957, p.244). Thus communication encompasses terms like transference, counter-transference, projection and projective identification. They are all communications, sometimes conscious, but mostly unconscious. To my mind this version of communication is a significant and helpful contribution to theory. Foulkes says: 'All phenomena in an analytic therapeutic group are considered as potential communications. This dynamic way of putting it eliminates the need for the usual concept of the repressed unconscious, defences and so forth, which is necessitated in a psycho-analytic orientation' (Foulkes 1973a, p.226).

The other description of communication is more prosaic and breaks down the continuum of the *field* into parts called transmitters and receivers: 'no process has fully become a communication until there are signs that it has in fact been reacted to, that it has linked a transmitter and a receiver. The process need not be conscious, but it probably is partly conscious as soon as it deserves the name of communication' (Foulkes and Anthony 1957, p.244). Now Foulkes and Anthony can't have it both ways: on the one hand they say that it has to be partly conscious to be called a communication, and on the other hand they say that the process need not be conscious and it is still a communication! Do they mean that some aspect of the communication is inevitably conscious or pre-conscious? Surely the astonishing thing about an unconscious communication is that the whole process takes place unknown to the ego, the communicating self. Both the transmission and the reception take place and are registered unconsciously! One could say of unconscious communication *that it is out of sight, but not out of mind*. They compound the error a few pages later when they say: 'Communication is everything happening... *which can be noticed*, it is everything sent out and received with response whether consciously or unconsciously' (Foulkes and Anthony 1957, p.259; emphasis added). It is possible that Foulkes and Anthony mean that there has to be the *possibility* of the communication being noticed by a third party – but that does not really address the criticism, as earlier in the same volume they say that communication does take place without consciousness: '...it must be remembered that what is dynamically unconscious is also at the same time subject to the primary process. It belongs to the system *ucs* that is to say it is cast in a primitive symbolic language. The language is understood unconsciously, and transmission – *communication* – *does take place without consciousness*' (Foulkes and Anthony 1957, pp.27–28; emphasis added).

To recapitulate, in this latter description of communication, they have said three contradictory things: (1) communication takes place *without consciousness*; (2) communication *is partly conscious* as soon as it deserves the name of communication; and (3) communication is anything which can be *noticed*. I think that these contradictions arise because they have tried to reduce the rich and sophisticated notion of a communicational field into its components. In fact they have attempted the very thing that Foulkes is so insistent is a mistake – the abstraction of a unity into parts. Why have these contradictions occurred? And why are they invisible to Foulkes and Anthony? Possible reasons will be gone into in the section entitled 'Levels of perception'.

Levels of communication

Foulkes and Anthony broke communication down into different levels, some unconscious and some conscious. They redefined the therapeutic task in the language of communication.

> In thinking of mental levels we may picture them schematically as steps on a staircase. Below a certain step...the mental content is, as a rule, 'unconscious' in the analytic sense, and is expressed in 'primary' language... On the top level of the staircase is clear, logical communication in words. At this level the 'secondary' processes of the mind operate. (Foulkes and Anthony 1957, p.259)

They equate verbal communication with the therapeutic process itself: 'communication is a process which moves from remote and primitive levels of the psyche to ever richer and more articulate modes of conscious expression, and...it is closely bound up with the therapeutic process' (Foulkes and Anthony 1957, p.246). They liken this process to that of dream analysis, of moving from the manifest to latent levels of meaning, and call this process 'translation': '...group-analytic theory recognizes this translation as part of the process of *communication*' (Foulkes 1964, p.111).

One can see then what a powerful conception the notion of communication is: (1) the need for it precipitates the mind; (2) it is the glue that binds a group together; (3) it is an ever existing network, fluctuating and flowing between the nodal points in the group; (4) therapy itself is a manifestation of the changing form of communication. 'We might describe the route taken from the autistic nature of the symptom to the more and more articulate recognition and formulation of the problem underlying that symptom as an important landmark of the therapeutic process itself' (Foulkes 1964, p.52).

The highest level of communication is said to be language. Foulkes elevates language to a sublime height, giving it great weight and significance.

> When we select language rather than action as our chosen instrument of therapy in the group we are choosing *the most perfect instrument of communication* which the group possesses. ... It is an instrument forever on the anvil, continually under the

hammer of new experience and feeling arising in the individual and the group.
(Foulkes and Anthony 1957, pp.244–245; emphasis added)

The reason why language is given so much weight is because it is a social artifact. According to Foulkes, when something can be voiced in language, then it is available to the entire network. And by definition, this availability is equated with health. When the meaning is blocked up somewhere in the network, when it cannot for some reason be put into language, then, by definition, it is equated with ill health.

The ultimate aim of therapy is to help the patient verbalize the conflict, to help the patient *translate* his symptom into a social medium, language, and thus make it available to the network. 'The group, through processes of progressive communication, works its way through from this primary, symbolic level of expression into a conscious, articulate language. This *work in communication* is the operational basis of all therapy in the group' (Foulkes and Anthony 1957, p.28).

Illness as the location of disturbance

The central role allocated to the instincts in traditional psychoanalytic theories is taken in Foulkes' theory by the notion of communication. Health is defined as the free flow of communication through the network, the community. From this it follows that ill health is a disruption in the free flow of this communication: 'mental sickness has a disturbance of integration within the community at its very roots – a disturbance of communication' (Foulkes and Anthony 1957, p.24).

Ill health is thought of as a disturbance in communication, a blockage that gets located in a particular individual or configuration of individuals; effectively, the disturbance is *located* in a particular place. 'The neurotic [and psychotic] disturbance is bound up with deficient communicability and is therefore blocked... The language of the symptom, although already a form of communication, is autistic. It mumbles to itself secretly, hoping to be overheard; its equivalent meaning conveyed in words is social' (Foulkes and Anthony 1957, p.260). When autistic meaning is converted into social meaning, then communication flows again and health is restored. '[The therapeutic process is] directed towards increasing transformation from autistic neurotic symptom formation to articulate formulation of problems which can be shared and faced by all in common' (Foulkes 1964, p.42).

Health and the therapeutic process are equated with communication: 'to become conscious, to verbalize, and to communicate are integral parts of the therapeutic process. It is extremely probable that we are describing a single process' (Foulkes and Anthony 1957, p.246).

A point that Foulkes emphasizes again and again is that both health and disturbance are things that belong to the group as a whole, the network, and not just the individual; '...the disturbance which we see in front of us, embodied in a particular patient, is in fact the expression of a disturbed balance in a total field of interaction which involves a number of different people as participants' (Foulkes and Anthony 1957, p.54). Psychological illness may be redefined as a perturbation, an anomaly in the communicational field.

This is in contradistinction to Winnicott who thought that it was the coming together of healthy individuals that made for a healthy group. Foulkes is saying that whether individuals are healthy or not will be almost completely dependent on the state of the group to which they belong.

Levels of perception

When complexities are reduced, then they inevitably give rise to contradictions. There is an analogy for this to be found in the world of modern physics. When we try to understand the quantum universe in ordinary language, we are startled by incomprehensible and impossible descriptions of reality in which somehow a thing manages to exist in several different places *at the same time*, or a thing exists and does not exist *simultaneously*, and so forth. Ordinary language born out of our four-dimensional world inevitably fails when we try to use it to describe realities more complex than that for which it was intended – indeed as do our minds fail even to imaginatively comprehend such realities.

It seems to me that Foulkes' notion of a communicational network, a communicational field, is exactly such a complexity, beyond our normal way of experiencing things, a higher order of reality.

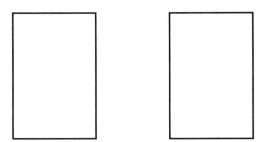

Figure 2.2

I would like here to draw an analogy from the world of geometry to make a point a little more clear. Take two rectangles (see Figure 2.2).

From a two-dimensional point of view (of a two-dimensional being living on the flat paper), these two rectangles look quite separate and unconnected. But now let us allow ourselves the privilege of looking in three dimensions at the page and the same rectangles (see Figure 2.3).

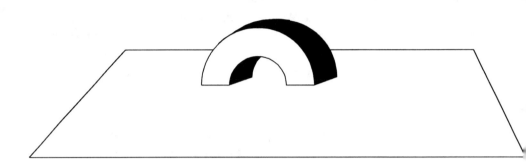

Figure 2.3

We discover in this particular case that if we take account of the third dimension the rectangles are joined – more, they are part of the same unity. In the two-dimensional world, to say that the two rectangles are part of a greater whole sounds nonsensical, whereas in three dimensions it is self evident.

This gives us a way of thinking about what is meant when we say that the isolation of individuals is illusory. In the psychological equivalent of the two-dimensional world (our normal experience), people *look* separated out from each other. In the equivalent of the three-dimensional world, the language of the 'field', they are part of a greater whole. The psychological interconnectedness of individuals is in a realm that is outside our experiential possibility, as well as beyond our language. Physicists might intellectually comprehend that there are more spatial dimensions and greater levels of unity, but these levels are forever out of their *experiential* reach.

This idea gives us a different, and more sympathetic, way of understanding the two versions of Foulkesian theory. The radical theory is announced from a higher level of complexity, the dimension beyond lived experience – the level of the group. The more orthodox theory is announced from within the known region of lived experience – the level of the individual. Language has evolved within the 'orthodox' frame – that is, the realm we experience. Thus attempts to use this language for a job for which it was not intended are bound to give rise to problems and contradictions. We can now give two sorts of explanations for the contradictions in Foulkes' thinking. First, his attempts to describe complex reality with 'ordinary' language are inevitably partial and precarious; it is not surprising that he often collapses back into the known world, the experience of individuals separated from each other in space. Thus, as we have already seen, the fact that language is structured through binary oppositions means that one is limited to words like internalization and externalization. A language form outside binary structures does not exist. Foulkes perhaps came close with his term 'permeate'. Second, this also gives us a more benign way of understanding the repetition in Foulkes' writing. These are places where he is endlessly circling an idea, trying to get to a new way of thinking – perhaps having an inkling of something else there – but the tools that he has available mean that he is unable to make the experiential leap into this more complex region.

However, radical Foulkes has managed to describe something about this more complex level of unity: the notion of the communicational network. From this perspective one can say that it may look and feel to us that we are a set of disconnected individuals, each having nothing to do with the other. Radical Foulkes would say that this is indeed an illusion, and in fact we are all intimately connected through being part of a greater whole – the group. Rather fancifully we could say that the relationship of group analytic theory to psychoanalytic theory has the potential to be in a similar relationship to that of quantum mechanics to Newtonian mechanics.

To change the language, the power of the notion of the communicational field is in the fact that it is a systemic conceptualization. In systems theory one cannot ask what is the cause and what is the effect. For example in a dysfunctional couple, say, one partner drinks and the other nags. In linear thinking one might construe that the one who drinks does so to get away from the one who nags, in effect we would be saying that the drinking is *caused* by the nagging. Or one might reverse the causal link and say the nagging is *caused* by the drinking. A systemic way of viewing the situation is precisely that – systemic. Cause and effect are rendered meaningless. One says that the system is dysfunctional, and so what one tries to address is the system as a whole. So it is with the complexity of the communicational field. To reduce it to receivers and transmitters is to reduce it to a linear way of thinking, to cause and effect, and it is this that gives rise to the contradictions we have come upon earlier.

Foulkes made much of the Gestalt notion of 'figure-and-ground', as a helpful way of thinking about thinking about groups. Foulkes says that in the mind, sometimes the individual is in the foreground (figure) and the group is the background against which the individual is viewed. At other times it is the group that comes to the front of the mind. One can apply this same attitude to the two Foulkes to some degree. Sometimes Foulkes speaks from the perspective of the individual – orthodox Foulkes – and sometimes he speaks from the perspective of the group – radical Foulkes. Sometimes one Foulkes is figure and the other ground, and sometimes the other way around. However if one viewed the two Foulkes in only this way, then there is a danger that one excuses and glosses over the many contradictions and inconsistencies in Foulkes. Contradictions that are not to do with the perspective, but are contradictions *per se*.

The matrix

The term that Foulkesian group analysts tend to reach for more than any other is that of the matrix. This notion has come to hold a central place in Foulkesian group analytic theory as it is redolent with impressions of the interconnectedness of existence. On the surface it looks like an idea that belongs to radical Foulkes, but as we look deeper we will find that really the idea belongs to orthodox Foulkes.

The three concepts, community, communication and matrix, slide into one another in Foulkes' writings. One cannot consistently distinguish between the three things, particularly when, as here, all three terms are used in the same sentence: 'The *network* of all individual mental processes, the psychological medium in which they meet, *communicate*, and interact, can be called the *matrix*' (Foulkes and Anthony 1957, p.26; emphasis added). This is the first problem.

They go on to say: 'This [the matrix] is of course a construct – in the same way as is for example the concept of traffic, or for that matter of mind'. So whatever else 'matrix' is, it does not exist *per se*. In many places Foulkes emphasizes that the matrix is not something that can be 'found' in any sense, and that it is a theoretical construct; for example: 'The Matrix is the *hypothetical* web of communication and relationship in a given group' (Foulkes 1964, p.292; emphasis added).

Perhaps the most clear and succinct definition of the matrix given by Foulkes is this: 'By matrix is meant a common communication ground which is shared' (Foulkes 1990, p.291). The analogy drawn is: 'The social matrix can be thought of as a network in quite the same way as the brain is a network of fibres and cells which together form a complex unit...' (Foulkes and Anthony 1957, p.258).

This much of the matrix belongs to radical Foulkes. But as time goes on, the matrix becomes elaborated into two further entities – the foundation matrix and the dynamic matrix. As these entities gain weight in his theory, they become increasingly concretized, less hypothetical, and more the property of orthodox Foulkes. To my mind this elaboration of the notion of the matrix is a retrogressive theoretical step, as it inexorably leads Foulkes back to the nature/nurture duality, a duality that he has tried so hard to overcome in statements like: 'Group-analytic method and theory do away with pseudo problems such as biological versus cultural, somatogenic versus psychogenic, individual versus group, reality versus phantasy. Instead we endeavour to use concepts which from the beginning do justice to an integrated view' (Foulkes and Anthony 1957, p.27).

In essentialist ways of thinking, nature is often allocated the role of the constant – something universal, something unchanging. Nurture is allocated the role of a variable, something contingent, malleable, on the surface, and therefore of less importance. We have seen that Foulkes has been at pains to emphasize that although he prioritizes nurture, for him it is not a surface phenomenon. He has said: 'the social aspect of human behaviour is basic and central, and not of a peripheral, comparatively superficial nature, not a later coming, additional, conditioning "outside" influence' (Foulkes 1948, pp.15–16). It seems to me that despite himself, he re-institutes the nature/nurture dichotomy, with 'nature' and biology inserted into the foundation matrix, and 'nurture' and culture inserted into the dynamic matrix.

This is how he describes the foundation matrix:

> I cannot on this occasion expand on the concept of the matrix,[12] beyond saying that it is possible to claim a firm pre-existing community or communion between the members, founded eventually on the fact that they are all human. They have the same qualities as a species, the same anatomy and physiology, and also perhaps archaic traces of ancient experiences. This pre-existing and relatively static part we call the 'foundation matrix'. (Foulkes 1971, pp.212–3)

Note the critical elements – it is said to be something 'relatively static' that is something unchanging, and to be pre-existing. Further, and importantly, the things that are unchanging are *biological* elements – human, species, anatomy, physiology.[13] *The foundation matrix is indeed Mother Nature in disguise.* It is not coincidental that he calls this the *foundation* matrix. In this passage he does not address how it, the foundation matrix, comes to be there in the neonate. It is 'just there', as it were, at birth. When he says 'pre-existing', then this is just the same as saying that it is inherited. But as we will see in the next passage, he is against this. The schism is compounded with his description of the dynamic matrix:

> *On top* of this [the foundation matrix] there are various levels of communication which are increasingly dynamic. This is called the dynamic matrix. In between are levels which in accord with the opinion of the observer are determined either more biologically or more culturally. What it really amounts to is whether certain values and complexes are more inborn, or, *as I believe, more transmitted by very early experiences* – transmitted by parents and family in the first place – who in turn transmit the values of what is good, what is bad, etc. in their culture... We must keep in mind that strict separation between all these levels of communication is

12   He does not expand anywhere else either!

13   At this time Foulkes still allows phylogenetic inheritance a role by speaking of 'archaic experiences'. Two years later he has jettisoned this idea, in favour of group dynamics: 'I am inclined to see human development more in the light of transmission than in terms of direct, inherited, archaic repetition' (Foulkes 1973b, p.238); and, 'The family conflict is not an archaic, inherited formation; it is relived in every family, *inevitably, by the very constellation of the family*' (Foulkes 1973b, p.238; emphasis added).

not possible, that they all operate at the same time in various admixtures. Nevertheless, for theoretical reasons…we can discern these two categories of regressive location, namely the relatively static and unalterable genetic foundation matrix, and the rest, which is, to a greater or lesser extent, subject to change within the ongoing dynamics of the group-analytic group.' (Foulkes 1971, p.213; emphasis added)

Thus nature and nurture, constant and variable, have been renamed as foundation and dynamic matrices: 'the relatively static and *unalterable genetic* foundation matrix, and the rest, which is…*subject to change*…'. The type of language he uses in his description of the dynamic matrix (particularly the phrase 'on top') leads backwards to a model of culture sitting on top of nature – and so he undermines his main claim that culture *permeates* to the core. Things are not at all clear. He appears to be hedging his bets, which leads to the odd proposition that although there are fixed (biological) elements, these are transmitted rather than inherited. Another way of putting it is this: he appears to be implying that the foundation matrix (biology) is transmitted by the dynamic matrix (social).

This part of his theory is riven with contradictions. Things are pre-existing yet they are transmitted, they are social yet they are biological, and so forth. The contradictions are born out of the retreat from the systemic notion of the communicational *field*, by trying to break it down into parts: 'fixed' and 'variable', 'inherited' and 'transmitted', 'on top' and 'below', and so forth.

A summary of the ideas of radical Foulkes

At this point it will be useful to gather up the radical elements of Foulkes' theory to see what they look like when put together.

1. He has prioritized the group over the individual.

    (a) He has said that the thing that needs explanation is the existence of individuals rather than the group.

2. He has said that the group is a contingent category – a construct, a reification.

    (a) He has told us that the group only makes sense in relation to that which is outside it: things need to be framed in order to be visible.
    (b) The 'whole' is always an artifact, an abstraction that is carved out of a greater complexity.

3. He has prioritized the whole over the part.

    (a) Thus dysfunction might appear to be *located* in an individual, but it is in fact a dysfunction of the larger group.
    (b) The greater whole informs what takes place in the part.

4. He has emphasized the interconnectedness of existence.

   (a) The part is always connected to a greater whole, and that to an even greater whole, presumably *ad infinitum*.

5. He has prioritized the external over the internal.

   (a) He has said that internal mechanisms are in fact internalizations of external group mechanisms and dynamics.

6. He has prioritized processes over constructs.

   (a) The 'mind' is made an interpersonal phenomenon.

7. He has prioritized the social over the biological.

   (a) The social is made the driving force behind all human interaction. It is the impulse to relate, to communicate, to belong.
   (b) The essential nature of humanness is to be related – to belong, to be a part of something.
   (c) The social is made part of both, the structure *and* the content of the psyche. At his most radical, he implies that there is no part of the psyche that is *a*social, and that the social penetrates right into the id itself.
   (d) The structure and content of the psyche, the shape it takes, is dependent on where one is positioned in the social hierarchy.
   (e) The structure and content of the psyche, the shape it takes, will vary from cultural group to cultural group.

8. He has prioritized transmission over inheritance.

   (a) All internal structures are internalizations of experience, and specifically group experience.

9. He has prioritized the social unconscious over the Freudian unconscious.

   (a) This follows out of the prioritization of transmission over inheritance.
   (b) He also says that what looks like elements of the Freudian unconscious, the life and death instincts, are in fact coagulations and polarizations of lived experience.

10. He has given communication a critical role in his theory of groups.

   (a) The group itself may be considered to be a communicational field, with the individuals as nodes in this network.

(b)   Ill health is thought of as a blockage in the free flow of communication, therapy is thought of as freeing the blockage, and health is thought of as free-flowing communication.

11. He has differentiated group analysis from psychoanalysis.

(a)   'Group psychology must develop its own concepts in its own right and not borrow them from individual psychology.' (Foulkes 1964, p.60)

Having set out the various elements of Foulkes' radical theory, I will now proceed to look at which theories prevail when he comes to describe clinical issues, that is, which of his theories he will use to try to understand what *actually happens* in groups and between people in general.

Application of the theories

We saw earlier that radical Foulkes has said that the very notion of a group is an abstraction. In contradistinction we have also seen in his discussion of 'community' that orthodox Foulkes ends up biologizing and essentializing some groups – particularly the family. This raises serious questions about how truly social his theory actually is. As we have seen, radical Foulkes has made much of his notion of the social unconscious by making it more fundamental than the Freudian unconscious, and so giving it a critical role in his developmental theory. Now, precisely because of the import given, we would expect Foulkes to use his new idea frequently in understanding group phenomena. Surprisingly, we find that this is not the case in his clinical descriptions: instead of the social unconscious we find references only to the Freudian unconscious.

The mystery of the absent social unconscious

Here is one example. Foulkes says that a fundamental problem that groups constantly have to deal with concerns parental authority. He says that the basis of the problem is '...represented in the primordial image of the leader, and corresponds to past, infantile and primordial reality' (Foulkes 1964, p.56).

All the elements he states are elements of the Freudian unconscious: past, infantile and primordial. One has to ask, but where is the social unconscious? What role does it play in the problematic with authority? A few pages later in the same book, Foulkes re-emphasizes that the basis for authority is *archaic inheritance – the father of the primal horde*: 'We can see...that the group can reanimate this archaic inheritance directly...[i.e.] the group on this level shows a need and craving for a leader in the image of an omnipotent father' (Foulkes 1964, p.60). Once again he has reached for Freud's idea – archaic inheritance. Moreover, *Foulkes has given a biological basis – father – for a social relation – need of a leader.*

Leaving aside any discussion about the veracity of the idea, it seems to me that renders his notion of the social unconscious redundant by never making use of it.

Another example occurs in this next passage in which he is drawing a parallel between dream processes and group processes: 'The manifest level comprises what actually goes on…adult, contemporary reality. The primary level refers to processes…which are predominantly unconscious: to primitive, infantile and primordial behaviour. Roughly these two levels correspond to the secondary and primary processes of the dream' (Foulkes 1964, p.56). The unconscious that he makes use of is the Freudian one. We can say this because the terms he uses all point in that direction: 'primitive, infantile and primordial'. He makes no reference to the social unconscious at all here. Has he forgotten it? Another example: 'The individual brings his authoritarian problem – his 'father complex' – into the centre of events from the very beginning…' (Foulkes and Anthony 1957, p.120). In this next passage, he not only neglects the social unconscious, he also abandons his other central idea, that disturbance is a difficulty of the entire network.[14]

> Human people live always in a social setting, from the cradle to the grave. A neurotic patient asks for help because he cannot live satisfactorily in his community, or because his community cannot carry on with him. *Because the forces by which he is run are anachronistic, according to an infantile and primitive pattern,* he cannot adjust to his social group, and because he is not aware of the source of these forces within himself, he cannot have insight. The main aim of a true therapy is therefore, to develop insight and adjustment, vital inner adjustment establishing harmony between the individual and his world – not conformity…
> (Foulkes 1964, p.87; emphasis added)

There are several comments one can make. First, there is *no* mention of the social unconscious. Second, he *locates* the disturbance in the individual, and more, he implies by the words that he uses – anachronistic, infantile and primitive – that the disturbance has come from the Freudian unconscious – which by definition is asocial. Third, the therapy suggested is completely individualistic, in which it is the individual that is to be adjusted to fit in with the network. Fourth, the distinction between conformity and adjustment is a moot point in itself. One person's adjustment is another's conformity.

With his group analytic hat on, Foulkes says, 'Freud has unearthed the human conflict which arises exactly between this dual biological and cultural inheritance of man… In group psychotherapy the group itself, as a token representation of

---

14   One might excuse it by saying that the original paper was given to the Congress of European Psychoanalysis Amsterdam in 1947, so in a sense it was before he re-invented himself as a group analyst. However, he knowingly published it in 1964, in a book on group analysis, with no comments. By this time he most certainly considered himself a group analyst.

the surrounding community and its culture, is for the first time called into the consulting room, into active co-operation within the treatment situation' (Foulkes 1964, p.156).

I have been unable to find a single instance of Foulkes using the 'surrounding community' or the social unconscious in an interpretation of clinical phenomena. It seems that when it comes to interpreting and understanding clinical events, Foulkes consistently reverts to his Freudian psychoanalytic ideas. True, Foulkes does describe group specific mechanisms and phenomena, but in his clinical comments, he always appears to understand them from an individualistic and psychoanalytic basis. Foulkes and Anthony (1957, p.250; emphasis added) say: '*All concepts used in discussing group behaviour should be concepts specifically derived from the study of groups.* The application of ready-made concepts from individual psychotherapy only serve to blur the sharpness of our observation and distort it, whereas the study of groups will help us understand the phenomena in both situations more clearly'. But it seems that Foulkes is actually unable to follow through his own assertion, and constantly falls into the trap of 'discussing group behaviour' with 'ready-made concepts from individual psychotherapy'.

Foulkes had derived the basis of 'authority issues' from the 'father complex'. And the 'father complex' from an 'archaic time'. It is curious that Foulkes does not reach at all for the actual external father to explain the 'complex'. In this respect he is much like Klein – projection and predisposition being of more significance than the external thing. He forgets his own thoughts: 'All this, it should be noted, can be shown to take place in historical times, and there is no need to jump at once to hypothetical assumptions of prehistoric life' (Foulkes 1948, pp.13–14).

When it comes to 'mother', it is the same as with 'father'. Below, he is discussing the reason for ambivalent feelings towards groups:

> the individual is torn between the mental fear of losing his identity…and the great fascination this has for him…the basic process is here is a repetition of the ego development in the very early stages…the emergence of the individual as a self, as a being of his own, from the total symbiotic unity with the mother. In consonance with this the large group very clearly symbolizes this all embracing, archaic mother who represents his whole world.' (Foulkes 1975a, pp.267–8)

In this passage he once again neglects completely the social unconscious and then falls foul of both his propositions, first, that one need not make allusion to prehistoric life (which he does by using the term 'archaic') and second, that one should not use notions from individual psychoanalysis for group phenomena.

Communication

The notion of the communicational field is one of the more important of the contributions that Foulkes made to group analytic theory. Although it is a very helpful tool for understanding some group phenomena, it cannot even begin to engage with others. For example this model makes no attempt to understand either the nature or genesis of the more violent emotions – hatred, envy, aggression, to name a few. These emotions are of course very pertinent to the subject of this book. As Nitsun (1996) has shown, Foulkes does not engage much with these elements. In other words the radical Foulkes has made no attempt to reframe these phenomena in the new language of group processes, and is content to think about them from within the classical Freudian frame, deriving them from Oedipal guilt and so forth. This is a serious omission in the theory of radical group analysis.

But let us pursue the topic nonetheless with the idea that communication is said to be *everything* that goes on between people, conscious and unconscious (Foulkes and Anthony 1957, p.244). They go on to give an example of the complexity of communication: 'we may sit opposite someone in the train who never speaks at all, and yet by his dress and posture, and by the colour of his skin, by his fidgeting, his tenseness, or his repose, he may communicate much to us which we can register in our minds and understand...' (Foulkes and Anthony 1957, p.244).

In what sense are these things communications? Presumably, on the most straightforward level they intend that it is possible to tell something by their dress about whether the person is rich or poor, and if he wears a pin-stripe suit or a boiler suit this might indicate something about his class and so forth. By the person's posture or tenseness one might be able to tell whether he is depressed or worried, happy or sad and so forth. So far so good. Now, in what sense is 'colour of skin' a communication? What might 'colour of skin' communicate? Speculating at the level of the most innocuous, we might suppose that Foulkes and Anthony are saying that 'colour of skin' communicates something about the person's alleged origins, something about his root group, his 'blood line', and thus something about 'not-blood line'.

Clearly 'colour of skin' is a marker of difference, and what it differentiates is something about belongingness. I think that what it is thought to 'communicate' is that the person either *is* one of us, or *is not* one of us. But in this sense is it a communication at all? I would say no. There are two further elements to be considered – 'deduction' and 'projection'. Deductions are inferences made by the conscious mind, guesses based on data, and so might be right or wrong. Projections emanate from the unconscious mind. Foulkes takes up this last idea in a discussion on 'location':

> we can tell immediately if he is angry... True enough one can be mistaken, but there will be special reasons why a mistake has been made, why we interpreted an expression...in a certain way. We can therefore never be completely mistaken – except in the 'location' of our experience. This is where observation such as

'projection', identification and projective identification come in. (Foulkes 1974, pp.278–279)

What this passage helpfully reminds us is that one never just reads a situation, but that one also reads things *into* situations. Thus all 'observations' are amalgams of three distinct phenomena: communications, projections and deductions. Communications emanate from the object, whilst projections emanate from the subject. Our conscious deductions are then constantly subverted and corrupted from within – by our unconscious projections. On this basis we can say that whatever an observer thinks is being communicated by 'colour of skin', they are almost certainly partly mistaken in the 'location' of their experience. The 'communication' is not just from without, but also from within. Something from the subject has been projected onto and into 'colour of skin' of the object.

If we challenged this observer, he or she might reply that all they are doing is neutrally noticing a difference. We then have to ask of them: 'But why do you notice it in the first place? What does that difference *mean* to you, what do you make of it? In effect, what do you *think* that it is communicating?' It seems to me that, through a variety of linkages, it leads inevitably to an inference about belongingness, and often rapidly leads to the common question: 'Where are you from?'

What has been said so far about 'colour of skin' must of course also be true of the other attributes that are listed – dress, posture and so on; one reads things into them. So what significance should 'colour of skin' have over and above the other attributes? In one sense, none, and in another sense, that of belongingness, plenty.

The argument depends of course on which attributes are critical in signifying belongingness. If 'men' were the attribute so designated, then one can proceed to allow innumerable differences to exist between men and they would all still belong to the category 'men'; and whatever similarities women may share with the men, they can never *belong* to the category 'men'.

Foulkes and Anthony (1957, p.157) say: 'In the most asocial and antisocial individuals, one can discern the wish [to belong], which is tantamount to saying that, fundamentally, man is a group animal'. As we have already stated, implicit in the notion of belongingness is the notion of not-belonging to something else. If Foulkes is right that there is a fundamental need to belong, then one literally needs something not to belong to, and skin colour is used willy-nilly to position the Self and Other, belonging or not.

It is the fact that skin colour has become a critical signifier of belongingness that perhaps gives it some of its intense emotional energy. We might well say from our conscious minds that in the contemporary metropolis skin colour says little or nothing about real belongingness, but this counts for little to the unconscious mind, or, as we will discover in the last section of the book, counts for little to the symmetric mind, where *one* difference, however innocuous and potentially meaningless, counts for *all* differences.

Hostility and aggression

We cannot complete any exploration of Foulkes without taking up notions of aggression and hatred. When Foulkes addresses hostility and aggression he uses the notions of the scapegoat and stranger anxiety. We will look at each in turn.

The scapegoat – in which the individual triumphs over the group

Scapegoatism began life as Dollard *et al.*'s (1939) Frustration–Aggression hypothesis, which was later renamed the Scapegoat hypothesis. This model potentially suits Foulkes' ideas, as it follows the idea that aggression is not innate. It echoes the thoughts of Fairbairn most closely, who has suggested that aggression is not an innate, primary phenomenon, but that it follows frustration. The theory suggests that when frustration cannot be expressed in *immediate* aggression then it is displaced onto a safer target. The Scapegoat theory suggests that this is *particularly* likely to happen when the frustration is caused by those in authority and power.

However what we find is that it is not radical Foulkes that has taken up this theory, but orthodox Foulkes. In fact Foulkes' use of this idea is peculiarly regressive and individualistic. Dollard's theory says that the aggression is an outcome of the interaction of the external with the internal. But Foulkes does not use the idea in this way – he reduces it to an internal model of discharge, thus allying himself with Freudian instinct theory.

I will quote the entire passage on scapegoats (Foulkes and Anthony 1957, pp.156–157), as it will be well worth going through it with a toothcomb.

> Scapegoatism is a regular phenomenon in all therapeutic groups, and this raises the interesting question whether or not every group needs, and out of its needs creates, a scapegoat upon whom it can project all its accumulated guilty feeling.

So they begin by talking about it as a group phenomenon, as something that is the outcome of a group dynamic. But then they continue:

> The choice of the scapegoat may depend partly on factors in the group and partly on certain elements present in the chosen individual. The group, in history and in therapy, attacks the scapegoat, because they are afraid to attack the person on whom their feelings are really focussed.

The attention has begun to move from the level of the group to the level of the individual. Which is not problematic in itself. However, when they go on, below, to explain where the aggressive feelings actually come from in the first place, 'the person on whom their feelings are really focussed', they abandon Dollard (and by implication Fairbairn) and his emphasis on *frustration*, and retreat instead to the mother–infant paradigm:

> Analysis of the scapegoat situation reveals this shift of feeling from the conductor, and the transference to him of the extremely mixed feelings *originally centring on the father.* (emphasis added)

We can see clearly here that the genesis of the scapegoat is made nothing to do with the group itself, the context in which it all takes place. Its basis is made Oedipal guilt, and infantile history. In their version the aggression is said originally to be aimed at the father; this is then shifted to the conductor, then to the scapegoat. They continue increasingly to individualize the model, getting further and further away from any thought for the group itself.

> Groups in which the phenomenon operates strongly contain individuals who have inherent difficulties in expressing their aggression and guilt in the open forum. They project their inner feelings onto some likely recipient, who submits to the projection for inner reasons of their own.

The most that can be said for their version of scapegoatism, is that although the phenomenon is said to occur in groups, its cause is something *inside* the individual. The basis of Dollard's idea is frustration; the basis for Foulkes and Anthony's model is projection. Once again they have missed the opportunity to utilize and elaborate the notion of the social unconscious, and have instead reached for the Freudian unconscious. Next, they go on to say that the choice for the scapegoat is isolation, being one of a kind. Some attribute, some difference, is used as the initial lever:

> The scapegoat may be selected in the first place on the elemental basis of being different. He may be isolated because of differences in age, sex, religion, class, race, etc. In a well selected group this is less likely to be the case.

But according to Foulkes and Anthony, these attributes are not of significance in themselves, they are mere triggers, conveniences. What is of significance is the internal need which is triggered:

> The phenomenon is precipitated when the urgent need for the group to punish meets an urgent need in a particular member to be punished. It is the conductor's task to help the group recognize its unconscious intentions and to forestall the extrusion of the innocent member.

They have repeated Freud's theory of instinctual aggression, and his idea that the object of the instinct is the most variable thing about it. One can see then that in fact Foulkes and Anthony's version of scapegoat phenomena is much less group-friendly than Dollard's. The cause for Dollard's aggression is frustration in the here-and-now, that is, something going on in the group. Whilst the cause for Foulkes and Anthony's aggression is the there-and-then of developmental history.

The point to note here is not an either/or one, of whether the cause of scapegoatism is the immediacy of frustration or whether its causes lie in internalized developmental history; no doubt both contribute to the phenomenon. The point of this discussion is to show the remarkable absence of the use of the here-and-now, as well as the absence of the social, by Foulkes and Anthony. *More, they have taken something that is potentially group specific and rendered it individualistic.* Here, they have abandoned the notion of context.

The stranger – in which 'difference' is turned into a 'similarity'

Foulkes and Anthony begin the subject with anthropology:

> The 'passing stranger' in anthropological literature was often seized and sacrificed, because he was a representative of the corn-spirit, or was thought to practice the magic arts...there were elaborate taboos on intercourse with him. The stranger was, therefore, looked upon as a potential threat. So it was with the history of the race. With the history of the individual, there is something not wholly dissimilar. (Foulkes and Anthony 1957, p.157)

One reason this is quoted here is to show how, despite their protestations about not needing to allude to prehistory, they constantly do.

Anyway, they continue by describing the 'stranger anxiety' – the phenomenon in which infants are friendly enough to strangers until the age of about six months, at which time they start reacting strongly to the presence of strangers – often with fear. They then say that the stranger response is gradually modified over time, but that it is still possible to discern its presence in adults.

As to the cause of the stranger response, things are confused in their writings. On the one hand the passage quoted above (1957, p.157) implies that because it was so with the history of the race, so it is with the history of the individual – prehistoric man's alleged hostile reaction to strangers re-emerges in the contemporary infant's reactions to strangers. This is the nineteenth-century theory of recapitulation (Gould 1984), which as we have seen is found in Freud too.

The other way that they attempt to address the 'stranger response' is to ask whether it arises out of nature or nurture. In order to do this they quote two 'scientific experiments' in each of which a new hen was introduced into a group of hens. The first hen was submissive, and behaved differently from the other hens, engaging in flight behaviour. Then by the tenth day she had blended in. The second hen was aggressive, and she engaged in fight behaviour, until she was defeated. After this point she engaged in flight behaviour until the tenth day, by which point she too had blended in.

Apart from the fact that they give no indication where this experiment took place, they make a serious error in their attempt at an analysis: they confuse the issue about who is the stranger. The 'stranger response' is about a response *to* the stranger, but instead, they discuss the other side of the coin: the response *from* the stranger. Leaving aside this glaring error in logic, their conclusion from this 'data' is that:

> There was thus a natural period of assimilation which was not affected much by events or personalities. Once assimilation was complete, the new hen entered a second biosocial phase during which her permanent status in the 'pecking order' was established; that is she was required to learn (from experience) whom she could peck and who could peck her. (Foulkes and Anthony 1957, p.158)

So Foulkes and Anthony give a twofold answer as to the genesis of the stranger response: they say that the period of assimilation is born out of 'nature', that is, 'not affected much by events or personalities'. The second part of the answer they give is that the hen finds its place in the pecking order through experience; in other words 'nurture'. These ideas might or might not be true, but they have nothing to do with the question that they set out to answer: an explanation for the stranger response itself: the strong reaction of the six-month-old *to* a stranger. They appear to have forgotten it.

It is clear enough that the argument they are building is fatally flawed and full of logical errors. Nonetheless they continue the argument in relation to people. They say that at some point each of us knows what it is like to be a stranger – very uncomfortable. When any other stranger appears at a later point, it reactivates these old uncomfortable feelings. Therefore, 'The persistence of strangeness is intolerable to the group' (Foulkes and Anthony 1957, p.159). Following this, they proceed to ally themselves with Freud's idea of narcissism. After some small discussion about the effect of the entry of a newcomer into a group, they conclude in the following way: 'At a deeper level, the advent of the stranger into the group probably harks back to an earlier situation, when the new baby was first introduced into the family. The jealousy reaction to this has complex determinants...' (Foulkes and Anthony 1957, p.159). There are several points to be made here.

First, they make no attempt to link this new idea up with anything they have said before, for example does this idea link in any way with the hen story?

Second, if they saying that the stranger response is based on a remembered jealousy *to* the new baby, then what is the six-month-old's reaction to strangers based on? These confusions arise, because they are confusing and conflating several things: the reaction *of* the baby, the reaction *to* the baby, whether it is the baby that is the stranger, or whether the baby is reacting to strangers, and so on. They appear to be forgetful of the fact that when a newcomer joins a group, then both are strange to each other; however their reactions need to be differentiated as they are not identical to the other. They do not keep this important distinction in mind and so proceed to collapse the responses of each into the other.

Third, if they are saying that the strong reaction of some adults to strangers is based on their childhood emotional memory of being displaced by a baby being introduced into the family, then it would imply that the youngest child, or only children, would not react adversely to strangers, because they would not have had an experience of being usurped; and of course this is not true.

So it seems to me that their theory of the stranger does not have much to commend it. In particular because they have reverted to the mother–infant paradigm, and completely ignored the group, the social in all its forms, conscious and unconscious. They have conflated all the complexities of 'strangeness', and tried to make generalizations that do not work. For example, they do not take up the issue that some differences activate stronger reactions than others; *in effect they are saying that all differences are equivalent.* They have fallen into this error because they have forgotten one of their primary axioms – that things can only ever exist in a context. To take up context is to take up the social, with all its complex emotional and power relations. It is this that must critically inform how a particular variety of 'strangeness' will be responded to.

An American in London

Foulkes and Anthony have a very benign view of hostilities and aggressions set off by differences. They think that there will inevitably be an initial negative reaction to a stranger, whatever the strangeness is. But that following this, the person is usually assimilated, and that this is natural and good. What they do not do is take up the *cost* of assimilation, either for the host group, or the newcomer.

They give a clinical vignette which describes the process of an American joining a cohesive group of English members in London. The group initially ignored the newcomer, which prompted the American to intrude belligerently and often. In the sixth session the American became quiet and compliant, and this continued for about six weeks. After this the American began 'to voice opinions that sounded quite familiar and acceptable to the group'. After this:

> His level of interaction increased, and he was soon very much part of the group, so much so that at one stage one of the members remarked, when he made a tangential reference to his nationality: 'Good heavens, I had quite forgotten you were American!' At this the group agreed that they never thought of him as such now. *He seemed to be just like them.* (Foulkes and Anthony 1957, p.140; emphasis added)

The cost of joining seems to be that he has 'to be just like them', that is, *become* one of them. The fact that Foulkes and Anthony do not elaborate or comment on the vignette, letting it stand and speak for itself, implies that they think that they are describing the vicissitudes of an *inevitable* course of events, that lead always to assimilation. They seem to think that whoever the stranger is, it will follow that eventually there will be assimilation and that this is a always a happy course of events, thus neglecting the cost and meaning of the assimilation for the stranger or the group.

Summary

We can boil down Foulkes' radical agenda to three elements: the central role given to the social, the significance allocated to communication, and the prioritization of transmission over inheritance. Ultimately, when we put the orthodox and radical Foulkes together, we see that he has not followed through his radical agenda. He uses the word 'social', but actually means 'external'. To truly give weight to the 'social' would be to give weight to *social relations* – both historical and contemporary. It is striking that in his discussions on authority, Foulkes never alludes to contemporary authorities – their shape and form. He even neglects the actual father in favour of the primordial father.

It seems to me that Foulkes holds to the notion of transmission over inheritance, however the contents of the transmitted are biological and archaic phenomena. One could say, although it would be overstating it somewhat, that ultimately Foulkes preserves Freud's theory, but says that the things that Freud thinks are inherited, are in fact transmitted.

Foulkes and contemporary group analysts (including myself) consistently reach for the mother–infant paradigm in their interpretation of group phenomena. It seems to me that the task of formulating a true group analytic language still lies before us – the task of creating a group analytic paradigm. And it is to this task that we now turn.

CHAPTER 3

Interlude Between Foulkes and Elias

Interlude – figuring out the ground

Foulkes has two masters – the psychoanalyst Freud and the sociologist Elias – and as we have seen he is constantly torn between the two. When Foulkes has followed Freud I have called him 'orthodox', and when he has followed Elias I have called him 'radical'. The term 'radical' has been applied to the aspects of his thinking that have tried to break free from individualism. But as we have seen Foulkes has been unable to follow through his radical agenda – partly because of the enormous difficulties of the task, but also partly because to follow through the radical agenda would reveal the extent of his discrepancy with Freudian theory.

Now, although it might be true to say that the dichotomy between the individual and the group, or between the internal and external, are reifications – abstractions out of an indivisible complexity – this has led Foulkes into an error. It has led him to suppose that therefore the view from Freud and the view from Elias are different perspectives on the same phenomena. It allows Foulkes to make it appear that the theories are complementary. He has done this by applying the notion of 'figure-and-ground' drawn from Gestalt psychology. Foulkes has used the 'figure-and-ground' idea to try to glue together two disciplines, psychoanalysis and sociology. He has used this to say that sometimes the individual is to the fore, is the figure, and the group is the ground against which the individual is seen. And sometimes it is the group that comes to the fore and the individual becomes ground. This much is true. The mistake he makes is in thinking that when the individual is in the forefront then Freudian theory is applicable, and when the group is in the forefront then Eliasian ideas are applicable. It is by this device that he gives them the appearance of being complementary to each other.

However, it seems to me that the two theories, *as they stand*, are not complementary but contradictory. This is because each is based on fundamentally differing hypotheses and assumptions. The Freudian model says that the social is the outcome of the internal drama. The driving forces here are the instincts, and it is their vicissitudes and sublimation that give forth culture, social life and knowledge as we know it. At its most overstated, in Freudian theory the social is an epiphenomenon of the biological. The Eliasian model, also overstated, is that of the social constructing the internal – where mind and personality are formed in the nexus of the social. The two emphases, as they stand, are mutually incompatible. It does not help much to say, as Foulkes does, that they are two sides of the same coin. This is because each theory says that one side of the coin creates the other. The dispute is about which of the two sides is to be given priority. Freud has one idea, and Elias another. This difficulty has to be overcome if the promise of Foulkesian group analysis is to be fulfilled.

Psychoanalytic developmental theories: a reprise

Psychoanalytic developmental theories begin their stories at some point near birth and the greater part of their focus is on the internal state of the infant. In contrast, sociological theories, at least the ones that are of interest here, begin with the environment, with society.

Things are of course not so neatly divided between the two disciplines. Some sociological theories (e.g. some varieties of Marxism) are crudely deterministic, saying that the plasticity of the individual is infinite and that the external straightforwardly impresses itself on the internal. Other sociological theories (e.g. those of Elias, Vygotsky, Mead, Burkitt) have a more complex picture of the mutual engagement and transformation of the internal and external.

Similarly, it would be a gross oversimplification to say that all psychoanalytic theories derive the social from the psychological, and do so in the same way. This is clearly not the case. For example Klein (1988a, 1988b), who is an instinctivist *par excellence*, allows the external a considerable role in the formation of the mature psyche. Her theory begins with a neonate who is almost completely instinct driven, and in particular driven by the anxieties aroused by the presence of the death instinct. In Klein's theory the external world is always more benign than the infant's expectation of it. This is because, initially, the infant projects out its death instinct into the world, and so turns it into a dangerous and frightening place. Through the maturational process, the infant incorporates its experience of the benign external world, and in the process modifies and moderates its internal world. This is no small matter. It seems to me that Klein actually allows the external world a much more significant role in the developmental process than is allowed for by either her disciples or her detractors.

Freud, as we have seen, has a very complex theory, based on the interpenetration of two conflicts. One of the conflicts is between the two endogenous instincts. The external world has no bearing on the genesis of this conflict, its basis being pure biology and so exclusively internal. However, the outcome of this conflict *does* spill out into the external world, where through the process of sublimation, society and cultural life are constructed. This now gives birth to the second conflict – this time between the internalized rules of society and 'nature, red in tooth and claw'. The bastion of the first being the superego, and of the second, the id. One can see then that in Freud, both society and the psyche are structured through a complex *interplay* of internal and external.

Winnicott (1982) begins to break with this tradition of starting a theory with the individual – and instead famously begins with the notion of the 'nursing couple'. He begins with two and not one. Unusually for a psychoanalyst he introduces the notion of a group very early on in the developmental process. He says that the child's first I AM moment is the construction of a group. He means by this that the infant 'pulls' together its fragmentary experiences to make a sense of wholeness, and that the coming together of these 'bits' is what constitutes the first group. After this promising beginning, in my opinion, his theory begins to slide towards an essentialism of true and false selves and so on. And although he gives the notion of culture a prominent role in his theory, it is the outcome of a process that takes place between infant and mother: play. His theory gives social culture little contribution to make to the structuring of the psyche itself. Having seen that an abstracted individual cannot exist as such, Winnicott prioritizes the nursing couple, and also the context of that couple: the family. He did not go beyond that to engage with the context of the family: society.

Fairbairn, on the other hand, struck out in a novel direction, and turned orthodox psychoanalytic theory upside down. Unlike the others he gave the external, the interpersonal, priority over the internal, the intrapersonal. His infant begins *on the outside*. His infant comes into the world ready to relate: 'libido is object-seeking and not pleasure-seeking' (Fairbairn 1943, p.78). For Fairbairn, healthy psychology is interpersonal. When things start going wrong for the infant (as they inevitably do) then the infant is driven inwards to construct its internal domain. Thus for Fairbairn, intrapersonal psychology is always psychopathology. What we find, however, is that although Fairbairn gives ontological priority to the external, his theory is curiously *a*social.

One can see then that in no sense can one say that psychoanalysis ignores the external. What we can say, however, is that apart from Fairbairn, they all give ontological priority to the internal over the external, and the individual over the social. And it should be remembered that 'external' does not always mean social. True, Freud does make a significant space for society in the psyche, the superego, but its institution is quite late in the story, at between three to five years of age. And whilst Klein's superego does start very early, its basis is not social but the death instinct. Further, Klein does not address the notion of society as such in her writings; what she allows is for a benign external to moderate the troubled internal.

Now out of his psychoanalytic predecessors, Foulkes has aligned himself with Freud (although it seems to me that Fairbairn's work is in fact much more sympathetic to Foulkes than Freud). The fact that Foulkes only ever takes up the second of Freud's conflict situations – between culture and instinct – leaves him with a problem. Freud's theory *needs* instinctual conflict to derive society and social life itself. Freud's is truly a heroic attempt at a 'theory of everything' that has its entire basis in this one conflict. This leaves a hole in Foulkes' theory. Foulkes ducks the question of how society comes into existence, making it a *fait accompli.*

From Elias, Foulkes has taken up several constructs – language, communication, figuration and history, to name a few. However, he has not taken them up quite as Elias meant them. Most importantly, Foulkes ignores the issue of social power relations, which plays a central role in Elias' thinking. By doing this, Foulkes has sanitized Elias – making him more complacent and comfortable, and less dangerous and problematic.

Now although it was not Elias' purpose to describe a developmental theory, his concerns being mainly the sociology of knowledge, it is possible to glean one from his writings. I do this in order to put it into a form more familiar to those in the psychotherapy world, so that the relevant aspects of the models – psychoanalytic and sociological – may be more easily compared and contrasted.

Part of the difficulty in proceeding with a description of Elias' views is due to the way he wrote. His thoughts in various places echo those of other thinkers and schools; in other places he violently disagrees with particular stances. However, he hardly ever makes any direct reference to them. He often takes a pot-shot at something, but obliquely, and one has to work out by reading between the lines whom he is attacking and why. This is a curious stance for a sociologist for whom context is central. It would seem that Elias is reluctant to engage with the sociology of his *own* knowledge. As to the reasons why – they cannot be pursued here.

Language is very important in Elias' theory. Many of his concerns and formulations are very reminiscent of the structuralists as well as the post-structuralists. But within this proximity, there are some fundamental and important differences between them. So before proceeding with Elias, it is necessary to give an abbreviated overview of structuralism and post-structuralism – in order then to be better able to position Elias.

An overview of structuralism and post-structuralism
The structuralists

Most accounts of structuralism (Eagleton 1983; Harland 1987; Selden 1989) begin with de Saussure who suggested that the structure of language structured experience. *Langue*, the language system as a totality, was to be distinguished from *parole* – the particular utterances that are made.

Language was broken into three interrelated components:

Signifier   ⟶   Word

Signified   ⟶   Idea in the mind

Referent   ⟶   Concrete Object

The relationship between signifier and signified was an arbitrary one, that is, the sound-name given to a thing could be anything. There is no reason why the thing we call 'tree' should not have been named 'port'. However, once named, then signifier and signified cannot be separated – the entity 'tree' and the word 't-r-e-e' are forever joined in the mind.

According to de Saussure, language itself consisted of a predetermined set of differences: 'The concepts are purely differential and defined not by their positive content but negatively by their relations with the other terms of the system. Their most precise characteristic is in being what the others are not' (de Saussure 1959, p.117). De Saussure thought that langue was a closed self sufficient system in which the signifiers held each other up, by 'leaning' on each other. For our purposes, the points we need to note out of de Saussure's theory are as follows:

First, langue exists prior to the individual, thus as one takes in language, one not only takes in a particular way of dividing and thus understanding the world, but also the values and attitudes to those divisions.

> The individual absorbs language before he can think for himself: indeed the absorption of language is the very condition of being able to think for himself... Words and meanings have been deposited in the individual's brain below the level of conscious ownership and mastery. They lie within him like an undigested piece of society. (Harland 1987, pp.12–13)

The meaning categories are transmitted intergenerationally as an interdependent whole, a process on which the individual can have little or no influence. De Saussure says: '[langue] is the social side of speech outside the individual who can never create or modify it by himself; it exists only by virtue of a sort of contract signed by the members of the community' (de Saussure 1959, p.14). Thus our notions of ourselves and the world we live in are said to be '*structured*' from without.

Second, the 'structure' is a *necessary* part of existence itself. This idea is contrary to individualism, and in particular the 'person centred' psychology of Carl Rogers (1967). According to him one works (through counselling) to rid oneself of these 'external' structures, to find one's true self within, a self that exists before and outside language. In de Saussure's system, there can be no meaningful notion of an individual prior to the absorption of language.

These ideas were taken up in sociology through Durkheim and in anthropology through Levi Strauss, among others. Durkheim argued that religious belief began with a division of the sacred and the profane (Harland 1987, p.22), and that this division arose in the first place as an attempt to order the universe. Durkheim argued that the function of taboos was to ensure that the sacred and the profane were critically and forever divided. One of the primary functions of taboo was to maintain *difference*. Durkheim also argued that the universe is divided *in order to unify the clan*. The totem was the clan's sign (name) for itself, and thus also signified that which was not part of the clan. The clan grouped and unified itself by naming itself. The totem constructed an 'us'.

Levi Strauss took these ideas further and argued that the totemic system itself was a kind of langue. By this he meant that the 'names' given constituted the entire system of possible thought. He then added a new component: he said that the differentiation bonded the parts into groups *in order to facilitate exchange between them*. These ideas anticipate some of Elias. Particularly, the notion that the totemic system created differences and thus interdependences, both within the clan, and between clans. As Harland puts it: 'Only man-in-association can survive'. Most importantly, Levi Strauss went on to say that the system of exchange was a form of *communication*: 'any classification lays a grid upon the world, and any grid upon the world makes communication possible' (Harland 1987, p.28).

Thus structuralism removes the *a priori* from the region of nature and embeds it in the social. Kant for example thought that we came into the world with ready-made universal categories in our minds – which ensured that we all categorized the world and our experiences similarly. Structuralism gives another answer – it says that we categorize the world and our experiences similarly, because the categories, concepts and differences are instituted in the structure of language itself – without which we would be unable to think at all. 'So, although the individual interprets personal sensory experience through classifications, categories and concepts, these are not universally given and fixed from birth. A philosophy of the social *a priori* thus avoids the pitfalls which beset innatist philosophies' (Harland 1987, pp.31–32).

Structural linguists like Jakobson (1962) pursued these ideas further. They argued that the deep structure of language was a binary one. And at its deepest level, the phonetic units themselves always occurred in pairs. 'In a child's mind the pair is anterior to isolated objects' says Jakobson. His hope was to show that all thought and categorization, however apparently complex, was built out of a series of binary oppositions.

The post-structuralists

The structuralists lived in a relatively stable world. The signifiers (names) were bounded, and in a sense, mutually exclusive entities. There was a one-to-one mapping from name to idea to thing. The post-structuralists destabilized this world by problematizing the signifier in two main ways.

First, they pointed out that one never actually gets to the signified in the mind. If one pursues a signifier, a name, to get to the idea of the thing that the name is said to represent, what one actually gets to are other signifiers, that is other names. Similarly, when we look a word up in a dictionary what we are led to are other words, which lead us to other words, endlessly. What looks like the signified, is always, at a deeper level, yet another signifier. This is the outcome of the fact that we are caught in the web of language and cannot step outside it. We are caught in an endless chain of signification.

Second, the post-structuralists problematized the binary structure of language, which is one of the linchpins of structuralism. The process of undermining binary oppositions is given the name 'deconstruction'. Eagleton explains that binary oppositions that appear self evident are a reflection of ideology. 'Ideologies like to draw rigid boundaries between what is acceptable and what is not, between self and non-self, truth and falsity, sense and nonsense, reason and madness, central and marginal, surface and depth' (Eagleton 1983, p.133). Now ideology is always invisible to the conscious mind. Ideology makes it appear that particular categories are 'natural' and inevitable ways of thinking and experiencing. The post-structuralists argue that whilst it might not be possible to think without these binary oppositions, they say that these oppositions falsely 'tidy up' things – and that things are never so neat. The process of deconstruction looks at the edges of these oppositions, finds a loose thread, and proceeds to unravel the structure to show it up for what it is not. An endearing example of this took place recently. A young friend[1] was completely unfazed when the great philosophical conundrum 'how do you know that the light is off when the fridge door is closed?' was put to him. He replied that he *knew it* was off, because he had recently opened the door 'a very little' in order to look. He had concretely deconstructed an apparent dichotomy, in which it appeared that the fridge door could be *either* open *or* closed. He found a gap between the polarizations, and then exploited it, proving that open and closed are not necessarily absolute states.

The structuralists have argued that binary oppositions are not found in nature but are an outcome of langue. The post-structuralists have argued that the binary oppositions are not to be found naturally in langue either. They would argue that langue is no more a given than biology. And that if one were to look deep into the structure of langue, of binary oppositions, then one would find there a history of power relations, one would find an ideology instituted there. Binary relations are instituted ideologies and ideologies by their nature are hidden. The post-structuralists have *made ideology the basis of langue and called it discourse*. For example Eagleton shows how the binary opposition man/woman *creates* the polarizations even as they are named:

1   Jack Sichel, age 11, personal communication.

man is what he is only by virtue of ceaselessly shutting out this other or opposite, defining himself in antithesis to it, and his whole identity is therefore caught up and put at risk in the very gesture by which he seeks to assert his unique, autonomous existence... Woman is not just an other...but...the image of what he is not, and therefore an essential reminder of who he is...one reason why such exclusion is necessary is because she may not be quite so other after all... (Eagleton 1983, pp.132–133)

Thus in a particular circumstance it seems 'natural' and self evident to carve the world up in a particular way – a particular 'us' and 'them'. As Althusser (1984) has said, ideology is profoundly unconscious for the rulers as well as the ruled. The post-structuralists would say that we have to face the hard truth that we are unable to transcend the dichotomous structure of our thoughts to get to an experience that is uncloaked by ideology. We can only ever exchange one ideology for another, we can deconstruct one ideology, but will inevitably find ourselves in another.

We are now obliged to engage briefly in a debate between the terms 'ideology' and 'discourse'. Whilst this might seem to be of remote relevance to the subject of groups, it will in fact be found to be of enormous significance at a later point, as post-Foulkesian arguments are built in the last chapter of the book.

From ideology to discourse

The term 'ideology' has fallen from grace in many contemporary academic circles, and has been replaced by the notion of discourse. And strictly speaking the term 'discourse' should have been used in the section above on post-structuralism. The oversight was deliberate, and made partly because Elias (who we go to next) uses the term 'ideology' and not 'discourse'. The other reason is that ideology retains a connotation with the politics of power, a connotation that is not always clear with the notion of discourse. To my mind they both have something slightly different to contribute, and so I retain them both.

Ideology and discourse are very similar in some of the functions they serve, but there are important distinctions between them. The differences are connotative rather than denotative, that is, the differences lie in the associations that people have to the terms, and this is in part due to the history of the terms.

The notion of ideology was born out of Marxist theory, where it was thought of as an all-powerful organizing force – the dominant ideology as it was called. According to traditional Marxism there was just one ideology in a society, and that was the one perpetrated by the ruling classes. Implicit in the notion of ideology is 'false ideology' and 'false consciousness'. In other words, the notion of ideology has buried within it the idea that there is a reality out there to be looked at, and that there are true and false ways of looking at it. This led to the simplistic formulation that bourgeois ideology gave a false and distorted perspective, whilst the proletarian vision saw the truth of things.

The notion of discourse counters the hegemony of ideology. Whereas there is just one dominant ideology, there are many competing discourses. Whereas ideology is grounded in the material conditions and is the sole property of the ruling classes, discourses are multivariant, allowing discourses of power, cooking, film, football etc. An important point is that one can never step outside discourse, all one can do is to step from one discourse into another. The notion of discourse will be elaborated on further in the last part of the book, as the need for its use arises. For the moment this is a sufficient overview of discourse, ideology, post-structuralism and structuralism. Sufficient that is, for the purposes of the Elias chapter, which is where we move to next.

CHAPTER 4

Elias

Introduction

To begin with I should explain why a book on an analytic theory of groups is about to give so much space and attention to a sociologist rather than a psychoanalyst. One reason is because of the influence Elias has had on Foulkes. But the main reason is that Elias engages with the fallacies within the individual/group dichotomy at a much deeper level than does Foulkes.

To take the group seriously is more than saying taking culture and the social into account. This attempt fails because one is led to ask questions such as how does culture get inside the individual, what are the effects of culture on the individual, and so on. These are important questions, but as we noted earlier, these questions begin too late in the story – they already assume a pre-existing individual who engages with the social, thus making them two different things. Elias goes behind these questions. His importance lies in the fact that his thought-provoking theories expose the fallacies constructed around the notion of the individual by probing the philosophy, history, psychology and politics behind the individual–group dichotomy. And unusually for a sociologist, he also engages with how these larger forces are institutionalized within the psyches of individuals. Elias, having no particular allegiance to Freud, is freer to develop the theme of interconnectedness in territories that Foulkes was unable to enter. Additionally, Elias begins to develop conceptual tools that go some way to overcoming the difficulties described in the section on Foulkes, the difficulty of finding a language of the field. Elias offers an alternative basis for a developmental model, one that avoids the solipsism inherent in instinctivist models of development. The subject matter of this chapter might seem remote and alien to the subject of group analysis, but in fact it is laying the ground on which a truly group analytic theory might be built. The point that continually stands out as one reads Elias is the centrality he allocates to the notion of social relatedness. It is this point that makes Elias so pertinent to the project that this book in engaged in – of taking the group seriously.

As for the structuralists, language is central to Elias' thinking. But unlike the structuralists, language for him is always grounded in human activity. In this sense Elias keeps closer to elements of Marxism – the importance they give to material conditions. But as we shall see, for Elias 'material conditions' are made broader than 'economic conditions' to include other elements like culture, status, power and so on. It seems to me then that Elias' ideas, as they mature and develop, are closer to those of the post-structuralists than anyone else.

The culmination of Elias' thinking is presented in his last work – *The Symbol Theory* – by which time his eyesight was failing, so it was dictated. Through Symbol Theory Elias seeks to bring many different things together – things that are normally thought of as belonging to different disciplines, and things that are normally thought of as polar opposites. Symbol Theory tries to be a unifying theory – unifying internal and external, individual and social, thought and speech.

Symbol Theory is an attempt at a 'Grand Theory', a Theory of Everything. It seeks to bridge all aspects of human existence, the particular and the general, the biological and the social, the internal and the external, the individual and the group.

First and foremost, Symbol Theory says that speech, thought and knowledge are different forms of the same entity – *symbol*; 'Language, reason, knowledge...to speak, to think, to know...all three activities are concerned with the handling of symbols' (Elias 1991, p.65). Second, he focuses on its location, and says that it exists in a place that transcends the usual internal/external dichotomy, as well as the ideal/material dichotomy. Third, the shape and form of 'symbol' is fabricated on the forge of social activity and power relations. Fourth, its 'shape' determines how one experiences the self, the world, one's relationships and one's experiences. And finally, the fact that this entity is grounded in social activity ensures that the dynamic is a recursive one, activity, experience, thought and structure, each feeding on the other, and so each in a continual state of transformation.

Let us begin the description of Elias' theoretical edifice with the notion of 'figuration'.

Figuration

Figuration is a notion that describes the interconnectedness of human existence. It is a term that is intended to transcend the individual–society dichotomy. Elias is trying to find a new language, one that goes beyond the individual–society dichotomy. For example, to say that the individual is embedded in the group is to give priority to the group; and to say that the society is an aggregation of individuals, is to give priority to the individual. The concept that is central is the clumsy phrase 'interdependent people'; and its clumsiness is the outcome of the structure of language. Elias (1978, p.125) says: 'the concept "individual" refers to interdependent people in the singular, and the concept "society" to inter-dependent people in the plural'.

Elias' notion of figuration relates to the relationship between the parts, and refers to the same thing as social 'structure', which is a description from the perspective of the 'whole':

> What we call 'figuration' with reference to the constituent parts is identical with what we call 'structure' with reference to the composite unit...the structure of societies and...the figuration or pattern of bonding of the individuals who form these societies...are...the same thing as seen from different angles' (Elias 1978, p.176)

Elias is at pains to undermine the individual–society dichotomy. He says that although individual and society are commonly counterposed as a matter of course, this polarization is not 'natural' by any means, but is contingent to this moment of history, and that it is the outcome of the 'civilizing process' which has transformed not only the structure of society but the personality itself. He says: 'the so called "environment" of the child consists primarily of other human beings... Society, often placed in mental contraposition to the individual, consists entirely of individuals, oneself among them' (Elias 1978, p.13).

If the argument were left here, then of course it would be extremely reductive. Like Mrs Thatcher he would be saying that there is no society, only individuals and families. What stops it being a reductive idea is the fact that the individuals are said to be *interdependent* – and hard on the heels of interdependence comes power relations, power which structures those interdependences. 'People make up webs of interdependence or figurations of many kinds, characterized by power balances of many sorts, such as families, schools, towns, social strata, or states' (Elias 1978, p.14).

To understand the notion of figuration, it is helpful to draw an analogy – albeit a rather bizarre one. It is as though we are each attached to every other with a series of elastic bands. This does not mean that our activities are determined by the group, rather they are constrained by the group. These 'elastic bands' are what Elias calls interdependencies. The critical difference between Elias and Foulkes here is that although both take up interdependence, the Eliasian notion of interdependence incorporates the notion of power, which Foulkes makes no reference to.

The significance and consequence of figuration and the network of inter-dependence is that thoughts and actions are inevitably constrained. It is this element that stops the notion of figuration degenerating into something re-ductive. Additionally, the fact that figuration constrains individuals is not to be taken to mean that it is residing outside and beyond human activity.

> The peculiar constraint exerted by social structures over those who form them is particularly significant. We tend to explain away this compulsion by ascribing to

these structures an existence – an objective reality – over and above the individuals who make them up. The prevailing ways of forming words and concepts...enhance the tendency in our thinking to reify and dehumanize social structures. (Elias 1978, p.16)

In this and many similar passages, Elias is attacking the school of structuralism, which, as we have seen, does indeed ascribe to language an objective reality over and above individuals. Elias is continually engaged in a balancing act that tries not to reduce society to individuals, nor make individuals mere pawns of society. He says: 'what we attempt to conceptualize as social forces are in fact forces exerted by people over one another and over themselves' (Elias 1978, p.17). However, although it is 'people' that constitute these 'social forces', the social forces are outside the direct control of any individual or group of individuals.

The notion of figuration strikes a fatal blow against the existentialist and humanistic idea that we are free to choose – free to choose our destiny once we have purged the ideas of others out of our heads. On the other hand neither is Elias saying that we are pawns of extra-human social forces – be they economic, linguistic, or whatever. This is why the word 'constraint' is so important. If one is constrained then this does not mean that one is powerless – it does not mean that one is without influence. This idea leads us to another critical element in Elias' theory – power relations.

Power relations

Power is another way of saying that humans are constrained by others – by people and things. There are many elements to the Eliasian notion of power: figuration, economics, knowledge and language. For the moment we will limit ourselves to the first of these.

One aspect of power is inevitably born out of the notion of constraint, which in turn is inevitably born out of the notion of interdependence. In other words the presence of power is an inevitable outcome of living together – out of the structure of life itself. The elastic band analogy should be remembered here. This idea strikes a blow against the liberal ideal, that somehow we can all live together in a sea of equality.

Power, Elias says, is a relationship. 'Power is not an amulet possessed by one person and not by another; it is a structural characteristic of human relationships – of *all* human relationships' (Elias 1978, p.75). Thus what is significant is the relativity of power between two groups or individuals, what is of significance is the idea of power differentials – in the elastic band analogy: how much pull one has compared to the other. Elias again: 'Whether power differentials are large or small, balances of power are always present wherever there is a functional interdependence between people' (Elias 1978, p.75).

Elias expands on the idea of power and constraint with the help of game theory. In a game like chess, the opponents are interdependent, in that they each need the other to play the game. Elias says that the opponents serve a *function* for each other. Further, the move of one player informs the move of the other player. The actions of one cannot be explained if taken in isolation. 'They can be explained only if one takes into account the compelling forces the groups exert upon each other by reason of their interdependence, their bilateral function for each other as enemies' (Elias 1978, p.77). The notion of power is predicated on the notion of function:

> Like the concept of power, the concept of function must be understood as a concept of relationship...when one person (or group of persons) lacks something which another person or group has the power to withhold, the latter has a function for the former...*people or groups that have functions for each other exercise constraint over each other.* (Elias 1978, p.78; emphasis added)

One can see then that power is intrinsic to all human relations precisely because we are related, that is interdependent. One of the novel things about this way of thinking about function and power, is that it makes one aware of the dependence of the master on the slave. Of course the danger here is that some might take this as an opportunity to 'equalize' everything – saying that the exploiter and exploited are both equally complicit in the situation – thus rendering the notion of moral responsibility redundant. It is clear that this is *not* what Elias means, because although no one is completely powerless, it is the power differential that primarily drives the situation.

Like other sociologists, the paradox that Elias is continually engaging with is that although society is made up of individuals it ends up being something beyond the individual.

He sets about addressing the paradox by building analogies with games at different levels. For example, he considers a chess game in which one player is overwhelmingly stronger than the other. The stronger player will not only have power over the weaker player, forcing particular moves, but will also have power over the structure of the game itself. The overwhelmingly strong player, be it tennis or chess, can dictate the entire course of the game, sending the opponent hither and thither at will.

Next, consider two players who are close in ability. Each will have less chance of manipulating the other, resulting in 'a game process *which neither of them has planned*' (Elias 1978, p.82). This sort of game process comes closer to resembling social process.

Elias then goes on to consider multi-player games in various configurations, one against many, many against many, where one player is much stronger, where all are more equal, and so forth. We won't trace all the intricacies here; suffice it to say that as the number of players increases the game becomes increasingly uncontrollable by any one individual, and in fact individuals come increasingly to be controlled by the game process:

> a game process which comes about entirely as a result of the interweaving of the individual moves of many players, takes a course *which none of the individual players has planned, determined or anticipated.* On the contrary, the unplanned course of the game repeatedly influences the moves of each individual player. (Elias 1978, p.95)

We can see here how although individuals come to be influenced and controlled by the game process, the game process itself consists of individual moves. This is the inevitable thing: constraint is the outcome of interdependence.

In the same way that one cannot exist outside relatedness and power relations, one cannot exist outside language. This idea will be taken up next under the more general term 'Symbol Theory'.

Symbol theory

Symbol Theory is Elias' attempt at resolving several ancient philosophical conundrums that all arise out of the Cartesian split between mind and matter (Descartes 1596–1650), and also out of the philosophy of Leibniz (1646–1716) who split every individual from every other, by proposing that individuals were monads, windowless entities, that imposed or imagined relations between things, whereas in fact there were none. An outcome of these philosophies were several fundamental questions.

First, there is this conundrum: how do we know that what is in our heads matches that which is out there in the world?

Second, there is the question: if something is not perceived, can it be said to exist? How would we know it exists?

Third, how does communication work? Or even, *does* it work? In other words, how is it that a person gets something from inside their 'head' to the inside of someone else's 'head'. And if it does get there, how do we know that the message that has been sent is the message that has been received?

Fourth (and Elias takes this question from Hume (1956)), how do individuals acquire the concept of a causal connection as a universal type of explanation? In other words, how is it that we all 'naturally' appear to know that there are cause-and-effect solutions, and that they are useful? From whence comes the young child's interminable why-questions? Elias thought that it was unlikely that every individual deduced this purely from experience. This is a particular form of another larger conundrum – what is innate and what is learnt, or as it is sometimes put, the nature–nurture dichotomy.

Elias' answer, in broad brushstrokes, was that the questions themselves arise out of mistaken divisions and false abstractions. In particular, these are the division between individuals, between individual and society, between internal and external worlds, between nature and nurture. Elias' Symbol Theory is his attempt to resolve these apparent paradoxes by viewing the terrain from a higher level of synthesis – much as I suggested earlier, with radical Foulkes (p.59).

Now although at the moment it might appear that we are a long way indeed from our concerns with psychotherapy and groups, this is not the case. For example psychoanalysis has felt the need to invent the communicational construct 'projective identification' to explain how particular sorts of thoughts and feelings somehow migrate from patient to analyst. This construct is predicated on an idea of individuals separate from each other. Whatever else might come out of this exploration, it will at the very least test these notions that have evolved in the context of individual psychoanalysis. The outcome might be that they are left as they are, or that one has to modify them. One might even decide, in the new context where the group is taken seriously, that the term is redundant.

Now, Elias was not so much a philosopher, more a sociologist. So he was not only concerned to correct the errors in logic, he was also interested in how and why these ways of thinking came about. What was it in the social *Zeitgeist* that meant that thought was 'driven' in this direction, a direction that increasingly widened the gap between mind and matter (inside and outside), between nature and nurture, and between individual and society?

The civilizing process

In the two volumes of his *magnum opus, The Civilizing Process,* Elias (1994) showed that the 'shape' of contemporary personality was not a universal, but that it evolved within a particular socio-historic figuration. He did this by tracing the 'Western' tradition from the Middle Ages to modernity through 'snapshots' afforded into the past by texts and pictures. He observed the progressive internalization and privatization of thoughts and feelings – beginning particularly during the Renaissance. He explained it in two main ways. First, he noted how specific behaviours were used by the nobility to differentiate themselves from commoners.[1] Among the behaviours that he describes are the progressive internalization and privatization of emotions and thoughts. Second, Elias linked these changes to the changing configurations of social power – in part a consequence of social systems growing larger, and in part a consequence of people from the 'lower orders' beginning to move up the hierarchy. As people from the lower echelons increasingly took on the attitudes, behaviours and etiquette of the aristocracy, the aristocracy were forced to continue to embellish and elaborate their way of being – constantly trying to distance themselves from

---

1   One is reminded here of the ideas of Durkheim and Levi Strauss that we have touched on. In particular their thoughts about the uses of totem and taboos to create and maintain difference.

the ever encroaching plebeian. And so it came about that things became increasingly psychologically hidden. The threshold of shame continued to increase so that less and less of one's thoughts and feelings were allowed to be visible.

Elias gives two conflicting explanations – one of which is that there is nothing intrinsic in the privatization of thoughts that made it particularly suitable for court life. The significant thing was not the 'content' of the difference, but that something, anything, was *used* as a difference in order to *differentiate*.[2] The other explanation that Elias gives is that as the network of power relations widened, connecting more and more people, it became *necessary* for behaviour to be circumscribed – that is, 'civilized'. Burkitt (1991) points out that Elias used 'civilized' in another sense too, which was to describe the process of the internal pacification of society by greater self regulation by individuals.[3] This then is another meaning of constraint – where the individual internalizes constraints. The fact that the individual now proceeds to live within these internalized parameters gives the individual the illusion of freedom.

Elias does not mean these personality adjustments in any shallow sense of adjusting one's behaviour whilst one's thoughts and feelings are kept under wraps. This would make the process very conscious. 'Rather what Elias wants us to contemplate is the entire restructuring of personality and the psychic economy in the process of historical change' (Burkitt 1991, p.174). The changes are not trivial, they are profound *structural* changes in the psyche. This is quite a different model from the Freudian one where one's 'nature' is in constant conflict with the rules of 'nurture'. In Elias, one's 'nature' is constituted through and by 'nurture'. As we shall come to see, things are even more complicated than this.

If things were left by Elias here, then there would be no place for conflict. This would be because if the inside were made purely by the outside, then by definition, the inside would perfectly match the outside; therefore there would be no difference between, say, one's aspirations and external possibilities, and so there would be no conflict. One would be made to fit one's place in society, and one would be content with it as one would be unable to comprehend anything different. One would not have the conceptual tools to do otherwise. Clearly there is conflict in all sorts of domains, intra-psychic, between people, between people and things and so on. Elias is cognizant of this and so his model avoids the trap of simplistically impressing the external on the internal, which leads to a crude materialism, and also avoids the trap of making the external some sort of function

2   For example in contemporary India, one of the markers of difference between the haves and the have-nots is fat on the body. Indian film stars and 'beauties' are very unlike their Hollywood counterparts. They are unashamedly plump – unashamed that is, in the current Indian context.

3   The second of the two explanations is not too far from the Freudian conception of the institution of the superego, as the place where the self regulatory mechanisms are located.

or reflection of the internal, which leads to a crude idealism. The way that he does this is through a novel description of language and knowledge that is formed out of social activity, and in a sense, impresses itself on both the external and the internal.

Knowledge

Let us go back to Hume's question which we left earlier, which is really three questions: (1) How do we come to know things? (2) How is it that we each come to think in similar ways? and (3) How much of what we do know are we born with, and how much do we learn? Elias eschews all answers that lean towards any kind of idealism – that is, answers that prioritize ideas above things, and mind above matter. For example, Kant agreed with Hume that this knowledge (that causal connections exist and are useful) could not arise purely from experience – and said that it could only be there if it was inborn, innate. Kant made particular knowledge 'a characteristic of reason itself' – due to the 'structure of the human intellect'.

Elias' answer to Hume is a sociological one: 'the term "cause" and its various uses are acquired through a process of learning by all normally endowed members of a contemporary language community' (Elias 1991, p.9). In other words, Elias agrees that the concept already exists prior to any particular individual's experience – but says that it exists in the structure and content of language. Language is the receptacle in which intergenerational experiences may be accrued and stored. And when an individual takes in a language, he or she takes in a particular way of thinking that is embedded in that language. Thus Elias (like the structuralists) has replaced the *a priori* in nurture, with an *a priori* in language. However, as it will emerge, unlike the structuralists and post-structuralists, Elias' notion of language is firmly grounded in *human activity*. Elias says that Descartes, Hume and Kant could not conceive of this more ordinary answer, because they were fixated at the level of the individual.

However, Elias is saying something much more than that our thoughts are structured by the language that we think in – he is also saying that our very psyches and personalities are also structured by language. How can this be? To answer this we have to go deeper into his Symbol Theory.

The tripartite structure of symbol

The intricacy of Symbol Theory, the fact that it is a 'general theory' that connects up many disparate things, means that one question inevitably draws in another and another. So however much one tries to simplify things, by taking one thing at a time, the discussion continually spirals out to include more than was initially intended. So the previous question: 'How does language structure our psyches?'

begs another: 'Why do we suppose that psyche and language are two different things in the first place?' The answer to this is that we make an automatic assumption that thought and speech are two different things. In a 'common sense' way, we assume 'I have my thoughts, and I use language to think them'. If we unpack this we find hidden within it an idea of thought existing outside and prior to language. The implication follows that language is just the tool used to express the thoughts. Elias would say that we have the illusion that: there is the mind, and *it* thinks *with* language.

Against this Elias would say that thought and speech are different aspects of the same thing – knowledge: 'Language, reason, knowledge…to speak, to think, to know…all three activities are concerned with the handling of symbols' (Elias 1991, p.65). Knowledge, Elias says, has been mistakenly broken down into three mutually exclusive functions: there is knowledge (the thing itself), how it is stored (thoughts) and how it is communicated (language).

It is clear that this tripartite structure is very similar, if not identical, to the holy trinity of the structuralists – the referent (the thing itself), the signifier (the word), and the signified (the idea).[4] He says:

> All three activities or products of people, refer to perspectives of symbols: *knowledge* mainly to the function of symbols as means to orientation, *language* mainly to their function as means of communication, *thought* mainly to their function as means of exploration, usually at a high level of synthesis and without any action at a lower level. (Elias 1991, p.71)

Knowledge as a social phenomenon

The important thing about knowledge is that first and foremost, it is social, it is communal, it is shared. This inverts Descartes' procedure of beginning inside his mind, and then wondering what else might he know outside of it. Descartes, the consummate armchair philosopher, closes his eyes and proceeds to ask some difficult questions, questions that can be reframed as 'how do I know, that what I think I know, is real?' His solution was to subject everything to scepticism,[5] that is subjecting everything in his mind to the test of doubt and seeing what survived it.

Elias thinks that Descartes has given himself a false problem, and this is so for two reasons. First of all, because Descartes has separated out knowledge and language, and so mistakenly imagines that he 'knows' things which he then puts into language. Language becomes the tool which he uses to 'put' what was inside

---

4   However, Elias makes no mention of either the structuralists or their terminology; it is as though they do not exist.

5   'The notion that the internal structure of this autonomous agency [mind enclosed within the head of every human being] impedes the human capacity ever to know whether what they perceive is real or merely a reflection of the autonomous thinking structure, the thing in the head, is a horror fantasy of highly individualized people.' (Elias 1991, p.82)

him (knowledge) outside. Elias would also say that the second error that Descartes made was to imagine that the individual was a monad – an enclosed entity – that somehow had to find a bridge into the external world. Elias (1991, p.94) puts words into Descartes' mouth: 'here am I – there is the world outside. How can I ever be sure that the pictures formed within me of the world without correspond to that world as it really is independently of myself?'

Elias' solution to the problems posed by Hume and Descartes forms the substance of his 'Symbol Theory', and is made up of several components.

Elias would say to Descartes, 'it is not that you have the thoughts first, which you then put into language – *your thoughts are already in language*'. Descartes might persevere and ask 'but how do I know that language is related to external reality?' Elias would reply that one can be sure of this to some degree, because language evolved in the context of human *activity*, in other words out of people's experience of their interactions with each other and their world.

The hows and whys of language evolution, for Elias, have their basis firmly in human activity. We have to begin, as we often must in this territory, with a paradoxical 'chicken and egg' question: which comes first, language or humans? Elias says that the mistake that the structuralists made was to actually answer the question – they say language comes first. He sets up a question with which to challenge the structuralists: 'If every human being, in order to become fully human, has to learn a pre-existing language, does one not have to conclude that language has an extra-human existence, that it exists in some sense independently of all human beings?' (Elias 1991, p.21). He answers his own question thus:

> The compelling force which a language has in relation to its individual users is not the result of an extra-human, quasi-metaphysical existence of language, but the fact that...[language] represents a unified canon of speaking which has to be observed by a whole group of people if it is to maintain its communicative function. (Elias 1991, p.22)

In other words, language arose out of a *need to communicate about each other and the world*. A need which, if met, would put humans at an advantage at the task of surviving.

'Both statements are valid: "every individual learns a pre-existing social language" and "social language requires individual speakers"' (Elias 1991, p.99). Elias says that this has the appearance of a paradox, for two reasons. First, because in order to answer the question one mistakenly looks for an absolute beginning, where one thing is put before another; and there is no such thing as an absolute beginning.[6] The second error is the fallacious proposition that humans have

---

6   This is true of all questions regarding beginnings. Beginnings are always arbitrary lines drawn in the continuum. For example, one cannot ask when the human eye really began. This is because the eye is not something fixed, it is a process of becoming. Our impression is that it has currently ceased evolving. This is

evolved their cognitive capacities independently of the world. This then 'creates' the problematic question of how the mind then engages with external reality. In fact, 'Human beings have evolved within a world. Their cognitive functions evolved in continuous contact with objects to be recognized' (Elias 1991, p.98). This last point says that thought structures and processes match the world to a large degree because they grew out of the engagement with the world. Putting it teleologically and anthropomorphically – because thought and language came from an engagement with the world, they give the appearance of being *designed* for the purpose of engaging with the world.

These remote philosophical cogitations have surprising bearing on the subject of this book – the relevance of the group. What this philosophical argument is doing is progressively embedding the individual in the larger social context, the group. The arguments are demonstrating how various mechanisms, thoughts and structures, that have the appearance of something private and individual, have their true basis in the communal, the group.

The genesis of thought (and language)

Whilst eschewing absolute beginnings, Elias does speculate that in earlier times 'participation in a hunting expedition entitled a person to participation in those aspects of the preparatory activities most closely related to what we might call thinking...thinking [then] had a much more interpersonal character than the standardized image of thinking operations...' (Elias 1991, p.81). There are several things to be noted in this passage: first, that what we call thinking is born out of concrete activity. Second, in the first instance 'thinking' took place *between* people, not inside them. Third, near the beginning thinking consisted of the manipulation of concrete substances rather than the manipulation of symbols. This last point is in fact very similar to Levi Strauss' notion that, in primitive times, the totemic sign system used concrete things as signs (say, emus), rather than abstract symbols – but that it was a language nonetheless. And being a language, it allowed communication and exchange to take place. 'By identifying with the emu, man makes a sign of himself, and enters as such into the discourse of his society' (Harland 1987, p.29). It is in this tongue-in-cheek way that we can say that our first thoughts were *actual* woolly mammoths.

The outcome of this is that language, by definition, contains representations of human experience as it has evolved in interaction. In other words, language *is* knowledge – they are one and the same. So Elias' short answer to Descartes is that the pictures/words in his head must correspond to the external, because they

not necessarily true. See Richard Dawkins for some interesting discussions on this subject – particularly *River Out of Eden* (1996).

grew out of the external and not out of his head. Elias would agree with the structuralists that it is true that we are 'stuck' in the realm of signifiers; he would also say that we can trust the signifiers to some degree, as they emerged out of activity. 'The fact that human beings depend for their orientation on the use of social symbols is perfectly compatible with the possibility to say that objects exist independently of human beings' (Elias 1991, p.97).

To recapitulate: language grew out of human activity, and it progressed from the concrete to the abstract: '...once the symbol is made abstract, emancipated from the concrete, then human action is freed from the domination of here and now stimulus' (Elias 1991, p.81). Elias suggests that the critical advantage gained through the ability to manipulate abstract symbols was that one could rehearse the consequences of one's actions – one could anticipate. This activity is the one we familiarly know as thinking.

The functions of symbol (that is, language, knowledge and thought) 'are directed towards the control of the social and natural world into which a person is placed' (Elias 1991, p.77). In other words language, and thus thought and knowledge, emerge so that one may better manipulate the environment, so that one is better able to satisfy needs. Surprisingly we find that this sociological formulation is very similar to Freud's psychological idea that the mind is activated in order to manipulate external reality better to satisfy the instincts. The difference between Elias and Freud here is that Elias' 'mind' grows out of a contact with the external world, whilst Freud's 'mind' (ego) is initially precipitated out of internal processes – the id.

Elias is making the important point that language and thought are different aspects of the *same* thing: 'This basic similarity, perhaps *identity* is...at the root of the possibility to convert speech into thought and thought into speech' (Elias 1991, p.81).

The invention of silence

According to Elias, thinking consists of the silent manipulation of sound symbols. The social psychologists George Herbert Mead (1863–1931) and L.S.Vygotsky (1896–1934) would agree with him, and say that thought is in fact an inner conversation – an internalization of the communication processes taking place in the social context. This is indeed a revolutionary way of thinking about thinking – at least to those of us who have previously considered thought and speech as two different activities, and of thought as an exclusively internal and private activity.

One reason that the linkage between thought and speech is hard to recognize is that thinking telescopes and abbreviates sound symbols. 'The telescoped manner of putting linguistic symbols through their paces is often linked to thinking in terms of images' (Elias 1991, p.69). Speaking is 'the handling of symbols in full dress', and thought is the 'flow of voicelessly produced sound symbols'.

Another of the striking elements of Elias' theory is that although the activity that we call thinking might well take place in an internal and private location, the activity itself is still a social activity. It is social on at least two counts: first, thinking consists of an inner *conversation*, and thus at least two structures have to be present. And second, the symbols that are used and manipulated in thought processes are first and foremost social symbols. 'Thinking as well as speaking relies on socially standardized sound-symbols. Both are social activities' (Elias 1991, p.82). In another place he says that 'the sound pattern has been socially stamped with...[the] message' (Elias 1991, p.59).

Like Piaget and Vygotsky, Elias noticed that young children talk aloud to themselves. Piaget thought that this speech was 'evidence of the fundamentally egocentric nature of childhood speech' (Burkitt 1991, p.146), which later became social communication. The direction here is the traditional one of beginning with the individual and moving outwards to the group. Vygotsky, on the other hand, thought that 'the child...[used] words to guide its own behaviour by talking aloud to itself as an adult would who was giving the child instructions' (pp.146–147). According to Vygotsky and Elias, the child talking aloud to itself gives us a glimpse of thought and thinking before it is internalized, long before it is made silent and invisible. Thus Elias says: 'Children are more inclined than adults to think aloud. In fact, thinking in silence without any overt form of speaking has to be learned...the voiceless forms of thinking and reading corresponds to a specific stage of social and individual development' (Elias 1991, pp.65–66).

These then are two of Elias' insights which will be critical to any reformulation of group theory. First is the social basis of thought and speech: 'Communication in the form of human speech...presupposes as the normal form of living a life in groups. *So does the activity we call thinking*' (Elias 1991, p.81). And second is the identity of thought and speech. He makes the interesting point that one usually says of a child 'that it is learning to *speak*'. According to him, it would be equally true to say that the child is learning to *think*. It is not just that the child is putting its experiences into words, it is also that the child is simultaneously using words to recognize, construct and name its experiences.

This section has focused on one aspect of Symbol Theory: the identity between internal activity (thought) and language. The next section continues the task already begun here, which is the linkage between knowledge and language, in other words, between language and the external world.

Language, knowledge and consciousness

Elias says that language has two functions, orientation and communication. To fully comprehend the profundity of this statement, we have to unpack it slowly. Let us begin with communication. The notion of communication presupposes that there is someone else there to communicate with. This rather ordinary seeming statement reminds us forcibly that the existence of language presupposes a social community with shared understandings:

> ...language can serve as the prototypical model of a social fact. It presupposes the existence not only of one actor, but of a group of two or more co-acting people. It fosters and at the same time requires a degree of group integration. In any given case a group of language speakers exists prior to the individual speaking act. A language, in other words, cannot be dissolved into individual actions, communicative or otherwise. It is as it were the prototype of a beginningless process. (Elias 1991, p.21)

This has to be so for language to work as communication. Words have to mean similar things to the speaker and to the listener – otherwise language would fail in its communicative function. This is not meant just on the level of speaker and listener having a similar understanding of, say, the word 'tree'. This is meant on a much deeper level, not only what is meant by 'tree', but also how one is to think about trees, are they good or bad things, useful or not and so forth. In other words, language also encapsulates shared attitudes and emotional valences. This last point reoccurs in the later discussion on orientation.

It is clear enough that communication is an interpersonal phenomenon. By definition, it presupposes something shared, and thus presupposes living within a community, a group. Within this territory, we have already begun to engage with the sub-question of just how much and what is shared, and answered that much more is shared, and at a much deeper level, than is commonly supposed.

Let us now move on to the second function of language, orientation. The way Elias uses it, orientation is another name for knowledge. Elias means two sorts of things by orientation. First, quite literally, language orientates one to the world, in effect describes positions and relationships. At its most basic, every sentence uttered is a description of the nature of the relatedness of each of the elements of the sentence to each other. '[Language] offers a separate name, a separate symbol for every experience within the reach of the group; it offers at the same time models of their relationship' (Elias 1991, p.70). At another level, a sentence also reveals something about the position of the speaker relative to the things being spoken about. Second, Elias also means that language orients each person to the world, in the sense of what to make of it: what is up and what is down, what is good and what is bad, what is right and what is wrong, and so on. This is the domain of emotions, which, traditionally, psychoanalysis has derived exclusively from a biological basis. It is thought that we are born with our emotional structures, a pre-given, which then get triggered and activated in various situations. Elias is saying that our emotional structures too are formed within the social context: 'symbols [exist] in the wide sense of the word including not only knowledge, but, for example, also standards of conduct and *sentiment*.' (Elias 1991, p.23)

The outcome is that language, symbols, knowledge, *places* each of us in particular positions in the world, in other words it orients us. 'Humans are located in the four spatio-temporal dimensions like all pre human events, but are in addition as human being located in a fifth dimension, that of symbols' (Elias 1991, p.47). It is tempting to think that with this notion of the fifth dimension of symbols, Elias is describing the internal psychological world. But this is not so. Symbol Theory incorporates psychology, but it is bigger than that; it also incorporates sociology, and goes beyond that too. The power of Symbol Theory is that it transcends the usual internal–external dichotomy – what is inside our minds is also outside our minds. Surprisingly, in making this statement we find ourselves in close proximity to Kleinian territory.

Through a combination of the notions of the fusion of the instincts and of projection, Klein would say that whatever one experiences of the world – out there – one will always find a part of oneself somehow embedded in it, and that this projected part of the self will critically colour one's experience of the external. In another language we could say that this is a description of the fact that subjectivity always permeates objectivity. Thus, in this sense, Klein too would agree that what is inside our minds is also outside our minds. However, Elias and Klein part company in the consideration of how this comes about. Klein's model owes a considerable amount to Leibniz's (1646–1716) philosophical view of the individual as monad, and also Kant's (1724–1804) philosophy of the *a priori*. According to Leibniz, individuals are windowless closed entities, each absolute in its separation from the other. As we have already seen, this gave rise to Descartes' conundrum which was: how does one then get from the inside to the outside? Leibniz's solution was the 'doctrine of pre-established harmony'. This is a version of the *a priori* in which God ensures that the internal states of each of the monads are inclined towards each other. The perception of causal relations between entities is said to be of illusory constructions supplied by God. Kant's solution was the proposal that one was born with *a priori* categories, in a sense 'pictures' of the world, and that it was these that allowed one to form a bridge from the inside to the outside. Klein says, like Kant, that the infant comes into the world loaded with *a priori* categories, and also the instincts. The Kleinian infant begins building a bridge from the internal world to the external world in three ways: first the *a priori* categories (e.g. a picture of the breast) that it is born with lead it outwards in particular directions. Second, the infant 'throws' out parts of itself, which it then proceeds to find there. Third, one of the things that the infant projects out is the death instinct. Once this is done then the infant's experience is that of being attacked and threatened by a malign external world; here the infant experiences the external world coming towards it. It is from these tenuous beginnings that a progressively elaborate bridge is constructed. So although it is true to say that Kleinian theory mixes up the internal and external, it is in a very particular way, and differs according to the stage in the developmental process. So at the beginnings of life, the direction is almost exclusively from the inside to the outside. Here the inside is found on the outside. Whatever is found in the external world at this stage is said to be a projection of the internal world to a large degree. As the developmental process continues, then parts of the external world are progressively incorporated into the internal world. The main point however is that in the Kleinian (and Freudian) view there is a gulf between the internal and the external which has to be bridged.

In contrast to this, Elias' Symbol Theory does not suppose that there is a gap to be bridged. For him existence *is* interdependence. The idea is so fundamental it is hard to describe its significance. Perhaps a parallel from physics will help. The existence of any object presupposes that it exists in space, and so also presupposes that its gravitational field will interact with the gravitational field of every other object in the entire universe. There cannot be one without the other. It is not a matter of choice, they all exist simultaneously. Human existence is similar – we begin as we must, in the web of symbol. And, as in the gravitational analogy, the nature of our existence immediately connects[7] us to others. Our movements are immediately shaped and constrained by the presence of others. By the same token the mere fact of our presence has immediately modified the symbolic (gravitational) field.

It is as well to re-remind ourselves that Elias does not mean that language *determines* one's attitudes and views, but that it *constrains* it: '...a given language and particularly the mother-tongue, *pre-empts an individual's thinking*...it is not possible, within limits, to cut oneself loose from categories implicit in one's languages...' (Elias 1991, p.70; emphasis added).

If one limits one's focus to the constraining dynamic, then it appears that one might be able to cast off this constraint, be free of it, and *really* experience the truth of the world. This is an impossibility. The thing that constrains us, is also the thing that forms us. 'Being by nature endowed with the capacity for orienting themselves in the world by means of language symbols, they are also in need of symbols...in short they cannot become human without learning a language'

---

7   Here is a problem with language. The word 'connects' invites one to view separate entities which are then 'connected' by a wire or line or something. Another word is needed to describe the state in which one is part of the fabric of existence itself.

(Elias 1991, p.57). We can no more live outside influence than we can outside gravity.

We are beginning to get an idea of the enormity of this way of thinking about 'language' or 'knowledge'. In fact it is intimately tied up with consciousness itself. Elias instructs us that consciousness does not exist as an empty state prior to knowledge, which is then later thought to 'fill it'. He says: 'No consciousness without knowledge, no knowledge without consciousness. Consciousness is merely another word for the condition in which stored sound symbols, or in other words knowledge as a means of orientation, can be mobilized at will in the normal way' (Elias 1991, p.120).

Once again a parallel from modern physics is helpful. Contemporary cosmology asserts (with good reason) that 'space' within the universe appeared at the same time as 'matter' and 'time'. In other words the container and the contained appeared simultaneously at the beginning of the known universe. Before the Big Bang not only were there no 'things' there was also no space or time for 'things' to exist in. One cannot exist without the other. If there were no matter then space would collapse. I think that Elias is describing the notion of consciousness in this sort of way.

Elias also reframes the idea of the unconscious in a similar way: 'The Freudian term "unconscious" refers to a condition in which stored experiences, though they may be still effective as determinants of action, cannot be recollected at will' (Elias 1991, p.120).

The limits of thought

The arguments linking knowledge, thought and speech lead us in the direction of the startling assertion that what is not within language, cannot be known. If this is so then it prompts another question: if things that are not within language cannot be known, then how can anything *new* come about? How do new thoughts, experiences and ways of viewing the world arise?

One way round it is to say that language is infinite. True, parole is, but langue is not. It is true that within the constraints of a particular langue, there are an infinite number of permutations of the available words. This is parole. However, the critical thing is that one is limited to the words within a language, and the rules for their arrangements that are embedded within a langue – a particular way of seeing and dissecting the world. The important point that Elias is making is that language and knowledge are different aspects of the *same thing*. Language doesn't just 'hold' knowledge, language *is* knowledge. So how can new knowledge appear? For the moment let us leave the question hanging.

The genesis of knowledge (and language)

To say that language is knowledge is another way of saying that language arises out of the experience of the engagement with and in the world. This is different from the traditional conceptualization which says that language exists separately from the world, and then is used to describe it. Elias is saying that as language has evolved out of social and material activity, it already contains the world, it already represents it. To be more precise, language contains and represents *experiences* of the world. 'A language symbolically represents the world as it has come to be experienced by members of a society where it is spoken.' (Elias 1991, p.129) These experiences are accumulated and stored in the concepts of a language; thus language is also conceived of as a repository, a container for the accumulated experiences and knowledge of the world. One could say that language is in itself a *precipitate* of historical experiences and attitudes, and that these precipitates constrain the way contemporary experiences will be understood. '[Language] reflects the world at large and at the same time the group of people, the societies which use the symbols as means of communication'. (Elias 1991, p.129) The argument is recursive: not only does language reflect the world, it also informs how the world is experienced. This is the paradox; Elias puts it like this: 'A people's language is itself a symbolic representation of the world as members of that society have learnt to experience it during the sequence of their changing fortunes. At the same time a people's language affects their perception and thus also their fortunes' (Elias 1991, p.61). Elias is constantly trying to hang on to both sides of the polarity and tries not to collapse on one side or other: '...the language one speaks, which forms an integral part of one's personality, is a social fact *presupposing* the existence of other human beings and *preceding* the existence of any particular individual' (Elias 1991, p.21; emphasis added).

Burkitt's (1991, p.120) paraphrase of Karl Marx elegantly captures Elias' philosophical stance:

> humans make their own history but they do not make it under conditions of their own choosing: they make it under conditions handed down from previous generations, in the form of the mode of production and its dynamics. In this effort, the means of acting upon the world will be expanded, but under conditions inherited from the past.

Language as bridge between social and biological

Language has a tentacle in every domain. We have noted its equivalence with knowledge, speech and thought. We have also noted its footholds in the external and the social. As we have seen, for Elias, language is never supra-human. He does not follow the route of the structuralists and allocate language a life of its own, outside human experience. True, once langue exists, then it does exert power over individuals and constrain them, but that does not make it non-human. Just as language has a basis in the social, it is also grounded in the body. He says about the processes of thought, knowledge, language, that they are 'not entities on their own, but functions *bound to organs*' (Elias 1991, p.69; emphasis added). One is reminded here of one of Freud's thoughts that he never developed, that the ego was first of all a body ego.

Elias continually reiterates the point that the polarization nature/nurture is not particularly useful as it leads one into a series of intellectual *culs-de-sac*. Elias says that the social aspects of life are not against 'human nature', rather '...far from being polar opposites, in the human case biological and social processes, in order to become effective, must interlock' (Elias 1991, p.6). What he means by this is that the two, the social and the biological, go hand in hand, working *with* each other and not against each other. The biologically given predisposition to learn language needs 'to be activated and *patterned* during early childhood by a process of learning' in order to become functional. For language to become a manifest reality it needs the presence of other human beings.

To prioritize nature over society or vice versa is a pointless activity, as both are necessary for all elements of human life as we know it: 'human beings cannot be polarized and divided in this manner. Language...is one of the missing links between nature and society or culture. Humans...are made *by* nature *for* culture and society' (Elias 1991, p.84; emphasis added).

If we think about it from a Darwinian viewpoint, we can say that a multitude of aspects and attributes evolve randomly. Some of these 'survive' because they are useful. And by 'useful' what is meant is that they are good at surviving. Emotions or, to be more precise, the potential for emotions, must come about the same way. At their most basic they are a signal for the presence of danger or not-danger. Now Elias is constantly reminding us that it is a mistake to imagine either that things exist or grow in individuals prior to experience, or that things are made exclusively by experience. And this is as true of emotions as it is for any other experience. Elias would say that the biological potential to emote has evolved and remains because it is useful. However this potential has to be socially patterned to come into existence. The intriguing point is that social patterns too have evolved, and are thus aspects of nature. As he puts it, 'human society is a level of nature' (Elias 1991, p.85). This notion is central and permeates all of his work: he is saying that the things we designate as social and counterpose against the 'natural' are 'natural in themselves'. Our social systems and artifacts have not appeared out of thin air, but have emerged through an evolutionary process. The social exists and continues to exist because, at the moment, it favours the human species by giving it tools to organize and do better at spreading than other species. To be sure this propensity might also be the undoing of the species, *but that does not make it unnatural*. This is as true of humanity as it is of the untold other species that have become extinct.

Grunts and grins

In the interminable nature/nurture controversy, language is partitioned into 'natural' and 'social'. Elias goes along with this division for some considerable distance. He puts it like this: 'Humans are biologically equipped for two different types of communication, for communication by means of *species-specific* pre-language signals such as laughter and by means of *group-specific* languages' (Elias 1991, p.87). Elias emphasizes the fact that humans are the only species that has developed group-specific languages. He then makes the interesting point that the species-specific pre-language signals communicate information about the subject – I am frightened, happy, etc. – through smiles, grunts, cries of pain, and so forth, whilst it is the group-specific languages that allow communications to be made about not-self objects and phenomena. However even the pre-language symbols are not straightforward any more; the example he uses is that of the smile. There are many kinds of smile, the manipulative smile of the salesperson, the smile of a child, the wry smile and so on.

He speculates that one of the impetuses for the *variety* of languages emerging was inter-group competition. He speculates that as one group's language becomes more elaborate it allows them to communicate information in finer detail, and so gain advantage over their neighbours. Elias also considers two other reasons for the drive to differentiate, 'cohesion and creativity. His notion of cohesion is very reminiscent of Durkheim's suggestion that difference is instituted *between groups*, in order to bind and cohere the interiors of each group. The other reason is not so much a reason as such, more an explanation of why (put teleologically and anthropomorphically) the evolutionary process has thought it to be a sufficiently useful property to allow variety to evolve. This is taken up next, albeit rather obliquely.

Novelties and fantasies

It is time now to return to the question posed earlier, how do new thoughts and ways of experiencing the world and self arise? Remember, Elias has said that, 'One can say that what is without symbolic representation in the language of a society is not known by its members' (Elias 1991, p.3).

Elias' answer has several parts to it – one of which lies in the human capacity to produce a wide and variable range of sound patterns. It is this versatility that allows something new to arise: 'Without innovatory changes of the sound patterns of a language, innovatory changes of knowledge would not be possible' (Elias 1991, p.4). This is the baseline, and is another way of saying that if there is no name for a thing then it cannot be known, thought about or experienced.

It seems to me that this idea is overstated – because it conflates two different things, words and arrangements of words. The same words (names) used in different arrangements also give rise to something new. A good example of this is computer code. At its most basic, computer language has a vocabulary of two – on and off. Strings of these (on–offs) are combined to build a particular set of instructions ('words' if you will) which number from 50 or so to a few hundred. These 'words' are what constitute a particular computer language. A good programmer does not invent new instructions, but instead finds novel ways of combining existing instructions to engage in novel tasks and procedures. Another good example is DNA. DNA has a basic vocabulary of four 'words' – T,G,C and A. The variety of combinations of just these four words have given forth the multiplicity of life as we know it. Indeed it continues to throw up novel combinations – the eventual outcome of which is new creatures.

To this criticism Elias and the structuralists would say yes, there are innovations, but they are limited to what can be achieved within that language, that particular langue. For example one cannot step outside the grammatical structure of language; if one does not follow it closely enough, then a communication would make no sense.

Elias goes further; he says that the 'novel' can only emerge and become meaningful *within* the social context. Once again this inverts the traditional way of viewing things – the picture of the solitary genius who has a new thought all by him or herself – shouting 'Eureka' and running through the streets spreading enlightenment. Elias says: 'individual mental process alone is never enough to account for the presence in a language of any new concept attached to a specific sound-pattern. It can attain this character only when it has gone through the mill of dialogues involving and interweaving the mental activities of many people' (Elias 1991, p.56). One should remember that even Einstein's staggering insights were built on the work of previous theoreticians from physics, mathematics and chemistry. It took some time before they became part of the intellectual currency, and this only after dialogue with others in the field.

The next part of Elias' explanation of how the new arises brings him surprisingly close to some psychoanalytic ideas. He says that 'Humans…were by nature equipped with a *need to know*…the need to know is an aspect of the genetic constitution of humans' (Elias 1991, pp.74–75; emphasis added). This is exactly the same as Melanie Klein's notion of the epistemophilic instinct; she too thought that there was a drive to know. Whilst both Elias and Klein are in agreement that the drive has a biological basis, they diverge in how the potential comes into existence. Klein says that the instinct is activated by sexual curiosity, which occurs very early on in the maturational process, when the ego is still very weak. According to Klein, the problem for the infant/child is that it does not as yet have a language in which to formulate its curiosity, and so it feels persecuted by it. Additionally, this is also the time of anal and urethral sadism in the developmental process, and these sadistic tendencies get entangled with the epistemophilic instinct. The outcome in Klein's theory is that the epistemophilic instinct comes to be driven by sadism: '...the child...dominated by the anal-sadistic libido position...[which] impels him to wish to appropriate the contents of the body. He thus begins to be curious about what it contains...' (Klein 1928, p.188).

Elias' explanation of the hows and whys of this drive's existence is given in terms of evolution. Although he does not say so directly, he implies that it has evolved out of random mutations, and it survives as it is profoundly useful to the survival and growth of the human species. Fundamentally it helps give the species control over the environment and themselves. However, this knowledge is always partial – there are inevitable gaps in it. He says that these gaps are filled by fantasy knowledge.

The introduction of the notion of fantasy once again brings him close to psychoanalysis. However, for Klein, phantasy was the mental correlate of the instincts, whilst for Elias, fantasy is the outcome of the need to know. To expand, Elias says that not to know something is too frightening, so one papers over the gaps with fantasy knowledge, that is, explanations that emerge from the imagination. 'All that is known is known by its name. The nameless occurrence is frightening' (Elias 1991, p.96). Here too he finds common ground with the psychoanalysts, both with the notion of fantasy, and also with the notion that not-to-know causes terror.

So knowledge is always a combination of reality-congruent knowledge and fantasy knowledge. Elias does not suppose that there is an inevitable trend towards ever increasing reality congruence – it can go one way or another and is always in a state of flux. What is remembered and what is forgotten is not arbitrary, but always intimately connected to the social conditions of the time. Thus knowledge is never 'pure', it is always permeated by the ideology arising from the power structures of the time. In other words the state of knowledge always serves a hidden function – that of somehow bolstering particular hierarchies under the guise of truth or naturalness. This gives rise to the problem that 'emotionally fantasy knowledge can take deep roots in the lives of human groups. It can give to such an extent the impression of being reality-congruent that it blocks the search for more reality-congruent symbols' (Elias 1991, pp.57–58). One can view religious systems and the notion of God in this light; one can also view the varieties of psychoanalysis, group analysis and the notion of the unconscious in this light. So one never knows which elements of one's knowledge are reality congruent and which are fantasy based.

But whichever way it goes, knowledge is always the property of the group. 'People...learn or forget as groups' (Elias 1991, p.73). This gives rise to the intriguing idea that what is considered to be objective and true at any moment in time is the outcome of a sociological process. This process might be an enlightened democratic one, or it might be a more dictatorial one.

It as well to remember here the deep linkage and identity that Elias makes between knowledge and language. Thus through the very use of language, in speaking or thinking, one unknowingly perpetuates and perpetrates particular types of value-laden knowledge as truth. We think we know what is true, because it is known by others to be so.

To recapitulate the argument: the new can arise because there is a biological flexibility to accommodate the new, in other words the possibility of producing new sound patterns. The other basis for the new is the generation of fantasy knowledge, theories which might or might not be reality congruent. And fantasy knowledge arises because it is too dreadful not to know. In summary, knowledge has at least three separate functions: to control the world (Elias 1991, p.77), to avoid the terror of the nameless, and to bolster hierarchies. The other main point is that knowledge can never be other than communal.

A bird's-eye view

Elias' theory is built on two central pillars – Symbol Theory and figuration. The fundamental idea that underpins each of these is the concept of interdependence. One could summarize Elias' entire theory by saying that it consists of nothing more or less than tracking the consequences of interdependence. In other words, everything is connected in some way to everything else, and so everything affects everything. Put like this, his theory is based on a simple and straightforward idea; but as we have already seen, the consequences of it are not at all straightforward. Thus the two pillars are not separate and distinct, but different aspects of the same thing, and so interdependent on each other.

One could say that the *philosophical* aspects of his theory are contained in the notion of 'Symbol Theory', which ties together thought, speech and fact through a sophisticated idea of language. An outcome of this process is that a number of dichotomies are rendered redundant: the internal and external, nature and nurture, and mind and body. He has shown how elements have been abstracted and allocated to one or other side of the dichotomies, and are then perceived as being in conflict with each other. He has then demonstrated how they are in fact not in conflict but interdependent on each other. In other words, they *need* each other. This shift from conflict to mutuality is not at all a complacent hippie ideology of pseudo-mysticism of love and connectedness embracing us all. *It leads actually to the politicization of the psyche.*

This follows from a consequence of interdependence which is that what is *able* to be thought, said and known is not just a function of intellect but also a function of the 'power relations' between people and groups of people. This can be described as the *socio-political* dimension of the theory. It is important to remember that the notion of power, an aspect of figuration, does not exist 'outside individuals, but merely results from the interdependence between individuals' (Elias and Scotson 1994, p.172).

The ultimate consequence of interdependence is that it leads in a circle back into Symbol Theory, to say that the structure of the mind itself, the entity that thinks the thoughts and feels the feelings, is not something that one is just born with. Elias says that the structure of the mind is not a universal, but is contingent, and partly determined by the themes that exist in the socio-political dimension. This is the *psychological* dimension of his theory.

The breadth of vision of Elias' theory is staggering, moving as it does between philosophy, politics and psychology. The sheer magnitude of the task that Elias engages with is surely the equal of Freud's. Both of them set out to derive and understand *all* of human existence – nothing is off limits. The difference between them is that at the core of the Freudian schema lies 'instinctual conflict', and at the core of the Eliasian schema lies 'interdependence'.

From self to selfcentredness: new age psychologies

One theme runs through all the discussion so far; that is the social nature of humanity. As we have seen, Elias does not mean by 'social' something which is in conflict with 'nature', but very much as a form of nature. This is the genetic source of all that emerges – the socio-political and the psychological. At this point it will be helpful to summarize the different ways in which this point is made by Elias.

First and foremost, the very existence of language, its very emergence, presupposes life in a group, a participatory community: 'language can serve as the prototypical model of a social fact. It presupposes the existence not only of one actor, but of a group of two or more co-acting people' (Elias 1991, p.21). Elsewhere he says, 'The structure of language reflects...very clearly, not the nature of the human being, nor the individual person seen in isolation, but human beings in society' (Elias 1991, p.68). He bases this on the fact that every statement makes clear the relationship of the sentence-elements to each other. 'It reflects the recurrent social need to express clearly in a socially standardized symbolic form the position in relation to the sender and the receiver of a message to which the message refers' (Elias 1991, p.86).

The fact that human beings also live in the fifth dimension, the realm of symbols, also leads inexorably to the idea of relatedness. 'All symbols imply relationships. They indicate how the people who use a particular symbol layer connect the world and its various aspects and items with each other' (Elias 1991, p.129).

All through his work, Elias is explicitly and implicitly arguing against philosophies that give 'the impression that every human being is by nature fitted for living alone as an isolated individual' (Elias 1991, p.51). The deification of the individual is most apparent in the excesses of some humanistic and new age psychologies. For example, a key speaker from the humanistic tradition said in his talk at the United Kingdom Confederation of Psychotherapists (UKCP) conference in 1997: 'the most important conversation a therapist has is with himself, and the most important conversation that a client has is with themselves' (Rex Bradley, a member of the Humanistic and Integrative Psychotherapy Section of the UKCP). This bizarre statement follows out of an ideology that says that human beings are asocial, that their 'true' nature is something outside human relatedness. In fact the suggestion is that relatedness somehow corrupts this true internal self. Under the guise of being a liberationist philosophy, it is in fact an expression of a completely solipsistic and self centred ideology – as long as I'm all right, Jack, I have no responsibility towards you. To be sure, it is an attempt to moderate the excesses of the superego, but the solution proposed is to deify the id.

The modern fantasy is to agree that early people lived in groups or even herds. This group primacy is accommodated by the device of naming it primitive; primitive people live in groups – which are said to be primitive social structures. The fantasy continues, that now, in modernity, we are individuated, and manage somehow to live outside and beyond groups. Moreover, those cultures and peoples that explicitly live in groups (extended families and so on) are considered to be still primitive. The notion of individuation is the fantasy that the more evolved the person, the more autonomous and free he or she is of the constraints of society and community – 'they' might live in groups, 'we' certainly don't, 'we' are free to choose. Margaret Thatcher is noted for stating the most extreme version of this ideology, that 'there is no such thing as society. There are only individuals and families'. By implication and inference Rex Bradley and Mrs Thatcher are in the same camp.

It does seem that some appear to have much more autonomy than others. Not only in what they are able to do, but also in what they are able to think, to feel and to say. How is this? The Thatcherite might answer that these people are just constitutionally better endowed, and so *naturally* do better than the others. The humanistic answer might be similar, saying that this person does better because they are more in touch with their 'true' self, or in harmony with their energy, or some such formulation. These arguments are myths, they reflect a particular ideology. Or to use Eliasian language, it is fantasy knowledge. Undoubtedly some people are better constitutionally endowed than others, but that is not the whole story.[8] To be able to make further headway in this argument, we have to take up the notion of 'ideology', and take up the consequences of Elias' theory in the external socio-political world. We will now move on to describing the socio-

---

8   There are hereditary members of the House of Lords that are energetic and astute, and there are hereditary members that make Bertie Wooster seem like Einstein; the issue is that despite their evident differences in endowment, they are both members of a ruling hierarchy.

political dimension of Elias' theory, and see how this dimension impacts on the psyche.

Dirty talk: politics

In the world of psychotherapy, politics is a dirty word. It is often said or implied that there is no place for politics in the consulting room, and should it intrude, then it is a displacement from a 'deeper' internal psychological issue. One hears much the same sort of thing in other arenas as well, for example, 'keep politics out of sport'. Implicit in the often made criticism that sport (or whatever) is being politicized is the idea that politics is secondary to existence. What Elias' work shows is that politics, that is power relations, are part of the fabric of human existence, and that it is not the politicization of events that needs to be questioned, rather it is the impulse to de-politicize that needs to be examined.

As has already been said, to take the group seriously, is to take the social seriously. This in turn means that one has to take social *relations* seriously, and this cannot be separated out from power and therefore political relations. Thus to take the group seriously, is always to take the political seriously.

The socio-political elements of Elias' work are encapsulated in a book written with Scotson and entitled *The Established and the Outsiders*. This work takes Scotson's observations of a community near Leicester in the late 1950s and early 1960s, and frames them in a general theory of inequality, a theory that has its basis in Eliasian ideas.

The community was given the pseudonym of Winston Prava, and consisted of three 'zones'. The first of these was predominantly middle class, and the other two working class. The two working class zones were distinguished by the fact that one of them was 'established' and had been there for some generations. The other working class zone was a new construction – where the outsiders took residence. The work focused on what took place between the inhabitants of Zones Two and Three. One of the fascinating things about this study is the fact that a neutral observer, new to the situation, would have been hard-pressed to distinguish the inhabitants from each other. None of the usual categories of difference existed between the two zones – class, religion, colour and so on. The distinguishing feature was solely that one zone had a history – and the other did not.

Nevertheless, the surprising thing was that the dynamics between the two groups were found to contain all the kinds of things that one normally associates and *explains* as consequences of other differences – say 'race' or religion, and so on. The thesis of their book is that 'difference' is used to sustain power differences. They found that it was not the presence of difference that caused hatred, but that differences were used to stir up hatred, to *preserve* power differentials.

The institution of power

The elementary fact that one group is more established in an area leads to some surprising and significant consequences. To describe a group as established means that it has cohesion and an internal order and hierarchy. This order and cohesion is not one that is explicit in any way; it is somehow structured into the nature of the internal relations of the group, and it implicitly organizes the relationships of the group to other groups. The fact that 'one group has a higher cohesion rate than the other...[then] this integration differential substantially contributes to the former's power surplus' (Elias 1976, p.xix). Better cohesion means better organization, and so allows them to exclude members of the new group from participation in the existing structures of power very efficiently. The new group, by contrast, is not yet a group, and so lack the basic elements of cohesion (Elias 1976, p.xviii). One could say that the newcomers, being in parts and fragments, had no central identity, no name for them jointly to belong to. Thus they were in a vulnerable state – vulnerable to being *given a name*, a bad name! 'Lacking cohesion, they were unable to close their own ranks and fight back' (Elias 1976, p.xxii).

The significance of time

To say that a group are 'established', is to locate them in time. This underlines the important point that whatever is taking place, is taking place in time – that is, it is a *historical* process. This means that one will not be able to understand what is taking place if one does not contextualize the events. To contextualize is to locate the events in *space* (to relate them to other contemporary events and structures), and to locate the events in *time* (relate them to what has happened previously). If one does not view a situation as a moment in a *process*, then one has to derive explanation somehow from inside each group. Let us schematize the situation to make the point clearer. Group A is acting in a hateful way to Group B. If we now ask questions of this hatred, how does it come to be here, why is it being expressed in this way, etc., then where do we look for answers? If we leave the context aside, then the only data we have available from which to construct an explanation are the internal elements of the groups themselves, or the contemporary dynamics between the groups. In such a situation one is forced to reach for answers like the death instinct, or the aggressive instinct, group prejudice and so forth. Elias and Scotson argue against the 'present conventions of thinking, [in which] *history has no structure and structure no history*' (1994, p.21; emphasis added). Thus if history is not taken into account, and a contemporary racism, or other violence between two groups, is looked at in this light, then it is not thought of as part of an ongoing process and instead becomes a reified thing. If one ignores process then one will look for causes *inside* the groups and inside the individuals, and use other constructs like splitting and projection to explain the effects of these internal phenomena.

We can see then how this notion of process undermines a purely psycho-analytic analysis, as that emphasizes internal elements of the groups. However, the notion of process also undermines a purely Marxist analysis that explains the structure of the situation exclusively through access to the means of production. Elias stresses that it is the fact that the older group had had a longer period of residence that is essential to the analysis. This time factor allowed the old to organize and cohere. This reveals 'the limitations of any theory which explains power differentials only in terms of monopolistic possession of non-human objects, such as weapons or means of production, and disregards functional aspects of power differentials due purely to differences in the degree of organ-ization of the human beings concerned' (Elias 1976, p.xviii). Thus some of the power differentials are the outcome purely of the *structure of the situation*, in time and space. Notice that Elias is not replacing the Marxist analysis or the psychoanalytic analysis with a structural analysis. He is saying that, as analyses, they are partial and limited if they take no account of time and space.

The term 'cohesion' is intimately connected to a sense of 'we'. Thus to think that a 'we' has come about because of certain shared attributes, cultural, racial or otherwise, is to begin at the end of things. It is more true to say that the elements are found to be contemporaneously shared *because* there has been time enough to build up a collection of shared attributes:

> they [the old families] had undergone together a group process – from the past via the present towards the future – which provided them with a stock of common memories, attachments and dislikes. Without regard to this diachronic group dimension, the rationale and meaning of the personal pronoun 'we'…cannot be understood. (Elias 1976, p.xxxviii)

More dirty talk: ideology

If we accept that there are inevitable power differentials between groups, then we may move on to examining the structures and mechanisms that are used to maintain the advantage of the power differential. Often enough these mech-anisms are overt and consist of brute force and physical violence. These are explicit and self evident although the perpetrators of the violence have a variety of ways of rationalizing their actions. For example Paulo Freire says:

> with the establishment of a relationship of oppression, violence has *already* begun. Never in history has violence been initiated by the oppressed. How could they be the initiators, if they themselves are the product of violence?… It is always the oppressed [who are blamed]…who are [said to be] disaffected, who are 'violent', 'barbaric', 'wicked', or 'ferocious' when they react to the violence of the oppressors. (1972, pp.31–32)

However, in Winston Prava, as in all 'normal' societies, the mechanisms are invisible and so more insidious. If one accepts as axiomatic that the more powerful seek to preserve their power differentials, then everything else follows seamlessly from that. For example Elias says that the differences between the two groups was not self evident: 'it was at first surprising that the inhabitants of one area felt the *need*...to treat those of the other as inferior to themselves...' (1976, p.xvii; emphasis added). The answer of course is that the 'need' is predicated on the wish to preserve the power differentials, and so it is not surprising at all. One of the critical elements in this process is the institution of the polarity inferior–superior over the arena and players. There are two main elements to this process, two terms that are not normally put together – ideology and gossip.

The structure of ideology

Currently ideology is not part of the vocabulary of either psychoanalysis or group analysis. Presumably because it is considered to belong to the domain of politics. As I hope eventually to demonstrate through Elias' Symbol Theory, it will be necessary to institute the term in the centre of any psychotherapeutic project, giving it a weight equal to that of the unconscious. There are a variety of definitions of ideology – some of which we have already come across. Earlier we quoted Eagleton (1983) who says that ideology is a particular way of viewing the world – a way that is defined by the more powerful. Rose, Lewontin and Kamin (1984, pp.3–4n) put it like this:

> Ideologies are the ruling ideas of a particular society at a particular time. They are ideas that express the naturalness of any existing social order and help maintain it. The ideas of the ruling class are in every epoch the ruling ideas; i.e. the class which is the ruling material force of society is at the same time its ruling intellectual force. The class which has the means of material production at its disposal has control at the same time over the means of mental production...

Elias and Scotson (1994) describe ideology as a weapon. One aspect of ideology is the construction of particular binary oppositions – and perhaps the most fundamental of binary oppositions is 'us' and 'them'. Which particular binary oppositions will come to the fore, and the forms they take, will be dependent on the function they are to serve. Now, ideology is always invisible to the conscious mind. Much like elements of the Freudian unconscious, ideology too drives and determines behaviour in invisible ways. Ideology is a means of preserving the current social order by making it seem natural, unquestionable, by *convincing* all the participants that it is so.

In using the term 'convincing' we find that we have somehow migrated from the domain of socio-politics to the domain of psychology, to the mind and its state. This is an example of the point made earlier, that because in Elias' theory everything is connected to everything else, the argument constantly spirals out into unintended arenas. So for the moment let us just note the fact that the discussion which begins with the notion of power ends up in the psyche, and take it up more fully a little later.

Returning to the discussion on ideology, we now have to ask: how does it work? Ideology has been given a prodigiously powerful role: it is said to organize society and the minds of the people that inhabit it. How does it 'convince' people? What are the mechanisms through which ideology is transmitted? Where and how does it reside?

It is part of the all pervasiveness of the notion of ideology, that one cannot even ask a straightforward question, without immediately chopping it up – deconstructing it. We are obliged to engage with these questions at a more fundamental level before we can proceed to answer them. Let us take just one of the statements: 'ideology organizes society and the minds that inhabit it'.

This sentence as it stands leads one to think that ideology *causes* the state of mind of the individual. This is true to a degree, but one also has to remember that the argument is circular, and that the mind, in a manner of speaking, causes ideology. It is a limitation of the structure of language that this circularity cannot be encompassed in a sentence. In effect, a sentence cuts the circle at a particular point, and turns it into a line. The cut turns the intricacy into a linearity, with a beginning cause and a concluding effect. The 'cut' invents a beginning.

One can see that even this act, the choice of where to cut the circle, is an ideological act. It has given forth a particular opposition – a cause and an effect. Causes are always more value laden than effects, they carry more weight and significance in the mind. By cutting the circle here, in saying ideology organizes society and mind, one finds that one has prioritized the external. If one were to cut the circle in another place and say that individuals make ideology, then one has prioritized the internal. There are not only entire socio-political systems that are based on this differentiation, there are also entire psychoanalytic systems that may be differentiated on this basis. The point is that the circle *has* to be cut somewhere, and the powerful thing about ideology is that it makes particular places seem the 'natural' and unthinking place to make the cut.

So keeping in mind this caution,[9] let us proceed to answer these questions, which were: how does ideology work? What are the mechanisms through which it organizes society and the minds that inhabit it? The answer that Elias gives is a surprising one – gossip.

---

9   That is, in the following sentences it will appear that ideology is an autonomous agency; this is only partly true.

The mechanism of ideology: stigma and praise

Ideology helps keep people in their place by making it appear that the places that they inhabit are the natural ones. In other words by making it appear that the more powerful *belong there*, and the less powerful *belong elsewhere*. And the way of doing this is to say that the more powerful are in positions of power *because* they are superior, and the others, who are not in positions of power, are not there *because* they are inferior. One can see the beginnings of how a series of binary oppositions are being layered, like pastry, each over the other – each reinforcing the other. There are a number of binary-pairs or polarizations that one finds recurring in so many different situations that one is tempted to ascribe to them a universal characteristic. Whether they are universal or not, they are certainly very generalized. For example some 20 years ago, in Freire's descriptions of the mythologies perpetrated (in his language) by the oppressors about the oppressed, I was astonished to find many perceptions that were familiar to me as a child growing up in middle-class India. Perceptions that were and are held as self evident truths about the servants and the poorer people in general; that they were dirty, untrustworthy, greedy, stupid, selfish, and thoughtless. 'We' of course were the opposite of this. One had to be in an ever vigilant state, because given half a chance 'they' would murder, rape, spoil or steal. I was to discover these same themes recurring in the works of Albert Memmi (1974) and Frantz Fanon (1982) in their descriptions of Algeria, and of course in folk discourse in contemporary Britain. At that time it was an intriguing discovery to find these apparently personal experiences echoed on so many different continents. The disciplines of sociology and anthropology have given these phenomena detailed attention in the works of Durkheim, Levi Strauss, and Mary Douglas (1991) to name just three. These self-same mechanisms were found by Elias and Scotson in Winston Prava, for example, '[The outsiders are] regarded by the established group as untrustworthy, undisciplined and lawless' (Elias 1976, p.xxv). The mechanism of stigmatization is not only a contemporary international phenomenon, it is also perhaps as old as humanity itself. For example Elias (1976, p.xxv) quotes an Athenian aristocrat: 'the natural characteristics of an aristocrat are discipline, obedience to the laws...while the natural characteristics of the common people are an extreme ignorance, ill discipline and immorality'.

Elias is clearly aware that 'the sameness of the pattern of stigmatization [is] used by high power groups in relation to their outsider groups all over the world – the sameness of this pattern in spite of all cultural differences...' (Elias 1976, p.xxvi).

To summarize the relationship between ideology and gossip:

1. The sets of binary-pairs (dirty–clean etc.) may be thought of as the *content* of ideology.

2. The *purpose* of ideology, it will be remembered, is to preserve the *status quo*.

3. And one of the means through which this is *implemented* is gossip.

4. The *structure* of gossip layers binary oppositions one over the other, in a value-laden direction: clean–dirty, good–bad, clever–stupid, generous–greedy, and so on.

5. The *result* of this layering is that 'charisma' is attributed to the more powerful 'us', and stigma to the less powerful 'them'.

'Stigmatization…can have a paralyzing effect on groups with a lower power ratio… Other resources of power superiority are needed in order to sustain the power to stigmatize, the latter is itself no mean weapon' (Elias and Scotson 1994, p.xxiv). Thus one sort of power resources is used to set up the power differential, and following this, gossip and stigmatization are used in the service of maintaining that differential.

The fifth column

Rather poetically, Elias and Scotson describe the existence of gossip mills, milling and processing information – but in a highly selective and partisan way. Events that did not fit the ideology or mythology were ignored, whilst those that did were emphasized and distributed along gossip streams and channels. 'Gossip is not an independent phenomenon. What is gossip worthy depends on communal norms and beliefs and communal relationships' (Elias and Scotson 1994, p.89). The gossip streams were full of praise-gossip concerning the established, and blame-gossip concerning the outsiders. They found that on the whole the 'streams' contained much more of rejecting and blame-gossip, and rather less of praise-gossip.

The fact that the established were cohesive, and had a close-knit structure meant that their gossip streams flowed readily along tried and tested channels. Whilst in the outsider territory (the Estate as it was called) there was no such structure, and so the flow of counter gossip was much more sluggish and so less effective.

However, the effectiveness or not of gossip depended on much more than the establishment of communication channels. For one thing, their study found that stigmatization was effective only when there was a sufficiently large power differential between the more and less powerful groups. Stigmatization was only effective when there was a power structure to back it up; without a power structure the counter gossip was ineffectual – in the vernacular, 'it was pissing in the wind'. One could put it like this, that stigmatization worked, that is the stigmatized took it on, because 'evidence' could be found for it in the world, in the sense that the outsiders were inevitably less well off than the established. This is a kind of behavioural model, where the message is reinforced by external reality, and so is driven into the psyche.

However, the psychoanalytic and perhaps humanistic challenge to this would be to say that the stigmatization works because there is something internal in the stigmatized that makes it effectual. The language that psychoanalysis would couch this in would be terms like 'self-esteem', 'ego-ideal', 'splitting', 'projection', and so on and so forth. For example, Adler (1938) talks about the 'inferiority complex', and Freud hints that the sense of inferiority has its basis in an early sense of loss and castration, and also the development of guilt. Foulkes, it will be remembered, said that the scapegoat had within them a 'need to be punished'. Elias would agree with the idea that stigmatization is effective because 'the established groups usually have an ally in an inner voice of their social inferiors' (1976, p.xxiv), but would give the 'inner' voice a very different aetiology to that of psychoanalysis.

First of all, Elias says that there is a strong emotional linkage between power superiority and human superiority: 'the logic of the emotion is stringent: power superiority is equated with human merit, human merit with grace of nature or gods' (Elias 1976, p.xxiii). He does not go into why this equation should be there; however, as we will discover in the last chapter, Matte-Blanco's ideas will give us a way of explaining the apparent inevitability of the linkage. For the moment let us just take Elias and Scotson's (1994) empirical findings as they stand – the discovery that power superiority leads to a *feeling* of human superiority, and contrawise, power inferiority leads to a *feeling* of human inferiority:

> the more powerful groups look upon themselves as the 'better' people, as endowed with a kind of group charisma, with a specific virtue shared by all its members and lacked by others. What is more, in all these cases *the 'superior' people may make the less powerful people themselves feel that they lack virtue – that they are inferior in human terms.* (Elias 1994, p.xvi; emphasis added)

There are two critical points to be underlined. First, for the stigma to stick, it has to be delivered from an established position of power.

> Attaching the label of 'lower human value' to another group is one of the weapons used in a power struggle by superior groups as a means of maintaining their social superiority. In that situation the social slur cast by a more powerful upon a less powerful group usually *enters the self-image* of the latter and, thus, weakens and disarms them' (Elias 1976, p.xxi; emphasis added).

In other words, power is needed to *drive* the stigmatization into the psyche. This power is a result of the figuration between the two groups, their interdependence, their relationship.

The second point is this: the effects of stigma and charisma are not surface ones, they actually structure the psyche at a profound level; as Elias says, they enter the self image. At first sight, this kind of an idea might appear to be anathema to psychoanalysis, but in fact there are already many precedents for it in the psychoanalytic orthodoxy. The most well known of these is the institution of the superego as elaborated by Sigmund Freud. Another example is the notion of the internalized aggressor as introduced by Anna Freud (1936).

In fact Elias' version of the inner voice is not unlike Sigmund Freud's version of the superego. Freud's superego emerges as a consequence of the resolution of the Oedipus complex. As we have already described, initially the superego consists of identifications with parental figures, and later social and cultural injunctions are added. To repeat the quotation once more here:

> a child's superego is in fact constructed on the model not of its parents but its parents' superego; the contents which fill it are the same and it becomes the vehicle of tradition and of all the time-resisting judgements of value which have propagated themselves in this manner from generation to generation... Mankind never lives entirely in the present. The past, the tradition of the race and of the people, lives on in the *ideologies* of the superego, and yields only slowly to the influences of the present and to new changes; and so long as it operates through the superego it plays a powerful part in human life, independently of economic conditions. (Freud 1933, p.67; emphasis added)

The passage is repeated here because, to my mind, it gives us, with Elias, new opportunities to build bridges between psychoanalysis and sociology. The passage has a modern ring, particularly as it allows ideology a legitimate presence in the psyche.

Influence: rethinking the superego

Now, among other functions, the Freudian superego acts as judge and conscience, organizing and limiting experience and behaviour. In Elias, the basis of conscience is, in part, group opinion. Psychoanalysts and group analysts might well balk at this idea. Traditionally conscience is given an almost divine status, unsullied by material events; it is often regarded as something deeply and profoundly internal and individual. Against this Elias says, 'Group opinion has in some respects the function and character of a person's own conscience. In fact the latter, forming itself in a group process, remains attached to the former by an elastic, if invisible chord' (1976, p.XL). This is indeed taking the group seriously. And it has some significant consequences for the practice of all psychotherapies, individual and group. If one follows this model of conscience, which is another name for an aspect of the superego, then one is led to say that group psycho-therapy seeks to confront the patient's problematic conscience with the one that is evolved within the culture of the group. Many will find this is a shocking and alien prospect, because in the normal way of thinking, one of the tasks of therapy is said to be the reduction of the ferocity of the superego. Something all psychotherapy is very wary of is of the therapist *influencing* the patient. The model (overstated here) is of the therapist empathetically but neutrally observing, commentating and interpreting anomalies and things hidden. The observations set off their own resonances and repercussions which result in a shifting and adjusting of the structure and content of the patient's internal world. *Influence* too is a dirty word in psychotherapy. However, an outcome of the Eliasian model of conscience is that the question of whether or not one *ought* to influence the patient is made redundant. In fact influence will be an inevitable and integral part of therapy. One could even say, that the success or failure of therapy can be measured by the amount and type of influence that has taken place. It seems to me that a consequence of giving the external more and more weight, is that we are inevitably confronted with the notion of influence. This means that one not only has to acknowledge the existence of influence in the psychotherapeutic process, but that one has to find a way to theorize it and incorporate it explicitly into the theory and practice of psychotherapy. This is one of the uncomfortable outcomes of taking the group seriously.

To reprise some of the main points of this section: conscience is born out of a group process, and so although we may experience it as residing inside oneself, it is in fact a property of the group. Further, the possession of power has a central role to play in the shapes that conscience and self image take up. One could say that conscience consists of the internalized attitude of the group to each and every known phenomenon, and this includes the image of the self. Thus ideology not only contributes to the formation of self image, ideology also contains an emotional response to that image, and both are incorporated.

> They [the established] can often impose on newcomers the belief that they are not only inferior in power but inferior by "nature" to the established group…and *this internalization by the socially inferior group…as part of their own conscience and self-image* powerfully reinforces the superiority and the rule of the established group (Elias and Scotson 1994, p.159; emphasis added)

Thus the stigmatization works because in part it is reinforced by explicit external evidence in the state of things, living conditions and so forth, and is also reinforced by internal forces which agree with the stigmatization. The outsider is caught in a double whammy.

A critical difference between Elias and Foulkes which has emerged here bears repeating. When Foulkes says that within the scapegoat there is a 'need to be punished', he is in a sense explaining away and naturalizing the attack, implying that the person is a born victim in some way, perhaps something to do with the endogenous instincts. In contradistinction to this, Elias is saying that if there is a 'need to be punished' (which is another way of describing the internalization of stigma), then it is a function of the position one occupies in the power differential. So no matter what the constitutional qualities one might have, it is not possible to leave out the power differential from the equation in the understanding of self esteem.

A criticism that might be made here is that Elias is homogenizing all differences in each of the groups. But Elias would agree that there are differences in each group – they are not all the same, but he would say that emotionally the participants *experience* the two groups as homogenous. This is the added and fatal twist of the knife: 'They [the established] can often enough induce even the outsiders to accept an image of themselves which is modelled on a "minority of the worst" and an image of the established which is modelled on a "minority of the best", which is an emotional generalization from the few to the whole' (Elias and Scotson 1994, p.159). This idea of the emotional generalization anticipates the ideas of Matte-Blanco, and also echoes those of Freud and primary process thinking, where parts are the equivalent of wholes. Once again these trajectories have to be abandoned until the last section of the book.

In the meantime, Elias does give gossip a critical function in the maintenance of the fantasy of homogeneity, which will be elaborated on next.

Ironing with gossip

The established feel threatened by the outsiders. Elias gives two reasons for this, one internal and one external. The internal reason is almost the same as Freud's notion of the narcissism of minor differences in which difference is said to *cause* aggression and hostility. Freud said, 'This self love works for the preservation of the individual, and behaves as though the occurrence of any divergence from his own particular lines of development involved a *criticism* of them and a demand for their alteration' (1921, p.102). And Elias says: 'The very existence of inter-dependent outsiders who share neither the fund of common memories nor, as it appears, the same norms of respectability as the established group, acts as an irritant; it is perceived by the members of the latter as an attack against their own we-image and we-ideal' (1976, p.XLVI). Like Freud, Elias says that the rejection and stigmatization of the outsiders by the established is in a sense a 'counter-attack', because the powerful group have already *felt* attacked, and so attack in turn. But there is a critical difference in the two attacks – the attack that the established experience is not based in reality, it is not concrete, it is a fantasy. Whilst the attack perpetrated *by* the established, rejection and humiliation, is concrete and real. Thus the stigmatization through gossip is in this sense a counter-attack. However the point that the counter-attack is real and manifest in contradistinction to the imagined initial attack, should not be forgotten.

The second reason given by Elias is grounded in the pragmatic external world and is simply that the established fear for their power base. Thus they defend it by ensuring through various strategies that the outsiders are excluded. One of these strategies is the dissemination of ideology through gossip – the ideology being that the outsiders are in innumerable ways inferior and so not deserving of a share in the power base. Of course things are not straightforward and stable – there is always the threat of disruption, either from within the ranks of the established or from the outsiders. In consequence of this, the boundary between the two groups is constantly being patrolled by the gossip merchants, ensuring that the 'we' stay good and the 'they' stay bad. So one of the tasks of gossip is to iron out heterogeneity as and when it appears, by ignoring facts that counter the ideology, and emphasizing facts that feed into the ideology. This whole strategy is not at all a conscious one; through their work Elias and Scotson concluded that the strategy was truly unconscious.

Another way of describing the situation is this: the gossip streams construct powerful emotional barriers between the established and the outsiders, to disable the possibility of migration: 'this emotional barrier accounts for the often extreme rigidity in the attitude of established groups towards outsider groups…' (Elias 1976, p.xxii) The aetiology is significant: it is not the emotional barrier that causes the division, but the emotional barrier is constructed to facilitate the maintenance of the division and so the retention of the power differential.

We can see here that Elias has *almost* repeated Freud's two theories of aggression. Elias' two theories consist of one where difference causes hatred, and another where difference is used to maintain a power differential.

Another function that Elias and Scotson attribute to gossip is that of social control, of both the in-group as well as the out-group. One way it did this was to expose a person of the in-group if they had dealings that were deemed inappropriate with the out-group. The person was stigmatized and marginalized by the in-group, and the mantle of group charisma was withdrawn from them. The effect of this was to enhance group cohesion and also to work against any integrationist tendencies.

The ideology was so strong that even 'twenty years after the arrival of the evacuees, the older residents of the "village" still spoke of people from the Estate as "foreigners", saying that they "couldn't understand a word that they say"'. The power was such that it seemed that once an outsider, always an outsider. And given that the outsiders were denigrated, the impulse towards integration from the established was limited. In addition, the fact that to some degree the outsiders believed the ideology meant that they tended to stay in their place, and this too worked against integration.

The linkage of gossip with ideology means we can say that not only does gossip maintain differences, it also sets about creating them.

A Socratic argument in which Elias is tested

At some point someone might ask of Elias: yes, I can see how gossip and ideology work to maintain the *status quo*, but how did the more powerful get to be there in the first place? Is it not a tautology to say that the ruling classes create ideology, and also to say that ideology keeps the ruling class in place? Elias would give two different answers: the first of which is that the more powerful got there by virtue of simply being there longer. The second answer he would give undercuts the first one: he would say that the argument has the appearance of a tautology, because one is mistakenly looking for an absolute beginning, and that the two elements of the tautology are in fact two different ideologies. Using the earlier analogy – the same circle is cut in one of two places, each giving rise to a different line; one line gives priority to the idea that ideology is *created*, and the other gives priority to the idea that ideology *creates*. The questioner, slightly confused, might continue thus: in this instance, in Winston Prava, the established, being there longer, were the more powerful. But if one looks at any colonial situation, or in fact any successful invasion, then the established end up being the less powerful. How is this? Elias would answer that it is because they have better access to the means of violence, and once victorious, they monopolize the means of violence. Ideology then steps in and disguises the violence of the state as 'justice' or 'law', whilst the violence of the less powerful is named 'crime' or 'terrorism' – this is another binary opposition. The recalcitrant questioner counters this by saying: but surely they won because they were better strategists? In other words the questioner has applied the binary opposition superior–inferior to victor and vanquished. The Eliasian (and post-structuralist) riposte to this is that the questioner has inverted the process. It is the victors that define themselves as better. The notion of 'better' has been applied after the fact; it is not that one group won because they are better, but they are named better because they are victors. One might well be a better strategist and yet be defeated for any number of other reasons. The questioner, finally catching on to this way of arguing, then might say, yes but haven't you just replaced my cause and effect with your cause and effect, my ideology with your ideology? And here Elias is forced to agree with him, and so one is forced to raise the analysis to a higher level of synthesis. The new synthesis will inevitably be a new ideology – albeit an ideology that addresses the contradictions in the earlier ideologies. Elias' attempt at the new synthesis is contained in his 'Symbol Theory', which is where this chapter began. We have come full circle.

CHAPTER 5

Biology

Introduction

On the whole, in relation to individuals, groups are usually given a bad press in all sorts of ways. In the world of psychotherapy, group therapy is seen by some to be a poor relative of individual therapy. In the world of politics, the group is often thought of as a mob. In the domain of morals, groups are considered capable of acts that are more heinous than any individual might contemplate (cf. Le Bon). In psychology, the notion of individuation says that the group is more primitive than the individual. In psychoanalysis groups are said to be emotionally more primitive than individuals, and capable of less intellectual differentiation and sophistication than individuals.

The issue is made complicated by the fact that there is a dispute as to the nature of the individuals that constitute the group. The two extremes of models are represented in the philosophies of Hobbes and Rousseau. Hobbes (1981) thought that at our core we are nasty and brutish and that left to our own devices we would end in a 'Lord of the Flies'[1] world. Meanwhile Rousseau thought that left to our own devices, in our natural state, we would exist in a world of natural harmony and mutual regard. And by 'natural state' Rousseau meant *individuals* in isolation in 'nature' – the noble savage.[2]

Famously, Freud encapsulated forms of both philosophies in his model of the two instincts, initially as libido and aggression, and later as the life and death instincts. It is as though in the Freudian psyche, Rousseau and Hobbes are engaged in an eternal battle, the vicissitudes of which generate all of human life as we know it.

---

1   The novel by William Golding.
2   '…man in a state of nature, wandering up and down the forests, without industry, without speech, and without home, an equal stranger to war and to all ties, *neither standing in need of his fellow creatures nor having any desire to hurt them*, and perhaps not even distinguishing them one from another…' 'Discourse on the origin of inequality.' (Rousseau 1913)

Thus there is no straightforward mapping of good and bad onto individual and group. Hobbes and Rousseau are describing versions of human *nature*, essentially bad or essentially good. In the current *zeitgeist* it would appear that Hobbes has won the day. In other words it is not uncommon to find the ubiquitous man on the Clapham Omnibus asserting that, *really* we are nasty and brutish, and that this element needs managing and controlling if we are to live with each other. To my mind, this is the view taken up by Melanie Klein, and it finds its expression in the emphasis she gave to the death instinct in infant developmental theory.

The Hobbesian view found allies in economics as well as biology. Two particular strands of biology, evolutionary theory and genetics, found much in common with Hobbes. In a reading of Darwinian evolutionary theory the catchphrases here were 'competition', 'the survival of the fittest', the war of all against all. With the advent of genetics and the discipline of sociobiology, came the new catchphrase 'the selfish gene'. It seemed that Hobbes and nature had finally won out over Rousseau and nurture. Hand in hand with this victory was the victory of individualism over any notion of group or community. Thus it seemed that biology tolled the final death knell for any idea of cooperation and mutual regard. Individuals were brutish at their core, and if they happened to get into a group then it was thought they became even more brutish and primitive. The more benign model says that the good bit about a social group is that it *civilizes* the individual by controlling the Hobbes within, but at a cost, which is injury to the 'natural' state. In psychoanalytic language this injury is called neurosis.

Given this history, it might seem rather perverse to introduce evolutionary and biological notions into a book that seeks to 'take the group seriously'. As Plotkin (1997, p.77) says, Darwinian evolutionary theory is all about '*individual* variation, *individual* fitness, *individual* selection'. Thus it would appear that biology is anathema to an idea of groups as a 'good thing'. As we have already seen, this must have been Foulkes' view, and this led him to ignore the biological basis of Freud, by avoiding altogether engaging with the notion of intrapsychic conflict. Foulkes compensated for this by giving more and more weight to the external and the social.

However, as I hope to demonstrate in this chapter, we will discover in contemporary biology, and especially through particular readings of genetic theory, game theory and evolutionary theory, a surprising ally for the notion of groups.

But as the reader has perhaps detected, there are a number of dichotomies that either have been, or have the potential to be, conflated here. There are at least seven dichotomies – nature and nurture, biological and social, internal and external, constant and variable, given and learnt, individual and group and finally, good and bad. In folk psychology, and many 'scientific' psychologies, it is usually the first element of each pair that are thought to 'belong' with each other, and are given more value and weight than the second element. The first three are directly linked, that is, it appears to the common sense view that biology is inside and society is outside. This view continues that that which is inside is one's true nature and constant, a given. And that which is outside is a variable and is the social. This polarized set of dichotomies is then usually mapped onto the polarization of individual and group. Elias' work has shown how and why these dichotomies have arisen in historical time and space. It is not pertinent to the task of this chapter to track the intricate overlappings of each pair of dichotomies. For our purposes it is sufficient to note that a conflation of the numerous dichotomies has taken place, and that it is this conflation that makes one mistakenly think that biology is the antithesis of the group. So whilst Foulkes has eschewed the biological basis of psychology in Freud, we will find that it is possible to re-engage the biological, but from a different, more contemporary vantage point.

Hot air and desire

In 1976 Richard Dawkins' eponymous volume, *The Selfish Gene*, gave rise to much controversy, not only in the field of biology, but also in other disciplines such as social psychology, anthropology and sociology. The thesis of the book seemed to lead back to a biological determinism, where one's thoughts and behaviours were said to be *determined* by one's genes. This was the new discipline of sociobiology – and it was one in the eye for the notion of nurture.

As it stands, the notion of a *selfish* gene is used as an anti-group formulation. This is because the polarization individual–group has another mapped onto it, selfish–altruistic. To explain: in folk psychology it is understood that if the motives for some action are self serving, then it is a selfish action. And if the action is for the benefit of the group then it is thought to be altruistic. Sociobiology told us that the selfishness is located not just in the individual, but deep in the individual, the gene. Thus we appear to be getting further and further away from the group, where society and nurture appear to be increasingly irrelevant.

To my mind the term *selfish* for genes, is a misnomer, and it is this which gives rise to a fundamental misunderstanding. Once we deal with the notion of selfishness, what we will find in the world of genetics is not an enemy, but an ally for the notion of the group. This then is what I will take as my first task, to criticize Dawkins' use of the term 'selfish', in order to dispense with it, and then get on to the other more useful things that biology has to offer the notion of the group.

It seems to me that by calling the gene *selfish*, Dawkins has anthropomorph-ized a statistical process, and by doing so has undermined his own thesis. To state the issue in as neutral a language as possible: out of a given set of genes, for a variety of reasons, some manage to replicate themselves, and others do not. The first mistake now is to say that some of the genes have 'survived'. This is an emotive word, as is its antonym, 'failure to survive'. Dawkins (1996, p.3) says, 'It is not success that makes good genes. It is good genes that make success... Each generation is a filter, a sieve: good genes tend to fall through the sieve into the next generation; bad genes tend to end up in bodies that die young or without reproducing'. By using the words 'good' and 'bad' Dawkins embroils himself in a moralistic language that needlessly confuses the issue. This is ironic, as one of the things that Dawkins is constantly seeking to do is to emphasize the statistical nature of 'survival'. For example he says: 'DNA neither cares nor knows. DNA just is' (1996, p.155). In another book he says: 'Natural selection is the blind watchmaker, blind because it does not see ahead, does not plan consequences, has no purpose in view' (Dawkins 1988, p.21). Now, despite this, Dawkins' arguments are teleological, that is, he writes in a way that gives the appearance of *intention* to the gene, as though the gene *wants* to survive. For example, 'All the organs and limbs of animals...are the tools by which successful DNA sequences *lever themselves into the future*' (1996, p.175; emphasis added). Genes do no such thing. They do not 'lever themselves into the future' and they do not *use* tools. They *happen* to find themselves in the future. As Plotkin says (1997, p.80): 'Evolution is a giant statistical machine'. Dawkins himself has said that a gene does not *care* for its survival. If one gene replicates where another does not, then it is the outcome of a random and statistical process. A gene does not *seek* to survive, it either manages to replicate or it does not. A gene does not *seek* to do better than its neighbour, as though it were in competition with it; as Dawkins put it, the gene neither knows nor cares.

This is the error of imputing to genes a purpose. A gene no more seeks to survive, than hot air desires to rise. One could say that hot air *desires* to rise, and rudely pushes the cold air near the ceiling out of the way, and takes its place; thus hot air *competes* for the space near the ceiling because it is more desirable. This is clearly anthropomorphic, and clearly ridiculous. Because the gene is a 'living thing', to impute it a purpose seems less ridiculous. To be sure, the outcome might look to the eye like competition, like selfish behaviour, but the gene is no more selfish for 'surviving', than hot air is selfish for taking perhaps the best seat in the house, near the ceiling. Thus by Dawkins' own argument, the term 'selfish' is redundant in this context. The situation is this: out of a given set of genes, after a period of time, the descendants of some will inevitably be found to exist, and others not. This is true, but to then go on to say that the ones that continue to exist are 'better' at surviving, and to call them therefore 'good genes' is a mistake. The 'goodness' or 'betterness' is defined after the event of so-called survival. It *happens* that some survive, it is not the outcome of design.

Order and chaos

The tendency to impute design and desire where none exist is to be found in many places. As meaning-making animals, we are constantly driven to ask 'why' questions, we look for purpose. It is difficult not to impute purpose to both animate and inanimate events.[3] By the same token it is very difficult to conceive that order might arise spontaneously out of chaos, with the result that we have to invent gods to serve this function.

But this indeed is what the mathematics of chaos theory tells us: chaos feeding on chaos, incredibly, gives birth to pattern. This is a completely counter-intuitive finding. A well-tested example of this occurs when a video camera is focused on a blank television screen, one that it is connected to, with the result that the camera is seeing what it is sending. In other words, it is a feedback loop.

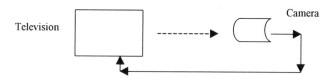

Figure 5.1

Of course the TV screen is not actually blank, it has 'chaos' on its screen – an infinite number of dots randomly going off and on – noise. So the camera is seeing this chaos, which it is then showing to itself. Once the system is functioning, then an astonishing thing occurs – the screen starts showing flowing and fluctuating patterns. The pattern has come from nowhere – from chaos recursively feeding on chaos. Another more commonplace example occurs when one inadvertently gets a microphone in front of a speaker. The 'order' which this creates is, it has to be admitted, a painful one.

Evolution, both animate and inanimate, is an expression of order emerging spontaneously from chaos. Once some particular division has begun, then the mere existence of something constrains what follows. The accumulation of changes over time gives the appearance of design and motivation, but this is ultimately an illusion. For example, in the inanimate domain, physicists tell us that the order that emerged in the early life of the universe, right after the Big Bang, was almost an arbitrary order. It is likely that on another occasion matter and space would have formed very differently from the one that is familiar to us.

---

3   This is another version of the question posed by Hume – how do we get the idea that there are causal connections between events?

Similarly with the evolution of life: Steven Jay Gould in his book *Wonderful Life* (1989) demonstrates the unpredictability and unrepeatability of the evolutionary process. The point is that existence, animate and inanimate, is the outcome of a statistical process, and so is *unrepeatable*. The magical thing is that the engine of statistics, over a long period of time, generates pattern and order out of chaos. Rather fancifully, the procedure is not unlike the Rumpelstiltskin fairy tale, where the princess spins gold out of straw. For example, Dawkins (1996, p.96) convincingly shows that the eye could have evolved 'from scratch fifteen hundred times in succession within any one lineage'. Indeed it has 'evolved at least forty times independently around the animal kingdom'. No grand designer here, no watchmaker, but yet miraculously, a watch.

This same idea, of order emerging from chaos, finds expression in many other places – two of which are: in economics, and in the Eliasian idea of 'constraint' as an outcome of figuration. The Eliasian idea was discussed in the previous section, and will be developed as we go along. The economic idea we will not be able to follow up at all here, but for those interested I would recommend Ridley's (1996) book *The Origins of Virtue*.

The cooperative gene

Given Dawkins' infamy regarding the selfish nature of the gene, to read him is to find something surprising – that the selfish gene could equally well be called the cooperative gene. Dawkins' descriptions of DNA and the structure of organisms in general are redolent with terms like 'community', 'collective' and 'team'. How can this be? Each individual organism is said to behave as though it were looking after its own interests first and foremost. On top of this it is said that the constituent elements of each organism give the appearance of behaving in exactly this same 'selfish' manner. So how do notions of community and team enter the biological picture?

Two sorts of answers can be given to this question, one concerns levels of description, and the other concerns the notion of 'survival'. I will take each in turn, and begin with the notion of description.

Not one but many

It seems to me that rather than notions of individualism and selfishness, not only is the notion of the group more appropriate, but it is actually being used by contemporary biologists to describe biological events at all sorts of levels. The first and most profound of these levels is that of the so-called individual organism.

This is the startling insight of biology: *there are no individuals, only groups*.

What is meant by this extraordinary statement? The biologist Lynn Margulis poetically says that even the individual 'cell…[is] an enclosed garden of bacteria'

(Dawkins 1996, p.53). The parallel with atomic physics is pertinent. No matter to what level one atomizes matter, the electron, proton and so forth, they are found to be made up of coagulations of more fundamental particles; and the most fundamental of particles, when they are found, consist of forms of energy, space and time. Similarly in the world of biology – every individual organism is found to be a coming together of more primitive levels of life. Dawkins (1996, p.52) again: 'A single animal or plant is a vast community of communities packed in interacting layers, like a rain forest...every individual member of every species being itself a community of communities of domesticated bacteria'. These are the words of a hard-nosed biologist, the creator of the notion of the selfish gene. What is germane to the subject of this book is that at whatever level one chooses to examine an organism, at a lower level, it will always be found to be a *collaboration* of more primitive forms of life. *Life must collaborate* if it is to live.

Ridley says:

> ...each single organism is a collective. It consists of millions of individual cells, each in its own way self sufficient, but also dependent on the whole...even cells are collectives. They are formed from the symbiotic collaboration between bacteria...[inside the bacteria] and inside the nuclei of your cells are...chromosomes, carrying...genes... Chromosomes are also collaborations, not individuals: collaborations of genes. (1996, pp.15–17)

Here, Ridley describes the process in the other direction, from the simpler to the more complex: 'Genes team up to form chromosomes; chromosomes team up to form genomes; genomes team up to form cells; cells team up to form complex cells; complex cells team up to form bodies; bodies team up to form colonies'.

One can see then that biology has deconstructed the notion of the individual – literally, concretely and completely taken it apart. This is as true of human beings as of other forms of life. 'Hamilton [a biologist] himself recalls the moment when it dawned upon him that *his body and his genome were more like a society than a machine*' (Ridley 1996, p.19; emphasis added). Hamilton realized that he, an individual, was not a unitary organism but, 'Instead, it was beginning to seem more a company boardroom, a theatre for a power struggle of egotists and factions... I was an ambassador ordered abroad by some fragile coalition, a bearer of conflicting orders from the uneasy masters of a divided empire'.

To my mind these ideas deliver a lethal blow to notions of individualism and essentialism. Thus we find that Margaret Thatcher's statement, that there is no society, only individuals, is completely reversed. Instead what we find is that there are no individuals, only societies; indeed, as Ridley has said, the so-called individual *is* a society: 'each single organism is a collective. It consists of millions of individual cells, each in its own way self-sufficient, but also dependent on the whole...' (Ridley 1996, p.15).

Ideology

Plotkin (1997) argues that the criticisms made of sociobiology as being racist or misogynistic and so forth are untenable, because 'no...scientific discipline is any of these things', although there might well be individual scientists of any discipline that have pernicious socio-political views. Thus, Plotkin says, the model itself is value free, and so dismisses the criticisms as 'silly claims'.

If this is indeed the case then there is a paradox here to be understood, which is: why do Dawkins and other sociobiologists keep emphasizing the 'selfish' nature of the gene, when as I have argued it could equally well be described as cooperative? To my mind the choice of emphasis is a clear example of an ideological choice. And in saying this, what is meant is that there are no neutral positions that have the privilege of being outside the network of values and thoughts of society; nothing, be it an object or an idea, has the privilege of existing in a vacuum cut off from the rest of existence. I am in good company with this view: it is pure Elias. If one takes the related nature of existence as basic then one cannot ignore these sorts of criticisms, and indeed one is obliged to take them seriously if the premise of this book is to have any meaning at all.

The biologist and neuroscientist Steven Rose (1997) argues the same point in his book *Lifelines*. He incontrovertibly demonstrates that the gene of the sociobiologist is a theoretical construct in that DNA and RNA are inert and useless if they are left on their own. They only replicate when the surrounding environment is right, when particular enzymes are present, and so forth. In other words, the gene, the fundamental particle of the geneticist, is not fundamental at all, or at least only partly so; the other 'fundamentals' reside in the enzymes, the temperature, the medium and so forth. Thus one could say that life at its most fundamental level must cooperate with other entities if it is to exist. The unitary individual entity, existing in Rousseauian solitude is to be found nowhere at all. Plotkin would concur with the latter idea when he says that 'inheritance is more than genes' (1997, p.65).

However, a problem remains unaddressed. And the problem is this: it might well be true to say that the various parts of any organism, from the simple single cell to more complex entities like humans, are working together. The questions which remain then, are why and how is it that the parts came to work together? Why does the selfishness of one not overwhelm the felicitousness of the many? One aspect of working together can be called cooperation and another altruism. The two can be thought of as different aspects of the same thing, and as they are interlinked it will not be possible to separate the discussion on each. However, the way the questions are put will reveal different aspects and emphases of the problem.

Altruism and cooperation

Let us begin then with this question: given that organisms are said to behave 'selfishly', that is, looking after their interests over and above everything else, how is one to explain the presence of altruism? There are numerous examples of animals (including humans) behaving in a way that gives the appearance of sacrificing themselves for the good of the group, or doing others 'favours' when there is no apparent pay-off. One answer suggested by some biologists (e.g. Wynne-Edwards 1962) was that natural selection worked on the level of the group – but the idea as it was formulated then was soon found to be flawed. It sought to explain individuals that, say, remained sterile and so did not pass on the genes. It was suggested that they acted in this way for the benefit of the larger group. This idea did not work because even if one assumed that such an altruistic group existed, the evolutionary machine was such that eventually a more selfish gene would mutate, and that the individuals carrying this gene would wipe out the more altruistic individuals. It seemed that selfishness and Hobbes continued to rule the day. Then E.O. Wilson (1992), Dawkins and others gave another explanation which was that the driving engine of evolution was not the organism, but the gene. Thus behaviours that looked altruistic at the level of the animal, were discovered to facilitate the survival of the gene. What this did was to drive the notion of 'selfishness' to a deeper level, by saying that what looks like altruism is in fact 'selfishness' at a more profound level. They argued that an entity only ever acted in an altruistic fashion when the action somehow helped its own genes replicate. But this is a pernicious way of reading things, because at the level of the gene, neither selfishness nor selflessness exists.

Consider: evolution is not a game, yet we can read it and understand it *as though* it were a game. If it were a game, then the aim of the game would be to survive into the next generations. Let us set up a thought experiment: here is a bucket of genes and a limited resource of energy. At some point in time we look to find that some have ceased to exist. The ones that continue to exist do so because they have some attribute that 'helped' them to replicate. Imagine then that, at some later period in time, through random mutation one of the varieties of genes gets a new attribute. Let us suppose that the effect of this attribute is to make it easier for it to replicate. The effect of this might be that this particular gene ends up being more prolific than the others.

What has been described is a sequence of events; there is no selfishness or competitiveness here. Over time genes randomly and accidentally accrue attributes and 'habits' that either facilitate their proliferation, or act against it. Neither one is good or bad *per se*. It stands to reason that the genes that will proliferate to the greatest degree are those that have attributes and habits that work in this direction. Interestingly, one of the 'habits' that is helpful to the genes' continued proliferation is cooperation of a kind. Two of the directions from which evidence for this comes are: first, 'facts' – that is, bodies consisting of disparate organisms working together do actually exist – and second, game theory. Game theory concerns itself with behaviour and strategy. In game theory not only economics, but also genetics and evolutionary biology, found common and fertile ground.

Game theory has been used to shed light on Ridley's question – if everyone is looking out just for themselves, then how does cooperative behaviour arise?

The problem was formulated in a game structure called 'The Prisoner's Dilemma', and the problem is this. Two friends are imprisoned in separate cells. Each is told that if he accuses the other then he will be set free, whilst the one accused will be very heavily punished. If neither accuses the other, then they will each get some punishment.[4] If both accuse each other then each will get an amount of punishment that is more than if neither accused the other. Put into numbers:

Both cooperate – stay silent – each gets 'The Reward':
3 points each.

If both defect – each accuses the other – each gets 'The Punishment':
1 point each.

If one defects and the other does not – the defector gets 'The Temptation':
5 points.

If one defects and the other does not – the silent one gets 'The Suckers Payoff':
0 points.

If one ordered the outcomes in relation to the number of possible points, they would line up as follows:
Temptation (5), Reward (3), Punishment (1), Sucker (0).

Because neither person knows what the other is doing, cold logic dictates that 'Whatever the other person does, you are better off defecting' (Ridley 1996, p.54). The logic of this is that if A defects and B does not, then A gets 5 points, and if B defects too then at least A is assured of 1 point. The logic is that of mistrust – the worst case scenario for A being that he says nothing and B defects – thus A would get 0 points. In other words logic dictates that in this game betrayal is the most sensible course of action, a guarantee of at least one point.

The game encapsulates the conflict between individual and collective interests, and may be described in another way: is trust a sensible course of action? Ridley gives an everyday example of the dilemma: 'all fishermen would be better off if

---

4   The psychoanalytic perspective is being deliberately left out of the picture for the moment, in order to look at these ideas in their own terms. What game theory leaves out is the place of fantasy – both conscious and unconscious. In other words the course of action that is decided on as 'right' will depend on what one *thinks or imagines* the other is going to do. And it is exactly this place that projection, transference (in the broadcast sense) and fantasy make their entry and complicate the issue.

everybody exercised restraint and did not take too many fish, but if everybody is taking as much as he can, the fisherman who shows restraint only forfeits his share to somebody more selfish' (Ridley 1996, p.56).

The essence of the prisoner's dilemma is this: the 'right' course of action is dependent on what the other does, and one does not know what the other is going to do. It is this simple twist that gives the game its complexity, and makes it more life-like.

But the way that the game was first played, as a 'one-off', was certainly not life-like. As it stood it seemed to give a rational validation to the Hobbesian notion of selfishness and self-interest over and above cooperation and altruism, the war of all against all. In this game only fools and bleeding-heart-liberals would trust, and they are bound to lose.

But then the game was modified to make it more life-like, by playing it repeatedly and not as a 'one-off'. Computers were used and mathematical 'entities' with differing strategies were programmed into it, to see which strategy did best. Additionally the 'artificial life' was allowed to 'remember' the outcome of its last interaction with each individual entity, which it then used to modify its current interaction. All sorts of strategies were tested, some that were nasty, greedy hooligans that always took for themselves (always-defect), some overgenerous (never-defect), some a combination of the two. When this game was played over a period of time, the surprising outcome was that it was not the nastiest strategy that won, but another called Tit-For-Tat. This strategy began by cooperating, but then continued by doing what the other did the last time. Much against common sense expectations, this strategy ended up beating the nasty ones outright. Cooperation makes rational sense! The critical element that allowed cooperation to win was the fact that the artificial 'life forms' were able to 'recognize' and remember each other. 'Reciprocity only works if people recognize each other' (Ridley 1996, p.69).

The strategy that eventually won the day had an odd name – Pavlov. Pavlov was an elaboration of Tit-For-Tat. Its strategy was: if your last move (cooperate or defect) worked, then repeat it with that particular entity; if you lost, then change it. An additional element in its programming ensured that Pavlov was not completely consistent; it occasionally also 'forgave' betrayals, and persisted in cooperating. And although Pavlov won the day, it was not in a straightforward way. If it was pitted against the 'always-defect' strategy, then it lost out. However it did come out top in a more complex scenario, where at first Tit-for-Tat overwhelmed 'always-defect'; once this problem was taken care of, then Pavlov was able to take centre stage. Thus Pavlov was 'cooperative' and yet not naïve, and in the end cooperation seemed to win the day again.

I have of course glossed over the complexities, but the point has been made: in the face of selfishness, cooperation emerges as a winning strategy. What is extraordinary is that this cooperation was not the outcome of the imposition of some moral injunction, but emerged spontaneously out of a statistical machine. This is indeed an astonishing discovery: that the cold number-crunching logic of computers comes to the conclusion that altruism eventually overwhelms selfishness.

A double whammy

Before moving on, we have to add here a caution that concerns the kind of argument that some sociobiologists are prone to, which is applying the insights gleaned from one level or arena to another without modification. For example, I think that Dawkins makes an error on two fundamental counts, and he does this by conflating levels of existence. First, the idea of selfishness and selflessness can only legitimately be used in the context of self-consciousness, they imply the possibility of choice and so forth. In no sense can it be said that a gene is self conscious, so the terms just cannot be used. Here Dawkins has taken something from a complex level of existence and applied it to a more primitive level of existence. Second, Dawkins uses the same reasoning that he applies to genes, for people. 'In a universe of blind physical forces and genetic replication, some people are going to get hurt, other people are going to get lucky, and you won't find any rhyme or reason in it, nor any justice' (Dawkins 1996, p.155). Genes exist in a statistical universe, whilst human beings exist additionally in a self reflective universe. Thus this kind of argument might well hold for pure statistical events like lotteries, or even aeroplane crashes, but not for when the hurt or good is deliberately caused by people to each other. The critical difference is that organisms have become more complex until they have become 'self conscious', that is, human beings. To my mind, at least at the level of human beings (and perhaps much before that), the game has changed, and one will need other additional ways of describing the situation. The gene is peculiarly placed, on the cusp of the animate and inanimate; although it is alive it is born out of statistics. This caution will be elaborated on in the next section of the book.

Dawkins is arguing a double whammy by imputing what belongs to human interaction (selfishness) to the level of the gene, and allocating that which belongs to the level of the gene (statistics) to human interaction. Thus if we are selfish, then it is because we are made so by our genes, and if horrible things happen to people then no one is complicit, because it is the outcome of statistics. Everyone is let off the hook. Given that Dawkins would not argue with the point that genes are subjected to statistical forces, he has after all said many times that DNA, the gene, neither knows nor cares, it is curious that he persists in calling the gene selfish. To my mind this cannot be other than an ideological act.

Trust

Let us now get back to the main argument. Ridley takes up the problem of why animals and humans on the whole do not take every opportunity to 'defect'. The winning strategies of the artificial life forms did so because they recognized other 'individuals', so why do we on the whole behave correctly even with strangers? He gives two sorts of answers, one psychological – at the level of human beings – and the other statistical – at the level of cells and genes.

To take the psychological one first. Ridley (1996, p.81) says:

> Reciprocal cooperation might evolve…if there is a mechanism to punish not just defectors, but also those who fail to punish defectors…[and] There is another…answer to the problem of free-riders in large groups: the power of social ostracism. If people can recognize defectors, they can simply refuse to play games with them.

These ideas are very reminiscent of Elias' (1994) findings as reported in *The Established and the Outsiders*. On the odd occasions when one of the established made some overture to one of the outsiders, thus in a sense 'defecting' from the belonging group, the gossip mills set to work, spreading gossip about the defector, effectively ostracizing him or her, literally not playing with them anymore.

The statistical part of the answer to the question, why do individual elements not defect more often, is to be found in evolutionary theory. The answer in part is that the actual state of things is not one of complete cooperation, and neither is it of complete anarchy, the actual state of things is one of tension between the two. It is a statistical truth that eventually one part of an organism will mutate in such a way that its behaviour might well benefit itself at a cost to the whole. However it is also a statistical truth that other elements in the organism will sometimes mutate in ways that control the potential mutiny of other elements. Of course there is no guarantee that this will happen – and if it doesn't happen then the organism ceases to exist. So statistically speaking, given any combination of entities, some will accidentally and eventually find, through mutation, that they work together, and some will not. It is the ones that do work that are the ones we know, but along the way there are an infinite number of experiments that did not work. Even now, in our bodies, there is the tension between the individual part and the greater whole. As Ridley says, when one cell in a body decides not to heed the instruction to stop replicating, then the descendants of that particular cell will indeed do better for themselves (temporarily) at a cost to the greater whole; and then, it is called cancer. This mutiny has a short-term gain, but long term it loses out. Thus over an extended period of time, the statistical machine of evolution will tend to iron out the destructive combinations, they will just cease to exist. Thus what we are left with are relatively stable structures, where the parts, on the whole, tend to work together for their mutual benefit.

Finding common ground: biology and structuralism

By asking the original question differently, we will find answers in new territories. Ridley asks a naïve and so interesting question – why do cells get together to form bodies, and why do bodies come together to form societies? The question is interesting because if Hobbes was right in saying that each organism is self serving, then we would expect societies to be constantly shattered by fragmentary forces. Hobbes said that therefore an equally strong government was needed to subdue and subjugate these antisocial forces. Meanwhile Rousseau had said that if 'man' was left in his natural state, then harmony and order would evolve of its own accord, in other words society would form of itself.[5]

Ridley elegantly demonstrates that both are right, and the clue to it is the division of labour. When functions get separated out, and different elements specialize, then exchange is not only possible, exchange becomes *necessary* to survival – exchange that is beneficial to both parties. This is true on all sorts of levels, from trade to biology, and is variously described as a 'non-zero sum' or a win–win situation. This was Adam Smith's insight: 'Smith saw that because of the division of labour, my selfish ambition to profit from trading with you, and yours to profit from trading with me, can *both* be satisfied. We each act in self interest, but we only benefit each other and the world' (Ridley 1996, p.46). Even at the level of the individual cell there is a division of labour, 'At the very beginning of life itself, the division of labour was a crucial step. Not only did individual genes divide and share the functions of running a cell, but genes themselves had already specialized in storing information, dividing labour with proteins, which are specialized to carry out chemical and structural tasks' (Ridley 1996, p.42). This then forms an element of the answer to the question, why biological elements come together to form groups, and why people form societies. And the answer is that by specializing in a set of functions, and then exchanging, *each does better for itself.* The other point is that once specialization has taken place, then exchange and cooperation between the parts are no longer a matter of choice, they are now a necessity and a matter of survival. In other words self interest is served through cooperation and exchange.

Surprisingly these ideas that have evolved within the discipline of biology are very similar to some of the notions developed by the structuralists, in particular, Levi Strauss. If we change Ridley's language slightly, we can reframe his thoughts and say that it is difference that allows for exchange. Exchange profits both parties, and so encourages them to work together. In other words 'community' is predicated on difference and differentiation. This is precisely Levi Strauss' insight – he said that human groups differentiated themselves into clans, in order to

---

5   However, the Rousseauian Society would be a rather peculiar one – of isolated individuals communing with nature.

facilitate exchange, and the system of exchange was in fact a system of communication, a *langue*. True, Levi Strauss is talking about the differentiation through
'naming' rather than 'function', but the two are interlinked. To take a very
concrete example: words name particular things, that is, words differentiate.
These particular words are then put together to form general sentences. Words
have to mean different things before one can join them up; if words were identical
one could make no communication. One could say then that in discourse theory,
there is a division of labour between words, and it is this division that allows for
the *society of words* to exist; society in this context being the equivalent of langue.
The same truth is being expressed in different languages in different disciplines.
In discourse theory Harland (1987, p.29) says, 'By identifying with the emu, man
makes a sign of himself, and enters as such into the discourse of his society'. In
biological theory Ridley (1996, p.41) says, 'When we look at the society of cells
that forms a body…we find a…complexity of specialized function. The division
of labour is what makes a body worth inventing'.

These are indeed remarkable affinities, between parts of evolutionary theory,
discourse theory, economics, the physics of cosmology, and the sociology of Elias.
And the affinity is this: each time, order is found to emerge spontaneously out of
chaos, sense from non-sense. They are all expressions of the mathematical theory
of chaos, and they make all need of a Creator or Design redundant. The term
'order' is another way of saying that things get related to each other, and this is
another way of saying that things end up working together, and this in turn is
another way of describing the notion of a group. But a group not in any simplistic
sense – there is no natural Rousseauian harmony – there is only tension. Every
collaboration consists of the tension between order and chaos, between the
collaborating forces and the fragmenting forces. And with this thought we find
that Freud with his conflict theory, was not so far off the mark after all. Thus
Ridley concludes: 'although Hobbes is right that we are vicious, not virtuous,
Rousseau is right that harmony and progress are possible without government'
(1996, p.46).

These ideas that order, altruism and cooperation can arise merely out of
structure, without help of moral injunction, gives us a way of deriving an element
of the superego, in a group specific way. One of the reasons that Freud 'invented'
the notion of a superego was that he thought that if we were left to our 'natural'
devices then there would be no end to our id desires – we would rape, gorge,
plunder, murder, and never be satiated. So we have to take something in,
something that will control and moderate these urges. Elias thinks something like
this too. There is much truth in this formulation. We can add to this formulation a
new component, which has its basis in the mathematics of chaos. The fact that
order can arise spontaneously out of chaos is an astonishing thought, but it is so.
Ridley (1996) gives several lovely examples of this. What each of them

demonstrates is that anarchy need not necessarily lead into a *Lord of the Flies* world. There are many examples of apparent anarchy breeding order, of lawfulness emerging out of lawlessness. The fishermen of Maine, (mentioned on p.137) are an example of order emerging out of nowhere.

One of the examples concerns the 'tragedy of the commons'. The story begins with Garrett Hardin (1968) (an authoritarian biologist) who argued that in medieval times common land was overgrazed and ruined because there were no regulations and no overall regulator. He supposed that being a free-for-all, it turned into a bun-fight which resulted in the ruination of the land through overexploitation. He contrasted this with privately owned land, where, he supposed, desires were moderated, and the land was able to be continuously worked. At least this was how Hardin saw it. This very interesting theory was marred only by the facts which did not cooperate with the theory. This was not what actually took place on common land, the reality was otherwise. The commons evolved a system of moderation and control of its own self. Ridley says that this system continues to exist today on the Pennine moors of northern England. Things started to go wrong once the land started to be enclosed.

Another example given by Ridley is from Bali. For over a thousand years the people have grown rice with an intricate set of rules concerning irrigation, terraces. The system functioned successfully for a millennium. The point that Ridley makes is that no one person 'invented' the system of checks and balances that allowed all to profit from a limited resource. 'Order emerges perfectly from chaos not because of the way people are bossed about, but because of the way individuals react rationally to incentives... All it requires is that each farmer copies any neighbour who does better than he did' (1996, p.238). It was after the Green Revolution that ecological disaster struck the area.

We can conclude that *sometimes* people behave sensibly, not because of a fear of an external authority, but because the structure of the situation leads them to behave in that way. If one were to revert to an instinctivist language, then one could say that we must also have instincts of sense and sensibility.

The evolution of culture

Surprisingly, the subject matter of the psychobiologist Henry Plotkin's book, *Evolution in Mind* (1997), covers similar ground to the subject matter of concern to Elias. Surprising (to me) because they come at the same territory from very different disciplines, biology and sociology. These disciplines appear to be the antithesis of each other, and yet they often arrive at very similar conclusions and speculations. For example, they both address, in some detail, Hume's question of how it is that the notion of cause and effect is so ubiquitous. They both discuss why culture comes to exist at all. It is with this latter question that we will begin.

Evolutionists would say that culture is an 'adaptation'. And by this they mean that 'it must confer on its owner some advantage over alternative forms in the population' (Rose 1997, p.230). In other words biologists would agree with Elias that 'human society is a level of nature' (Elias 1991, p.85). Meanwhile Elias agrees with them that culture and society are an outcome of the evolutionary process when he says: 'Humans...are made *by* nature *for* culture and society' (Elias 1991, p.84; emphasis added). It's all very well just saying this, like Foulkes that the social permeates the psyche. But having criticized Foulkes for not taking this any further, it is now beholden on us to ask the questions that he never did: why should 'nature' invent, as it were, 'culture'? What are the advantages that culture confers?

It is tempting to say that the existence of culture *presupposes* not only existence in a group, but also the existence of a mind with which to comprehend this culture. But if we do that then we will have lost all the ground we made with Elias, because to 'presuppose' means that groups and minds exist first, and that this is then followed by culture filling in the spaces between people, and inside people. Instead, we will find in this reading of evolutionary theory a strong echo of Elias' view that groups, culture, mind, are all concomitant.

> ...there never was a 'before' society. Human society is derived from the society of *Homo erectus*, which is derived from the society of *Australopithecus*, which is derived from the society of a long-extinct missing link between humans and chimps, which in turn was derived from the society of the missing link between apes and monkeys, and so on, back to an eventual beginning as some sort of shrew-like animals that perhaps genuinely lived in Rousseauian solitude. (Ridley 1996, p.157)

It is hard to over-emphasize the importance of a passage like this, written from the domain of biology. This is because traditionally, psychoanalysis has used a recapitulationist, and therefore mistaken, version of biology to sound the first note of the developmental drama. To understand this point it will be useful to make a small digression here into the territory of recapitulation.

Recapitulation theory

The palaeontologist Stephen Jay Gould takes the notion of recapitulation apart, verse and chapter, in his lucid volume *The Mismeasure of Man* (1984). Recapitulation theory is best known about through the gnomic formula: ontogeny recapitulates phylogeny. This is a statement of the belief that the development of an individual member of a species (ontogeny) will repeat (recapitulate) the evolutionary history of the species (phylogeny). Thus the fact that human foetuses begin their existence in a liquid is taken to reflect that evolutionarily we were once fishes. As the theory of recapitulation was elaborated it became progressively more insidious: 'Recapitulation required that adult traits of ancestors develop more rapidly in descendants to become juvenile features – hence traits of modern children are primitive characters of ancestors' (Gould 1984, p.119). It is as though we each have within us a tape recording of the evolutionary journey from amoeba to the current state of the species. The development of each individual consisted in part of replaying the phylogenetic tape. The theory would have it that whites, being more recent and modern compared to blacks, had more tape to play than the blacks. Thus the development of an individual black stopped earlier than that of a white. This meant that the traits of adult blacks (being evolutionarily more primitive) were to be found in the children of whites. It was said that the white children would grow past these traits, whilst the black development ended there. Individually they could go no further because as a 'race' they were further behind. The same argument was also used with gender. It was said that male children echoed the traits of adult women (also being more primitive). Interestingly, when the data tended not quite to fit the theory, for example white males tending to have hairier bodies than blacks and women, then the notion of neoteny was invented. Recapitulation would argue that as apes have hair, then blacks and women, being less evolved and so more juvenile in evolutionary terms should retain hair, whilst white men should grow past this. As this was not the case, 'neoteny' was invented to explain this phenomenon, and basically it reversed the tenets of recapitulation. Now, superior groups were said to 'retain their childlike characters as adults, while inferior groups pass through the higher phase of childhood and then degenerate toward apishness' (Gould 1984, p.120).

Out of the two rival theories, psychoanalysis took up recapitulation. Elsewhere (Dalal 1988) I have looked in some detail at Jung's explicitly racist use of the notion of recapitulation. Now, whilst orthodox psychoanalysis has in general *not* taken up the more insidious version of recapitulation, it has taken it up nonetheless. And it has taken it up literally in the sense of ontogeny recapitulating phylogeny, that is the development of the child is thought to follow a similar shape to the evolution of man (*sic*). To be more precise, the evolution of man *as it was thought* to have occurred. And here is the rub – they thought wrong. Of course they could not do otherwise, that being the state of knowledge at the time. The image of the social evolution of man was one that was thought to begin with a *solitary* Rousseauian individual communing with nature, who ended up in a Hobbesian society. This evolutionary fantasy was mapped onto the beginnings of each individual human life. It was thought that the human infant, like the first evolutionary entities, had no mind and was full of primitive animal instinct. It was thought that the infant began closed off from the world, in some sort of an autistic state, and later it built a bridge into the external world. Literally, of a movement from darkness into light. As we have seen these notions are self evidently to be found in many psychoanalytic developmental theories. For example, the attention

Freud gave to phylogeny, the primal horde, the autoerotic instinct, and so on. Recapitulationist notions are also to be found in the psychoanalytic developmental theory of Margaret Mahler (1952), who described the infant as beginning life in an autistic state, cut off from the environment.[6]

Thus psychoanalysis read an incorrect version of evolutionary history into the developmental story, an evolutionary history that prioritized the individual, the animal, the mute, and the asocial. Psychoanalysis used nineteenth-century biology to construct its notion of the human being. And this is why this digression is important to the argument of the book; contemporary biology completely disenchants all notions of humans beginning their evolutionary existence in pure solitude, cut off from the world. Thus, even if the theory of recapitulation were right (which it is not), then contemporary evolutionary theory would tell us that the neonate begins life as a social being. And indeed this is the case, as the infant observation studies of Daniel Stern (1985) and others have shown. However, it should be stressed, this does not validate in any way the theory of recapitulation.

Before we get back to the plot, we can also make some sense here of Foulkes' insistence (which he did not hold to!) that one should not make reference to prehistory in thinking about contemporary psychology. I would suggest that this was because Foulkes must inevitably have taken the then current origin myth as the truth – an origin myth that gave succour to individualism and so worked against his thesis. Thus, as it did not suit his argument, he tried to rule this evidence out of court. But as this chapter is in the process of demonstrating, present contemporary origin myths from evolutionary theory actually substantiate the notion of the social over and above the group. And it is for this reason that Foulkes is being overruled, and we are lingering in this not so hostile territory.[7]

The emergence of consciousness

Going hand in hand with the question of why culture exists, is the question of why we are self conscious at all? In other words why do we have minds? And why do we imagine that other people have minds? And why do we think that similar sorts of things go on in each others minds? And so on and so forth. We find ourselves once again with the old philosophers and their preoccupations. This time biology will try to provide the answers.

The most straightforward answer given by evolutionary biologists is that minds have evolved and been selected by the process of natural selection because

6   In the light of more recent evidence, she then changed her mind on this.

7   I think that it is for the same reason that Harry Guntrip (1961) spent so much of his time arguing for a psychoanalysis that had no basis in biology – because he too thought that the arguments from biology were against notions of relatedness.

they were found to be helpful to survival and replication. Although this is in a sense a truism, it is an important one nonetheless, notwithstanding its pragmatic nature. More detailed answers follow.

One answer follows out of game theory. Reciprocal cooperation, which self-evidently exists, can only work if one has a way of *recording* a memory of an interaction, whether it was beneficial or destructive. In other words, it is possible to think of the mind as an organ that has evolved to facilitate cooperation by being able to remember and recognize the Other. Elias says something similar through Symbol Theory, where he moots the idea that language is a storehouse of knowledge.

Another reason, also from game theory, comes from 'The Prisoner's Dilemma'. Remember that here, the 'right' thing to do was completely dependent on one's supposition of what the other was going to do, and that depended on what the other prisoner thought that the first prisoner was going to do, and so on, endlessly in a circle. At least it would be endless if there were no interruption – and this interruption has the name 'trust'. The notion of trust can have two meanings here, one is the more usual one of trusting the other person, and the second is that of trusting the outcome of one's own speculations and theories of what the other might do. Without trust, there would be no action. Thus just using armchair logic, we can safely assert that the possibility of trust has to be deeply programmed into us, and it must be as much a fundamental emotion as those beloved by some schools of psychoanalysis – hate and envy.

Another answer emerges from the assertion that human beings are social primates and never were anything other than social. The evolution of the mind is a substantiation for this assertion. And here we find the most critical of statements, which says that the mind evolved *in order* to facilitate socialization. This completely inverts the Rousseauian order of things where a solitary person and mind exists first, which is then used for socialization. Implicit in this formulation is the idea that the mind is now being used for something that it was not intended for. It is thought that in socializing the mind is, in a sense, going against its own nature – which is solitary, not unlike Leibniz's monads. Thus the mind is said to be deformed by this process. But now, having turned Rousseau upside down, we find his pockets and ideas empty. One element of the biological evidence for the co-existence and co-development of mind and society is found in the fact that the size of the human brain has doubled over the last two million years, which is about the length of time that humankind is thought to have existed. And many authorities correlate the increase in computational power with the increasing complexities of social life. There is other evidence that shows that the intellect of animals living in social[8] groups is greater than that of other animals. Plotkin describes this idea, the social function of intellect hypothesis, thus: 'Social primates, Humphrey[9] asserted, have "to be calculating beings; they must be able to calculate the consequences of their own behaviour, to calculate the behaviours of others, to calculate the balance of advantage and loss"' (1997, p.204).

All this is another way of saying that evolution has prepared us for social life. This not only contrasts with Freud's idea that the mind is precipitated in order to better help the instincts with their aim of discharge, it contradicts it. Instead of solipsism, biology gives us a relational model of the mind which is perfectly in line with Elias' and Foulkes' thesis that the mind arose out of a need to communicate.

Inheritance vs. experience

Once we have agreed that evolution has prepared us for social life, then we have to re-engage with another old saw – what is innate and what is learnt? In other words we find ourselves once more with Hume's question.

Foulkes, it will be remembered, decided to give up on all things inherited, and said that everything came from transmission. (In doing this Foulkes is following in the footsteps of Locke, the father of empiricism.) This is a rather extreme and therefore peculiar position to take. Why did he do this? I think that this was because although he paid lip service to the idea that nature and nurture were one and the same, he did not really believe it. I think that the Freudian part of him, orthodox Foulkes, supposed that nature was really at war with nurture. Moreover, he must have supposed that the war was actually lost – that nature won out over nurture. He must have supposed that if anything were actually inherited, then it must be things against the group, selfishness, greed, envy and so forth. So his way of managing the embarrassment was literally to banish it, and the way he does it does smack rather of wishful thinking. He baldly asserts that all things come from transmission and not inheritance, and never substantiates it.

Once again the findings of contemporary biology as well as experimental psychology come to the conclusion that fundamentally we are designed to relate. For example, it is clear now that infants are already programmed in some way with physics and psychology, as well as the potential to learn a language, and as well as relatedness. To expand: Plotkin and others argue that it is just too expensive in terms of resources to re-invent wheels each time a new individual comes into the world, so certain types of knowledge are wired into our brains. This view then gives weight to Kant's answer to Hume's question, over and above Elias' answer

8   In this ethological context, the 'social' group is distinguished from other sorts of groups like flocks of birds.

9   The psychologist N.K. Humphrey.

(and therefore Klein's answer over and above Foulkes'). And indeed there is much experimental evidence to substantiate this: for example infants are known to find drawings of schematic faces more involving than other similar drawings, they are also known to fix on eyes more than anything else. It is also well known that if a mother fixes her face and does not respond, then the infant finds this a very distressing experience. Relevant here are a group of experiments described by Plotkin (1997, p.191), which Baillargeon did with twelve and eighteen week old infants that demonstrate that the infant is programmed somehow to know[10] that they are looking at physically impossible events – and they 'know' this before they have had any experience of these events. The impossible events include 'knowing' that physical objects need support below them in order not to fall, and not to the side of them. They 'expect' the correct movement of a billiard ball after it has been struck by another, and so on. It is in this sense that infants have a kind of knowledge of physics, psychology, and cause and effect programmed into them.

Once more, things are reversed, in that what is found to be innate is information about the external world. One of the best known examples of innate knowledge is the capacity for learning a language. There were two sorts of answers given to the question of where languages come from. One side was represented by Piaget who proposed a cognitive and developmental theory, and the other side was represented by Chomsky who proposed an innate capacity to learn a language which was then triggered by the environment. Over the last two decades, the weight of accumulating evidence has knocked Piaget out of the ring (Pinker 1994).

Plotkin argues that 'learning and intelligence…is almost certainly nearly as old as multicellularity itself…collectives of cells that were specialized at inter-acting with one another' (1997, p.166). He then suggests that this ancient neural architecture forms the basis of a mechanism 'such that it can learn associations of what goes with what'. The evolutionists would say that a form of connectionist network evolved very early on, and was progressively refined as it was transmitted to later generations.

So on behalf of the biologists Plotkin answers Hume thus: 'the infant is born with neural structures already in place which give it a priori knowledge of the causal texture of the world' (1997, p.194). Plotkin then goes on to give an interesting twist to the story. He says that evolutionary knowledge cannot of course anticipate all eventualities of lived experience so 'evolution learns, so to

10   A word of explanation as to what is meant by 'know' in this context. Infant studies use habituation, that is, something repeated until the infant is 'bored' with it. Following this, something novel is added, and the way the infant reacts to this is measured. The level of interest or boredom is measured by particular sorts of physiological activities of the infant – eye movement, or how much or fast it is sucking and so on.

speak, of its own limitations. It learns that uncertainty can never be entirely eliminated, that the chance, the contingent, the arbitrary have always to be reckoned with...[and therefore] some relatively open learning ability is necessary'. Biology's full answer to Hume then is that first, knowledge about causality is wired into the brain, and second, it is necessary for this to be so for the human being to function as a learning animal, causality being pivotal to any learning process.

The return of group selection

As we saw earlier, the first attempt at formulating a model of group selection was found wanting. But now, with new understandings in genetic theory, the notion of the group makes a reappearance in evolutionary theory. There are two aspects to this, one insidious and the other promising. To begin with the latter.

Ridley argues that society and culture exist to bind groups together, to cohere them. And that this trait is favoured by the evolutionary machine because groups of people that cooperate with each other do much better at surviving than isolated individuals or groups of people who are selfish. Thus natural selection will inevitably favour the trait of cooperating at the level of the group. Plotkin puts it like this:

> Contrary to the generally held assumption that traits...that increase the fitness value of the group are invariably unstable and vulnerable to selfish mutations that favour the individual over the group – it is perfectly possible, especially in species like hominids where individual survival may be...closely bound up with living in a group, for traits that favour the group to have a higher fitness value for the ultimate survival of the individuals in the group than do traits that favour the individual at the expense of the group. (1997, p.229)

This argument is important to us because one of the things that is constantly being said against society and groups in general is that to live in a group, whilst it may well be necessary, is against our 'nature', precisely because of our biology which is said to be inherently selfish. The growing weight of the biological argument presented here reverses this, and says that to live in a group is in our nature. To use that dangerously teleogical word – we are *designed*, albeit accidentally, to live with other people.

The point is that we have always lived in groups – Rousseauian man has never existed. 'Humans are not solitary animals... It is likely that the small social group numbering perhaps ten or at most a few hundred people has been one of the few constants in our evolution' (Plotkin 1997, p.228).

Free will and determinism

Now to the insidious version of group selection. This comes directly out of sociobiology and its overruling dogma – that of the selfish gene. Here we also meet the central reason why biological notions have been anathema to those interested in the social, and those on the left of the political spectrum. In a curious and over-generalized way, the philosophy behind sociology has been seen as more conducive to those on the left of the political spectrum, and the philosophy behind biology as favouring those on the right wing. This has occurred because of the mistaken presumption that biology equals determinism, that is, that we are fixed at birth by our genes, and so we have a true nature, and that this nature is selfish; whilst sociology equals free will, that is, that nurture can make us anything we want. It is a debate about our plasticity. However, one of the central notions being developed through this book is that of *constraint*; this encapsulates both, determinism and free will, and is different to each. The point is that constraint is part of existence itself, and nature has no more privilege over it than nurture. This contention will be more fully elaborated on in the last part of the book.

The more insidious form of sociobiology argues that there are genes *for* things, like aggression,[11] homosexuality, greed, etc. and that biology *determines* all aspects of life: mind, action and body. We have already been building arguments against this idea in the paragraphs above. For example Rose and Plotkin both show that genes only 'work' within a context. In other words there is no such field as pure nature, no field as pure biology, environment is ever present. By the same token there is no such field as pure nurture, biology is ever present. We have also seen that the use of the term 'selfish' at the genetic level is not legitimate.

This version of sociobiology has been used to justify and naturalize the inequities of the world – it is an unholy celebration of Hobbesian man. This works in a pincer movement, and the unwary, the marginalized, is caught from both sides. On the one hand it is said that there is nothing untoward in wanting to hate and oppress, it is after all just part of our nature. An example is provided by Rose, Lewontin and Kamin: 'John D. Rockefeller…said at a business dinner, "The growth of a large business is merely survival of the fittest… This is not an evil tendency in business. It is merely the working out of a law of nature"' (1988,

---

11   There are indeed genes 'for' some diseases like sickle cell anaemia, but these are few. Most physical diseases are caused by a complex of a number of genetic chains in interaction with the environment. Moreover, finding a gene for a particular straightforward physical disease is one thing, and assuming from this that there is a gene for a bio-psycho-social event like aggression or depression is quite another. Rose (p.277) treats all attempts to find genes 'for' depression or aggression with suspicion. He says it is a way of avoiding looking at the social causes of such phenomena, which would make us all complicit, and instead seeks to blame problematic behaviours on bad genes. The sorts of things that some sociobiologists look to find genes 'for' is also telling. For example, Rose says, no one is 'researching the genetic "causes" of homophobia, racism or financial fraud'.

p.26).[12] On the other hand when the oppressed and marginalized protest, then their protest is defined as a genetic illness. Rose *et al.* give an example of this too:

> psychosurgeons Mark and Ervin argue in their book *Violence and the Brain* that as only *some* blacks in American ghettos participated in the numerous uprisings of the 1960s and 1970s, the social conditions to which *all* were exposed, cannot be the cause of their violence. The violent cases were those with diseased brains and should be so treated. (1984, p.20)

To understand the arguments it is necessary to explain the technical term 'fitness'. The biologist uses it in a very particular way to mean 'more likely to survive longer and reproduce more offspring'. It is used in the sense of the degree of *fit* there is between organism and environment. This is not usually understood, and so the term 'fit' is heard in the sense of being strongest, or brute force. Thus 'survival of the fittest' is heard as 'survival of the strongest'.

In any case, sociobiology sought to extend Darwin's notion of individual fitness to that of inclusive fitness. What was being suggested here was that individual organisms acted in ways that promoted the fitness of *shared* genes, in other words it led to an idea of kin selection, and from here it is but a short step to racism. This notion legitimized racism, as something encoded into the genes – it is natural to be racist because 'they' do not share 'our' genes. Against this inexorable truth, bleeding heart liberals everywhere are on a hiding to nothing. Or so it is said.

It seems to me that this central tenet of sociobiology can be defeated by a *reductio ad absurdum*. Let us begin by accepting the proposition as true, that individuals will act in ways that seek to promote their shared genes. The next question is: *which* shared genes?

The notion of the genetic basis for favouring one's kin over and above those not of one's kin, is racism pure and simple. To explain: the notion of kin selection is built on the assumption that the so-called 'racial' groups share a particular genetic pool, and that this pool is different from other racial groups. Thus it is said that the groups will react with *inevitable* hostility to each other, because it is so ordained by the gene. The word 'inevitable' is important, because what is being said is that our behaviour is *determined*, and so twist and turn as we might, we cannot avoid our biological fate.

However, one of the first findings of the new genetic science was the discovery that the genetic pool of any one 'race' was as big as humanity itself. The genetic information coded into a particular individual when compared to the genetic information in someone of the same family and someone of a far distant group, was found to be not dissimilar to either. 'The genetic variation between one

12   I am not using this quote here to argue that business is evil, I am using it here to show how the Darwinist idea is being used to rationalize particular sorts of behaviour.

Spaniard and another, or between one Masai and another, is 85 percent of all human genetic variation, while only 15 percent is accounted for by breaking people up into groups' (Rose *et al.* 1984, p.126).

These facts, which no contemporary biologist would dispute, make a nonsense of kin selection. Which ones of our genes are we going to favour? Are they suggesting that somehow we 'know', or the gene 'recognizes' a fellow gene in another person? And even if we allow this nonsense, then by what mechanism are some genes to be privileged over others? Remember most of our gene pool is shared with all of humanity – so why should not kin selection work with the 85 per cent of shared genes, by what mechanism and by what logic is it to be limited to the 15 per cent? When we add to this that one first of all has to carve up people into racial or ethnic groups before doing the experiments and counting of gene frequency, we can see that the groups have been already so divided. Thus if the 'races' were differently divided, then a different 15 per cent would be found to be common to them. It is well known now that the 'races' are fictions based on how they look – and it is this that reveals the speculations of kin selectionists for what they are: pseudo scientific rationalizations of their deeper and darker thoughts and emotions.

There are two more levels of argument we can marshal, one provided by Dawkins (1996, p.38) himself. He invites us to take part in a thought experiment: we each have two parents, four grandparents, eight great-grandparents, sixteen great-great-grandparents, and so on. If we proceed in this fashion to the time of Jesus Christ, and do this for each individual on the earth at present, then we would arrive at the extraordinary figure of a million million million million ancestors. This is clearly not the case. The resolution of the difficulty is simple enough: the

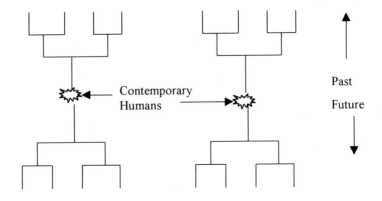

Figure 5.2

fact is, that actually, we all marry cousins from one to many degrees removed. Thus Dawkins says that between him and one other random contemporary person living in Britain, their most recent shared ancestor would probably have lived no more than a couple of centuries ago.

He suggests that the usual model of gene transmission as an ever branching tree (see figure 5.2) is incorrect, and more correct is one of a river with criss-crossing currents (see figure 5.3).

Instead of the ever branching tree, Dawkins proposes that 'a far more realistic model of ancestry and descent is the flowing river of genes... Within its banks, the genes are an ever-rolling stream through time. Currents swirl apart and join again as the genes crisscross down the river of time' (Dawkins 1996, p.40).

Dawkins then takes this notion even further and tells us about findings regarding mitochondrial DNA. This is a DNA that is transmitted only by females, and by tracking its genetic 'finger print' in contemporary peoples, biologists have shown that *all* of humanity have at least one common female ancestor, who lived between one hundred and fifty thousand and two hundred and fifty thousand years ago. Through tracking other sorts of DNA biologists also speculate that the most common male ancestor might have existed just twenty seven thousand years ago (Jones 1996, p.94). Genetic kinship is larger than some sociobiologists would have us believe. Thus if our genes did indeed select for kin – they would be rather confused as to who to leave out. Because what Dawkins has just shown is that *we are all genetic kin*, and quite recent kin at that.

Figure 5.3

The final and perhaps most damning point is this: Plotkin informs us that we share 98 per cent of our genetic material with chimpanzees, that is, we are 98 per cent kin with chimpanzees. So if kin selection were really an operational force, then surely it would encompass our closest cousins? Where does kinship begin and where does it end? Kinship, at a genetic level, is so ubiquitous, that it is rendered meaningless. These contemporary biological facts ring the death knell for the specious notion of kin selection.

Although the arguments in this section might seem at a slight tangent to the purpose of the book, their importance lies in the fact that it is now possible to reclaim the biological for the notion of the group. Up to now, Foulkes' claim that nature and nurture are one and the same thing has had a hollow ring – but how could it be otherwise when he had eschewed biology altogether? The importance of the arguments here have been to show just *how* nature and nurture might be connected, to give substance to Foulkes' dictum. It seems to me that those involved and concerned with the study of the social aspects of human life, have for too long thought of biology as the enemy of the social, and they have done this because of the strong mythology that has encompassed the subject. The linkages between the terms 'biology', 'inheritance' and 'internal' have frightened off those who would think about social groups. This is because it has been supposed that all things innate can only ever be pre-social or asocial, things like the instincts, and that what innate information there is must therefore be against nurture. In fact, what the new biology is increasingly coming to say is that information is indeed inherited, but this time what is being said is that the innate information is about the *external and social world*. Thus where once upon a time biology was used to substantiate individualism, it is now possible to use it to substantiate the social group.

Before we end this section, one last point needs to be mopped up. Having gathered together evidence that showed how culture and the social has emerged from the biological, Plotkin asks an interesting question. He asks, how is it that culture, evolved as it has been by permission from nature, might well contribute to the demise of man, that is, work against nature? In other words how is it that this *natural* thing, culture, might be bad for us? And by bad he means that it is quite possible that we might wipe ourselves out as a species through precipitating ecological catastrophes or blowing ourselves up and so on.

Plotkin suggests, with some others, that once the social and the cultural have emerged, then they have been partly decoupled from biology. This is the Frankenstein's monster idea: something is created, which then takes on a life of its own to turn against its maker. Whilst I would certainly concur wholeheartedly with the idea that the social has a dynamic and logic of its own, I think that it is both unfortunate and unnecessary to then attempt to decouple nature from nurture. Particularly given all the hard work that has gone into formulating their common basis. I think that this attempt to split nature and nurture is based on two fallacies. First is the idea that that which is 'natural' must be 'good'. This is clearly not true, but it is hard to break out of this habit of thought. Accordingly, some so-called 'natural' remedies of both occidental and oriental medicine are actually very toxic to the body, and not 'good' at all. The second fallacy is based on a Panglossian idea (Rose 1997, p.233) that the adaptations that evolve out of natural selection must be the best out of the possible alternatives. This is another version of the 'if it is natural it must be good' idea. This is clearly not the case – sometimes adaptations are useful and sometimes they are not. Sometimes they are useful for a time, and then as the context changes, these self same adaptations can end up working against the survival prospects of an organism. For instance, the camouflage colour of an insect works in particular environments – if the environment changes, then the colour of the insect will not only not camouflage it, it will work against it by announcing its presence to predators. One can say something similar about a cancer perhaps, when it initially manages to exploit its environment and flourish, but then the attribute that allowed it to flourish works so well, that it destroys its environment and thus itself. I do not by this analogy intend to say that culture and society are a cancer, all I intend to say is that notions of 'best' are only ever contingent and temporary. The other point, made by Elias earlier, is that even if the consequences of culture end up acting against us, this does not mean that culture has decoupled from biology, any more than, say, the peacock's tail is decoupled from biology.

A summary

Foulkes decided against *a priori* knowledge, and he avoided the biological basis of humankind. I have argued that he did this in part because he supposed that each of these worked against his project of prioritizing the group over the individual. He assumed, like many others, that biology equalled innate, biology equalled animal, and biology equalled individual. I hope that what this chapter has done is to undo these linkages and remove the possibility of individualistic philosophies having exclusive rights to the territory of biology. I hope that the chapter has made it more possible for sociologists, group analysts and the like, to engage with the insights of biology more freely, and make it their property.

Biology is exclusive Hobbesian territory no longer. Some of the misunderstandings were due to the anthropomorphization and conflation of terms used. Thus one cannot impute to 'nature' human attributes and call it cruel and selfish. Indifference does not equal malice: 'The butcher may not be motivated by benevolence, but that does not mean he is motivated by callousness or a desire to be nasty to others. The pursuit of self-interest is as different from the pursuit of spite as it is from the pursuit of altruism' Ridley (1996, p.45). To this we can add that nature is not self interested either, it just is.

The emphasis of this chapter has been on cooperation, altruism, and the like. Partly this has been compensatory, compensating for the enormous emphasis on cruelty and selfishness by certain readings of biology and psychoanalysis. A major criticism made of Foulkes by Morris Nitsun in his book *The Anti-Group* (1996) is that Foulkes' view of the group is too benign, and that he neglects to engage with the destructive and anti-therapeutic forces that can rage through groups. The same criticism might be made of this chapter, and to some degree it is true, but there is a reason for this, and it is to be found once more in the conflation of dichotomies. If we begin with the conflated dichotomies that doing something for one self is called selfish and doing something for someone else is called altruistic, then one can see that in seeking to emphasize the possibilities of relationships to others, one is led to emphasize cooperation and altruism. To my mind this is one of the reasons that must have led Foulkes to emphasize the benign side of groups. However, I would then want to differentiate this thrust of this chapter from Foulkes as well as Rousseau. What is being said here is that if order and cooperation arise, then it is not out of any innate goodness, but purely out of the structure and logic of the situation, out of the nature of the group, out of the nature and structure of relatedness itself.

Having derived cooperation as a 'natural' consequence out of the structure of groups, the work that this chapter leaves unfinished is that of deriving animosities and hatreds out of the same dimension. Nitsun uses notions from Freudian and Kleinian psychoanalytic theory to give explanation for the disruptive forces in groups, but these are all derived from the individual. And whatever truth there might be in that formulation, in the language being evolved in this book, I would say that it is 'orthodox' – that is, he does not derive animosities out of group specific modalities. The animosities within a group are given explanation by him in terms of the individual's internal structure and content: death instinct, projection, splitting and so forth. What we have to get away from are ideas that seek to polarize aggression by deriving it exclusively from an individualistic and instinctive domain. As we proceed we will see what possibilities there are to derive aggression from a non-individualistic and thus a non-instinctive basis.

Let the last words in this chapter be said by Ridley, who despite his mistaken use of the word 'selfish', encapsulates the ideas put forward here. If one removed the word 'selfish', then the passage would reflect exactly the thesis of the chapter:

> Our minds have been built by selfish genes, but they have been built to be social, trustworthy and cooperative... They come into the world equipped with predispositions to learn how to cooperate, to discriminate the trustworthy from the treacherous, to commit themselves to be trustworthy, to earn good reputations, to exchange goods and information, and to divide labour. (1996, p.249)

CHAPTER 6

Elements of a Post-Foulkesian Group Analytic Theory

Introduction

The work of constructing a group analytic paradigm that proceeds from the group, in contrast to the mother–infant paradigm that proceeds from the individual, has already begun in the previous sections of the book. The difficulties have been legion, beginning with the structure of language itself. As we have seen even to ask the question how is culture internalized, is to assume that culture starts on the outside and is then internalized.

At this point some might argue that the whole task, of taking the group seriously, is redundant in the sense that it is already being addressed in what are now being called the interpersonal schools of psychoanalyses. These seek to give considerable weight and significance to what takes place *between persons*. But here's the rub: it is between persons, that is, individuals. Implicit in the notion of something being 'interpersonal' is the ontological priority given to individual persons, and then to the things that happen between them. So interpersonal psychoanalysis will be very sympathetic to group analysis, and might well have much to offer it (e.g. Brown 1994). However, for the purposes of the current project, not only does interpersonal psychoanalysis not go far enough, it begins in the wrong place, with the individual and not the group.

So how are we to proceed? We are compromised even as we start to speak, as we start to use the very terms 'internal', 'external', 'individual', 'group', and so on. It seems to me that the main task before us is to see if it is possible to go some way to deriving a different way of speaking and *thinking*, of formulating phenomena in a way that does not make the notion of the individual at once central in a statement. Another task is to see if it is possible to formulate notions of health and ill health from the perspective of the group.

Individuals in groups: four psychoanalytic answers

Elias asked a question which is at the core of the issue: 'Society…[is often thought about] as an aggregation of individual people… Can anything be said about society which could not be found out from studying individual people?' (1978, p.95).

Freud's answer can be gleaned from this statement: '*a psychological group is a collection of individuals* who have introduced the same person into their superego and, on the basis of this common element, have identified themselves with one another in their ego' (1933, p.67; emphasis added). In other words, the individual is said to precede the group.

Melanie Klein is even more explicit: '*A group…consists of individuals in a relationship to one another;* and therefore the understanding of personality is the foundation for the understanding of social life' (1959, p.247; emphasis added).

Despite Fairbairn's dramatic theoretical shift from libido to relatedness, in the end he remains an individualist: '…all sociological problems are ultimately reducible to problems of individual psychology… "group psychology" must be regarded as essentially the psychology of the individual in a group' (1935, p.241). Here no italics are needed to make the point.

Winnicott too, having instituted the group-like notion of the nursing couple, answers Elias in the negative: 'Cultural influences are of course important, vitally important; but these cultural influences can themselves be studied as an overlap of innumerable personal patterns. *In other words, the clue to social and group psychology is the psychology of the individual*' (1958, p.15; emphasis added). He also says: '…the basis of group psychology is the psychology of the individual, and especially of the individual's personal integration' (Winnicott 1965, p.146).

Whilst these thinkers are undoubtedly partly right, in that individual psychology contributes to group psychology, implicit in all their statements is the idea that individual psychology arose somehow outside or prior to the group. To take the group seriously is to reverse the answers given by each of the psychoanalysts above, and say in effect: 'The clue to individual psychology is to be found in the nature of the group'. And if we reverse Klein then we would say: 'the understanding of social life is the foundation for the understanding of personality'.

It should be stressed here that to begin with the group is not necessarily to succumb to a simplistic notion of deterministic social forces, external to human life, somehow impregnating the psyche. But once again, even as we speak, we find that all we have done is to reverse the polarity and place group over and above the individual; we need to go further than that. One could say that the psychoanalytic thinkers quoted above are focusing on the notion of *individuals inside groups,* and so our task is to focus on the notion of *groups inside individuals* – and when the two are joined together then we will be some way to constructing a group analytic paradigm.

The external, the group, and the social

Before proceeding further with the exploration, a clarification needs to be made, a clarification that anticipates some of the argument that follows. In the paragraphs above sometimes the term 'social' is used, sometimes 'group', sometimes 'external'. What is the relation between them? It is a habit of thought that often lumps 'external' with 'social'. But this habit is predicated on the notion of the social as something outside that enters an already formed inside. In contrast to this is the fundamental Foulkesian and Eliasian notion that the social does not reside just outside in the spaces between people – it is everywhere. As we will see, Fairbairn too, who has placed great emphasis on the external, thinks of the external as an asocial space. It is the argument of this book that it is never possible to be in a place that is *a*social – outside society. On the one hand this is a banal truism, on the other hand much psychoanalytic theory and practice proceeds as though the fundamentals of the psyche and psychotherapy have nothing to do with social life. As we have seen, so does Foulkes at times. The clarification then is this: whilst 'social' and 'external' are not referring to the same thing, 'social' and 'group' are referring to the same thing.

This truism is at the heart of the book. To take the group seriously is inevitably to take the social seriously. More, the internal structure of the group is of itself that which constitutes psychological life, as does the interactions between groups. But now, having made this distinction between the inside and outside of groups, we find ourselves (with Foulkes) in considerable hot water. The 'hot water' is a difficulty in how to conceptualize the very idea of a group, and as we work towards resolving it, we will find ourselves in post-Foulkesian territory.

Belonging

Inter-group and intra-group

The curious thing about Foulkes' theory of the group, is that it purports to be a theory of what takes place inside a group, and not what takes place between groups.

> We are concerned only with groups in their psychological aspects, with psyche groups... We are...leaving out of account here the psychological relationship between groups, or between any particular group and the community of which it is a part, i.e. group dynamics. We are concerned with internal psychological processes, endo-psychic reality, intra-psychic mechanisms or dynamics. (Foulkes and Anthony 1957, p.25)

The question is, can they legitimately do this? I would say, not if they are to remain consistent with two of Foulkes' central propositions. The first of which is that the individual does not exist in isolation. It follows that that which is true at the level of the individual must also be true at the level of the group; the group cannot exist in isolation. And indeed Foulkes knows this and has encapsulated it in his second proposition – that ultimately, the group, any group, is an abstraction. He has stressed that groups can only be seen in relation to other groups: 'In order to see something whole we have, I believe, to see it in relation to a greater whole, so that we can step outside of that which we want to see' (Foulkes 1973a, p.230). What I have taken this to mean is that groups are always carved out of a larger constellation. And that whichever configuration is designated to be the group, there are always a myriad of other potential configurations which are also equally legitimate 'groups', existing simultaneously within the constellation. The configuration that is chosen as the designated group, the line drawn around it, is not so much arbitrary, more it is a motivated designation. We will come back to shed light on the motivation in a moment.

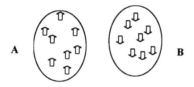

Figure 6.1

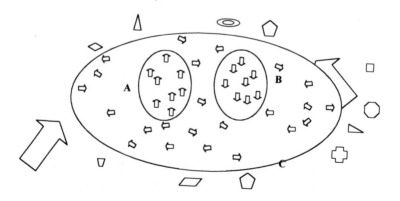

Figure 6.2

Logic then dictates that all phenomena are simultaneously both inter-group and intra-group phenomena. The difference is one of definition and perspective.

For example, the interaction between A and B from one perspective will look like an inter-group event (see Figure 6.1). And from another perspective, it will appear to be an intra-group event (see Figure 6.2).

Another way of putting it (using a Foulkesian term), is that in the first picture it appears that A and B belong to different categories, whilst in the second picture it appears that A and B belong together in C. Thus from one perspective A and B look like groups in their own right, and from another perspective they look like subgroups.

It seems to me that we can make considerable use of this 'anomaly'. The first picture is a template of 'difference' – in that A and B are differentiated. The second picture is a template of 'similarity' – in that A and B are both part of a greater world called C – the world of arrows of a particular size. Next, given that one always has the possibility of viewing A and B as either belonging together or not belonging together, then we have introduced some notion of 'choice' in the matter. In other words, what motivates the choice to see the two entities as either different or similar? We have begun to engage with an idea of a motivated designation.

Deconstructing 'belongingness'

Foulkes has said that there is a fundamental psychological need to belong, and that no sort of health is possible without this. Let us deconstruct the notion of belongingness:

1. To belong to one thing is not to belong to another thing.

2. The notion of belonging (say the case of A and B above) is based on some of the attributes of A and B being shared. In other words all we could say is that *in certain respects* there is a similarity between A and B.

3. In the real, that is experienced world, things are only ever more or less similar or different. Things are never ever identical, which is to say that two things are never exactly, precisely and completely the same as each other in each and every respect.[1] By the same token, neither are they ever irrevocably and completely different.

4. Take *any* two objects and we will *always* be able to find at least one shared attribute that will make for a similarity between the two objects.

---

[1]   There are only two places that I know of where things can be identical to each other. One is in the world of atom, where named particles are completely interchangeable with each other. One electron is identical to another. The other place is in the abstract world of mathematics. There is in fact a third place, which is a psychological space – this we will come to in due time.

We will also *always* be able to find at least one attribute that is not shared, so making a differentiation between the two objects. This is another way of stating the point above – which is that things are always similar to each other in some respects *and* simultaneously different to each other in other respects. In other words it is always possible to find a category that any and every combination of objects will be able to 'belong' to, and another category that they will not mutually 'belong' to.

Now we can make more sense of Foulkes' statement that groups are abstractions, and as we grapple with this idea, we will discover that the consequences of this are dire indeed. It seems to me that Matte-Blanco's (1988) theory of thinking is made for elucidating the complexities of groups. In fact, as we will discover, the group is literally a pictorial representation of his theory of thinking.

Overview of Matte-Blanco's theory

Matte-Blanco focuses on the mind as a classifier, as opposed to Freud who focuses on the mind as a system of various forces (Rayner and Tuckett 1988). Matte-Blanco builds his theory on the basis that there are two different systems of logic operating in the mind, asymmetrical and symmetrical logic.

Asymmetrical logic

Asymmetrical logic is the familiar logic of the everyday, rational world. It is 'asymmetric' in that things are distinguished from each other, and are located in relation to each other in space and in time. For example the sentence, 'Peter drinks tea', is asymmetrical in the sense that Peter and tea are recognized as two different things, which are in an asymmetrical relationship to each other; that is, it is not the same as 'the tea drinks Peter'.

The rules of this logic, when set out formally by mathematicians and philosophers, amount to a set of rules on sorting objects by referring to similarities and differences. To my mind these may be boiled down to three rules.

The principle of identity: X is identical to X. (By implication, anything not-X is different to it.)

The law of the excluded middle: a thing is either B or not-B; (a thing is true or not).

The relationship of parts to wholes: if a thing X is removed from a thing Y, the resultant is less than Y. (The formal version of the well-known fact that it is not possible to have one's cake and eat it too.)

This logic is that which Freud called 'secondary process'. Broadly, it belongs to the conscious mind and is a bivalent logic. What is meant by bivalent is that this mode of logic requires that at least two things are to be related to each other. To be related means to have a position in space and time – for there to be a before and an after, a left and a right, an up and a down, an in and an out, and so on. This is the logic of finite things, of things that have a beginning and an end, where things are recognized and known, thus differentiated. If an object exists here, then it does not exist there. A tree occupies a particular bit of space, and it exists in a limited bit of time. Asymmetrical logic is reflected in the structure of language. Thus, the rudimentary English sentence relates a subject through a verb to an object: that is, there are two things (subject and object) and their relationship (verb).

Symmetrical logic

This other logic is a logic whose rules jar with the world familiar to us. At its limit, in this logic, all objects are identical; Matte-Blanco uses mathematical terminology to say that in this logic all relationships are symmetrical. An everyday example of a symmetrical relationship is 'June is the sister of Sally'; the obverse is also true: 'Sally is the sister of June'. Another example is 'the cup is near the saucer'; it follows that 'the saucer is near the cup'. Now, the statement 'the cup is on the saucer' is asymmetrical, that is, it is not the same if the terms are reversed. The cup being on top of the saucer precludes the saucer being on top of the cup. So we would think. However, according to the rules in this new logic, the statement 'the cup is on the saucer' is identical to its obverse 'the saucer is on the cup'. To our rational minds this is a nonsense – it literally makes no-sense. At its limit, this logic homogenizes the entire universe; more, it collapses the universe into a single point in which there are no objects to differentiate, to place in relationship; there is no space and no time.

This logic is of course very similar to the Freudian notion of primary processes, which he says take place in the unconscious. The five rules of unconscious thinking as elaborated by Freud (1915b, pp.186–187) are: the absence of mutual contradiction, displacement, condensation, timelessness, and the replacement of external by internal reality. Thus in this realm things can collapse from one to another, change from this to that, slide from here to there. If one can't differentiate between two things, then they are treated as the same, as identical, and so interchangeable. Cause and effect become interchangeable. In this world the fact that Jill is bigger than Jack does not prevent Jack being bigger than Jill at the same time. If John loves Sally, then to him, in this logic, it is equivalent to Sally loving him. Freud says: 'There are in this system no negation, no doubt, no degrees of certainty' (1933, p.73). As is well known, we see revealed in dreams images from the unconscious, images that hold strange contradictions with no difficulty – the cup above the saucer, and simultaneously, below the saucer. The tiger becomes the same as fearlessness and so on. Here, it is possible to have one's cake and eat it too. Thus analysts who on hearing a dream in which, say, a mother shouts at a daughter, try not to get involved only with the content but also reflect on the structure of the dream: something is attacking something else.

A fact in this realm can be both false and true at the same time. This is the realm of the eternal, where things may happen without consequence. For example, in fantasy the infant kills the mother whilst in a hungry rage. Within this logic there is no surprise or conflict when the external mother appears alive a few minutes later with food. Interestingly, this way of viewing the phenomenon of the fantasized murder of the mother seriously undermines the notion of splitting – in fact rendering it redundant. The notion of splitting is based on asymmetrical logic, the suggestion being that the baby cannot tolerate its heinous act and so splits both itself and its mother into two – the good and the bad. The splitting is followed by repression. However, in the world of symmetric logic, there is no need to split – the contradiction that the mother has been killed and is also alive is comfortably accommodated. One needs to split in order to accommodate contradictions, but contradictions can only exist in asymmetric logic, thus in symmetric logic there is no necessity to split. In symmetrical logic Humpty Dumpty is constantly being put back together again with no difficulty.

In this logic, there is no difference between things, so they become identical. There is no space, so there is no relationship between things, they collapse into each other. There is no time, so things are eternal, and therefore unchanging. As a consequence of these rules, things that would be contradictory in the first logic are allowed in this one. The instances of this that will be of interest to us are as follows.

1. Because all things are equivalent, a thing ('X') and its contradiction ('not-X') are identical and therefore true at the same time.

2. Because all space is equivalent, a thing can be both inside and outside a room, or a person, at the same time.

3. Because there is no time, things can be alive and dead simultaneously.

4. Parts are identical to wholes.

5. Change can take place and at the same time things remain eternal.[2]

Table 6.1 tabulates the differences between asymmetric and symmetric logic.

---

2   This follows out of the curious mathematical attributes of infinity. If a cake is infinitely big, then one can take a slice and what remains is a cake that is still infinitely big. Infinity is so big that infinity minus ten million is still infinity, and infinity add twenty billion is still infinity.

Table 6.1

Asymmetric Logic	Symmetric Logic
Differentiated	Homogenized
Relative	Absolute
Gradation	Polarization
Time and Space	Timeless and Spaceless
Mortal	Eternal
Change	Fixed
Finite	Infinite

The structure of thought

Matte-Blanco differs from Freud when he says that all thinking, conscious and unconscious, is bi-logical. What he means by this is that both logical systems, symmetrical and asymmetrical, are applied at the same time in all forms of thought. The degree of mix of the two logics will be dependent on which level of the mind is doing the thinking. At the deepest level of the unconscious, it will be mainly symmetrical logic that will be utilized. The main point is that thinking is never entirely asymmetrical or symmetrical.

What is so interesting here, is that our so-called normal objective logical thinking has symmetrized logic embedded within it. To go further, it would not be possible to engage in the 'normal' logic without the use of this 'crazy' symmetrical logic.

The key thing to remember is that asymmetric logic differentiates whilst symmetric logic homogenizes.

For example one might say of a shoe shop that 'they sell more brown shoes than red shoes'. There are three elements in this statement: 'red shoes', 'brown shoes', and the relationship between them: 'more'. At the macro level of the sentence, it is asymmetric logic that is being applied;[3] that is, the obverse statement is not simultaneously true. However, if one looks within the category 'brown shoes' then we discover that for the purposes of the statement all the shoes coloured brown have been homogenized. For the purposes of the statement it

---

3   In symbolic logic the statement would be 'brown shoes > red shoes', i.e. it matters which side of the sign the terms are.

does not matter that some of the brown shoes are stilettos and others are brogues. For the purposes of the statement all the shoes coloured brown are identical, and all the differences between them are made meaningless, thus rendering them invisible. Also, for the purposes of the statement the similarities between the two groups (they are all shoes) are not emphasized. One can see that it would not be possible to make the more 'sophisticated' statement in asymmetric logic, if the internals of the elements it refers to were not first homogenized by treating them with symmetric logic.

We can now make a general statement and say that all thinking consists of fracturing the continuum of experience, of breaking it up into different parts, and relating those parts to each other. Thus between the parts, difference is empha- sized, and similarity is obliterated – asymmetric logic. Whilst within each part, similarity is emphasized and difference is obliterated – symmetric logic.

In order to make any meaningful statement it is necessary to homogenize the interior of the parts of the statement, to blind oneself to the differentiation that exists within each categorization.

A digression: Bion

The contrast in the lists of attributes belonging to the two logics unexpectedly reflects and echoes Bion's (1961) descriptions of 'basic assumption groups' and 'work groups'. And so this is as good a place as any to account for why Bion has not been given more space in a book on groups, and to correct this to some degree.

Bion's offering is a complicated one. On the one hand one could say that he takes the group much more seriously than Foulkes, and on the other hand the individual seems to disappear almost entirely. What remains are the internal forces operating in individuals. The picture that we are left with then is a curious one, of a group filled with psychological forces, but with no sight of the individuals that they are presumably emanating from. This is an outcome of his metapsychology that lies behind his theory of groups – a metapsychology which is pure Plato. As we proceed we will discover that it is a metaphysic that Elias has spent all his work arguing against. And it is here that we must begin.

In the Bionic metaphysic all things begin in the protomental state. This region is similar to Plato's heaven where the Ideal forms are said to reside. Bion's region is not in heaven, but in the mind, and it is where the physical and the mental are said to be undifferentiated. It is a psychological equivalent to the universe before the Big Bang. In Plato's philosophy there exists in heaven perfect entities. The entities that manifest in the world are but poor copies of the real thing. Similarly, in Bion's theory, all things that manifest in the world have their basis in this region. The protomental region is attributed an *a priori* existence, and one that is outside experience; Bion says that it 'transcends experience'. So, already Bion has parted company with Elias, for whom thought emerges from worldly activity.

To continue: within the protomental region are said to reside the prototypes of the three basic assumption groups. These will be described in a moment, the point to be noted here is that the use of the notion of prototypes here is very similar to Plato's use of Ideal. To be sure, Plato has the added dimension of perfection in his Ideal, a dimension that is not present in the notion of a prototype. But leaving this difference aside, the similarity is that each system has an all-encompassing universal region from which all is said to emerge.

Next, out of the protomental state there emerges emotion. 'Starting then at the level of proto-mental events we may say that the group develops until its emotions become expressible in psychological terms. It is at this point that I say that the group behaves "as if" it were acting on a basic assumption' (Bion 1961, p.101). On the whole, the emotion emerging appears to be distress of some sort, and its basis, according to Bion, is the 'questioning attitude'.

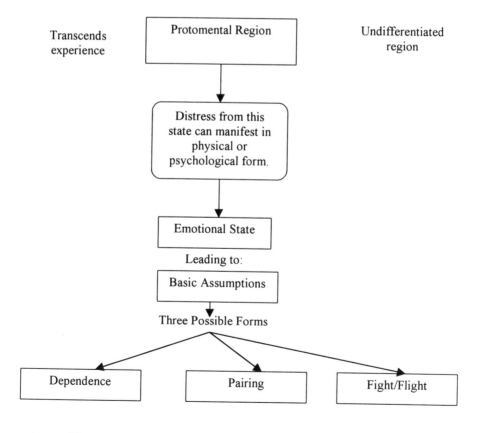

Figure 6.3

Now, we have to make a bit of a clumsy jump to reorientate ourselves. Bion is conducting this discussion in the context of a group that has met to examine itself. In other words, to learn about groups by experiencing a group. Thus the 'work' of this group, its task, is to look at itself. In general then Bion says that every group has a task, and when it is engaging in that task, then it is operating in a modality called the work group. But now, the group hits a problem. Bion says that the questioning attitude is regarded with dread by the group, and in part the dread is because 'the group approximates too closely in the minds of the individuals composing it, to very primitive fantasies about the content of the mother's body'. (1961, p.162) Thus the investigation is hampered, because to inquire into the workings of the group is to inquire into the secret and taboo recesses of the mother's body. The group defends against the dread by adopting a basic assumption, which is an emotional state that is in lieu of 'working'.

There are three basic assumption states (see figure 6.3), one of dependence, one of pairing, one of fight/flight. The pertinent thing about these basic assumption states is that they are all encompassing. The group and all the individuals are merged in one or other emotional experience, and are unable to think.

When we come to Bion's descriptions of the qualities associated with basic assumption groups vs. work groups, we find many similarities with Matte-Blanco's two logics. The qualities of the basic assumption group echo those of symmetric logic. For example Bion says: 'Participation in basic-assumption activity requires no training, experience, or mental development. It is instantaneous, inevitable and instinctive' (1961, p.153). The basic assumption group is a timeless, instinctive and emotional state, and in contrast to this the work group is bounded and mental. It seems to me that not only has Bion divided emotion from mental function, he has elevated thought as a good thing, and relegated emotion as a bad thing in that it prevents thought. I know I have overstated it somewhat, but nevertheless it does seem to me to be the general tenor of this theory. These ideas of Bion's are part of the larger cultural current which Elias has described so well. The current being the one that splits mind and matter, and deifies the former; a current that elevates what it imagines to be the unchanging over the transient, a current that seeks to flee from earthly form, which being both material and transient, is bound to decay. As we have seen, these currents have been institutionalized in various philosophies and religions, where notions of concept or idea or spirit have been elevated to a region outside of material existence, so that it may live forever. So when Bion says about the work group: 'The term embraces only mental activity of a particular kind, not the people who indulge it' (1961, p.144), it does seem to me that he is following in this general trend.

It is these sorts of ideas that make Bion's work on groups sound a discordant note in relation to the general tenor of the arguments being developed here. True,

Bion does say in many places that man is a group animal, but he then says that the animal nature is in constant conflict with the social nature. Additionally, he attributes all things that happen in groups to primitive mechanisms taking place *within* individuals, for example, 'I think that the central position in group dynamics is occupied by the more primitive mechanisms that Melanie Klein has described as peculiar to the paranoid-schizoid and depressive positions…[which are] the source of the main emotional drives in the group' (p.188). Groups on the whole are said to stir up primitive fears of being devoured and so forth. But the main point is this, that the driving force of group dynamics is made internal and individual: 'In my view, it is necessary to work through…the more *primitive anxieties of part-object relationships*. In fact I consider…[them] to contain *the ultimate sources of all group behaviour*' (Bion 1961, p.189; emphasis added). Bion agrees that individual and group psychology are one and the same, but makes the basis of their sameness that of the individual:

> the apparent difference between group psychology and individual psychology is an illusion produced by the fact that the group provides an intelligible field of study for certain aspects of individual psychology, and in so doing brings into prominence phenomena that appear alien to an observer unaccustomed to using the group. (Bion 1961, p.134)

Although many will disagree, these are the grounds on which Bion's theory of groups has not been given more of a role to play in the ideas being formulated here.

Increasing the complexities of belonging

Let us for the moment put Bion aside and return to Matte-Blanco, and apply this theory of thinking to the diagram above (Figure 6.2). We can say that symmetrical logic has been used to homogenize the *insides* of the groups A and B, whilst asymmetrical logic has been applied to the space *between* the two groups. However,

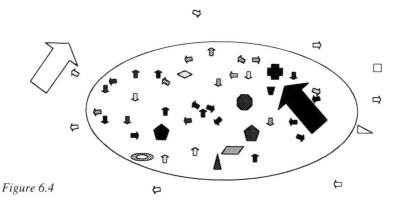

Figure 6.4

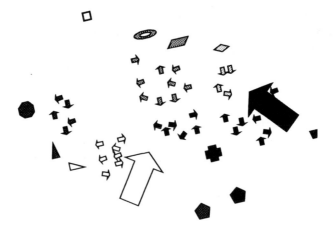

Figure 6.5

if we now look inside group A, we might discover that there are other differences there which we had not previously noticed, for example that the arrows are of different colours. These internal differences have been homogenized in Figure 6.2 by the application of symmetrical logic.

If we were now to use another attribute, say, 'coloured' or 'not coloured', to re-sort the same objects, then the picture would *look* dramatically different (see Figure 6.4). In effect, the use of the attribute 'coloured' has destroyed the previous grouping.

We are now bound to ask: is it not possible to keep both shape and colour in mind? If we try this, and keep two kinds of attributes in mind, shape (say number of sides) and type of colour, then we would have a very complicated grouping of sets and subsets, variously intersecting or not (see figure 6.5).

As one can see, it is getting increasingly difficult to say which belongs with which, and this is with just *two* attributes. In the real world any object will have an infinite number of attributes.

It is self evident that in complex situations, the brain simplifies things by picking out particular attributes and making them primary. This then is the cognitive component of motivation – a drive to simplification. We have yet to take up the other subjective and possibly emotional component – given that there is a drive to simplify, which particular attributes will be chosen to be made primary out of the multitude of possibilities?

Two essentialist fallacies

To help answer this question it will be useful to summarize the points so far with the help of two new simplified diagrams. In the first some shapes are sorted

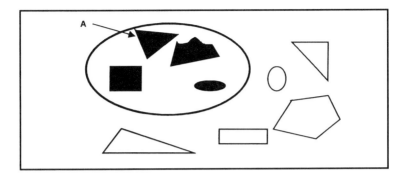

Figure 6.6

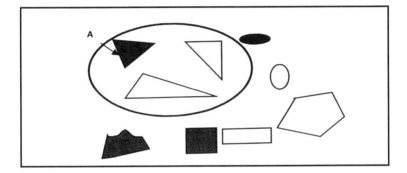

Figure 6.7

according to colour and in the second they are organized according to number of sides.

Looking at the two diagrams, it would appear that in Figure 6.6 the 'essence' of shape A, the thing that makes it belong to that group and differentiates it from all else, is its colour. Whilst in Figure 6.7 it would appear that the 'essence' of the same shape A, the thing that makes it belong to *this* group and differentiates it from all else, is the number of sides it possesses. Something tautological has taken place. The chosen method of sorting, colour or shape, has determined the 'essential' quality.

This is the mistake made by the essentialists – they, like all of us, enter the world to find it already divided, but they make the mistake of thinking that this is a natural and only division. We can see from the diagrams that 'essence' is partly a property of an object, but it is also a function of context. Context essentializes a particular property.

But having said that, there is the opposite danger that one will take context as 'a given'. But as Figures 6.6 and 6.7 clearly show, the appearance taken on by 'context' is determined in part by the chosen way of seeing, that is, the chosen way of sorting. To think otherwise is to naturalize and essentialize the notion of 'context'. The importance of the point is that there are many ways of sorting, none more intrinsically potent than any other. From this it would follow that the thing called 'essence' is not a constant, but really a variable that is a function of three things, the properties of the thing, the properties of the context, and the 'way of seeing'. The last of the three terms, the 'way of seeing', is in a sense the most fundamental, as it organizes and informs which properties of both object and context will be elevated and prioritized.

From these diagrams, one can clearly see the linkage between 'essence' and 'belongingness'. In Figure 6.6, it would appear that shape A *belongs* in that group, because of its alleged essence, its colour. Whilst in Figure 6.7 it would appear that shape A *belongs* in that group, because of its alleged essence, its number of sides. The admixture of essence and belongingness leads us inexorably towards the notion of identity.

To repeat the conundrum, given that there are a multitude of places in which one could legitimately be said to belong, in any given situation, what makes one or more sorts of belonging primary?

Identity parade

With the notion of identity, we begin to approach interesting territories. First, it is now clear that there are a multitude of legitimate answers to the question 'where do I belong?' Second, it will always be possible to find a grouping to which any two randomly chosen people will be found to belong. Third, it will always be possible to find a grouping to which any two randomly chosen people will be found not to belong to.[4] There is always a choice as to which side of the fence one is to focus on.

This then is the paradox: it would appear that on the cognitive level, the notion of identity is a contingent category; ultimately it is a reification – an empty category, apparently an arbitrary way of sorting. The empty category is variously 'filled' with the way of sorting (e.g. coloured or triangle, as in the diagrams above).[5] The other side of the paradox is that on an emotional and experiential

---

4   As we have seen in the chapter on biology, most of the DNA is shared by all humans. Certainly it is possible to find DNA patterns that are unique to each and every individual, but that does not mean that unique individuals have nothing in common between them.

5   Of course they are not really arbitrary at all, only in the realms of pure logic. In differing contexts we find particular 'ways of sorting' are experienced as critical. It matters little that one can point out that there are other equally valid ways of sorting. For example, in Northern Ireland it is the Protestant–Catholic divide that appears to be the only relevant one. In Chicago during the Watts riots

level, the feeling of belonging is substantial and critical to a sense of well-being, of psychological health itself.

The question then is this: *how is it that something that in a sense does not exist* per se *gives rise to something, a subjective experience, which does exist, and indeed, needs to exist.*

It seems to me that here, we are engaged in the difficult task of trying to correlate two very different things – the cognitive task of categorization and the emotional sense of belonging. Both of these come together in the notion of identity. So we can say two preliminary things about identity here. First, identity is a name, the name of a category. Second, identity is an internal sense of belonging to a name.[6]

Given that there are a multitude of potential identities, there must be a constant danger of slippage from one to another. In other words, there is a constant danger of 'loss of identity'. Any such threat is indeed an existential crisis. Suddenly, one sort of an 'us' might transmute into another sort of an 'us'. Suddenly, and perhaps terribly, one might find oneself belonging together with one of 'them'. How is one to cope with this? There are two different answers to be found for this question, one from post-structuralism and one from a reading of Matte-Blanco.

Identity crisis

As the reader might recall from Chapter 3, the post-structuralists have described the nature of existence in very similar terms to those above. The older idea of ideology was much more straightforward – it was either false and bourgeois, or true and proletarian. If persons were in the grip of false ideology then they were said to be alienated from their 'true nature', thus they had the advantage of possessing a true nature to be alienated from. The point about a dominant ideology was that it naturalized the order in the world – it made it appear that the current order and hierarchy was the 'natural' one. In a world organized by ideology, one knows where one stands, literally there *is* a place to stand, even if it is the wrong place. One knows, or at least there is the possibility of knowing, right from wrong – thus even if one is trapped within a false consciousness, it is possible to get to something more true. Ideology allowed the notion of a 'true reality' to

---

– colour; in parts of the Middle East – Arab/Israeli; in the Institute of Psychoanalysis – Freudian/Kleinian/Independent, and so on. What makes each of these attributes relevant in these contexts, is history. Whatever attributes the battle takes place over, the manifest terrain, ultimately it is always over control and power. This includes notions of 'blackness' and 'whiteness'. These thoughts will be elaborated a little later.

6   We are now forced into a further complication, which is to consider whether one *identifies* oneself or whether one is *identified* by some other. In other words, whether one is a subject or an object. Thus there is potentially a space of conflict – between the external categorization and the internal experience. This too clearly brings us into the realm of power relations. This point is linked to the previous footnote and, similarly, will be taken up later.

exist out there, and the 'correct' ideology was said to give one access to picturing and experiencing that true reality as it was.

The structuralists, although they began from a different place, also allowed more of a 'fit' between reality and experience. Signifiers and signifieds were firmly tied together. They said that we were structured from without by the Word, and the Word was Langue. I think that it is true to say that on the whole, the structuralists posited one system that each of us were part of. Loosely, we can map this model on what is called modernism (Frosh 1991), where things change rapidly but where one has the possibility of riding the tides of change – of accommodating the self to the changes, of accommodating the changes to the self. The rapidly mutating cultural frames, and the concomitant states of mind that these generate, might alter at a ferocious rate, but they are serial, that is, we are in them one at a time.

Post-modernism, and linked to that post-structuralism, robs us of even this last refuge. The buzzword here is 'discourse' – a sea of belief, speech and thought – that engulfs, permeates and fills everything. A particular discourse orders the world and its inhabitants, it defines and positions a particular sort of self in relation to the world, it defines and positions the Other. In this sense discourse does the same job as ideology, it naturalizes a particular world order and it constrains one's possible thoughts and experiences to within that discourse. But now, discourse and ideology part company. Whilst the notion of ideology implies that there is an external reality, the notion of discourse is completely self referential – there is no place outside discourse. Discourse is an endless chain of signifiers: words pointing to words pointing to words pointing to words – and we never get to the thing itself, or even the idea of the thing. One could say that discourse was a particular way of ordering a hierarchy of words. Unlike ideology, discourses are not only formed by the power relations, but also by other social and cultural currents. But then we find that something else has also happened – discourse has broken free of the material world. Thus there is no notion in discourse of a true reality outside of it. This is the paradox of discourse – it is born of the world, but no longer of it.

Instead of notions of truth, what we find are other competing discourses, other ways of ordering the world, other ways of defining subject positions. And here's the rub: there are many discourses operating simultaneously – thus there are many competing simultaneous claims on the sense of identity. There is no peace of mind here, no place of rest, discourses are being constantly subverted and disrupted by other discourses. Existence, the sense of self, the me, the us, becomes increasingly precarious and fragile, and so begins a terrifying slide into a kaleidoscopic unstable universe.

So, although travelling a quite different route, travelling through ideology and discourse, we have arrived back at the same problematic place – the problematic of identity. A place we had already reached at the end of the previous section through discussions on cognition and categorization.

We can now formulate a way of describing a solution to the post-structural predicament. This predicament is the fragmentary and slippery nature of existence and sense of self. We can put it in a psychological language: we find it impossible to exist in an unstructured universe – partly because to exist is to structure, and partly because of the intolerable existential anxiety that is evoked as we contemplate chaos, where meanings slide and evaporate, where nothing whatsoever is fixed and stable. This is indeed a post-structuralist anxiety – which is too much to bear – and one defends against it by retreating into the binarized world of structuralism. We cannot do otherwise. One could say that we defend against post-structuralist anxiety by a retreat into structuralism.

In other words, we end up imposing a tenuous order on this perpetually fluctuating reality by clinging to a particular discourse. We are caught up in particular ways of experiencing a self – a self that is dictated by particular discourses. We constantly try to shoehorn the multiplicity of existence into a unitary frame, *this* is me, that is not; I belong here and not there, we are a 'we' because of a such and such, and so 'they' are not 'us'. The frame continually threatens to burst, and let the cat out of the bag – the cat being the knowledge that there are untold versions and varieties of 'we', not just the one that I *feel* right now. And if the 'we' is so precarious, then what comfort is there for the 'I'?

One of the things that has been said about discourses is that they are in a sense closed systems – sufficient unto themselves. And so, having fled from the solipsism of the innatists, it would seem that we have found ourselves embroiled in a new solipsism, a solipsism of culture. Indeed this is one of the main criticisms made of these sorts of theories, but for the moment I want to make another point – which comes from the domain of mathematics. Earlier we touched on one of the supreme achievements of mathematics this century – the work of Godel and his 'incompleteness theorem'. This proved that no logical system can be both complete and self-consistent. In other words, if a system seeks to be complete, then one will always be able to find logical inconsistencies within it, and if the system is consistent, then it will not be complete, it will always have to make some reference to something outside it. These somethings are what are commonly known as axioms, something that one has to take as a given in order to proceed further.

If one brings this mathematical insight to bear on discourse, then we can say that discourse has and gives the illusion of something all knowing and all seeing, of something complete – but that this is a deceit. And it is a deceit that it hides from itself. One of the deceits is the appearance discourse gives of self sufficiency, of not being part of the material world. This gap between consistency and completeness is where deconstruction has the possibility of gaining a purchase, which it can then exploit to overturn the prevailing order. Another way of putting it is this: there is never any closure, only the fantasy of closure and always an impetus towards closure – towards the definitive narrative.

These ideas have been pursued here because it seems to me that they have a great affinity with Elias as well as notions of group, which are all about finding one's sense of self through participation and plural existence, and not through a retreat into individualism, which is but a fantasy of living outside ideology and discourse.

It seems to me that the model of a multiplicity of discourses disrupting and confounding each other is actually quite a good description of what takes place in groups. Participants form and recount their narratives from within particular discourses. One could say that each participant speaks a discourse which appears self evident, natural and almost *complete* to them. Participants seek the collusion of others to close things down, saying in effect: that is how it was then, and this is how it is, and that is how it will be. It is the other persons in the group who bring a tangential gaze to bear, whose other discourse has the possibility of finding the gaps and anomalies in the apparent completeness and coherence, and of thus instituting a deconstructive process. Hence, in this new language, a model of a functioning group would be that of competing discourses colliding with each other and finding each other out, disputing realities that seek out the chink in each others discursive armours to prise them open. In this way I think that the structure of group therapy reflects more closely the structure of life itself.

As a psychotherapist I am now bound to ask, but where are notions of health and ill health in all of this? What is to be thought of as therapeutic and what is not? In the post-modern age there are no easy answers to these questions, there is no more stable ground, no North Star to orientate us through the turbulent seas of discourse. Absolutes are lost to us – they have become fond memories of more comforting times. Are we then driven towards a relativism saying that neurosis, psychosis, and so-called normality, are just competing discourses, each with equal validity within their own frame? And what of Foulkes' notion that the 'normal' is constructed within each group by the differences contained therein, and that this norm is identical to 'health'? I think that there is some mileage in this proposition, as long as we are allowed to problematize 'norm' and 'health'. As we have noted, the problem with some versions of discourse theory is that it seeks to present itself as something divorced from the world. However, there are post-structuralists who think the contrary, Terry Eagleton, Michel Foucault and Edward Said to name but three (Selden 1989). Additionally, there is Elias and his Symbol Theory, which is firmly grounded in the external and the social. It is true that within discourse, one is constrained by the notions of that discourse. However, discourse is not free to take any shape – it too is constrained by the nature of lived experience, which is constrained in turn by *a combination of* the material and the ideological. In beginning with the word 'discourse' and ending with the word 'ideological', we have made a circle, but not a solipsistic one. We have made a circle that repeatedly cuts through the material and the ideological, continually transforming each. This idea is pure Elias.

Thus psychotherapy groups are not isolated rafts floating adrift in a vacuum, albeit rafts of competing but equivalent discourses, endlessly interpreting and interrupting each other's texts, self absorbed and self referential. There are at least two partial anchors: groups are full of people with lives in the world which brings its own constraints; and the group analyst refers constantly in his or her mind to his/her own dominant theoretical discourse. Although the group analyst's discourse is given an authority over and above other discourses, it too is tested, punctured and deconstructed by the processes in the group. And it is in the nexus of these conflicting forces that something is painfully given birth to, and that something is tested and reformulated continually in the forge of experience both in the group and also the world. Perhaps we can say that group psychotherapy has the possibility of freeing one from being stuck in one discourse, one experience of self and world, and opens up the possibility of connecting with other discourses, other ways of being and experiencing that one did not have previous access to. That conceivably is as much as can be said – there is no definitive health here, just flexibility, which perhaps is health enough.

The emotional need to belong

Radical Foulkes has said that one of the fundamental organizing principles driving and structuring human existence is the need to belong. This has distanced him from the Freudian schema which is instinct driven, and brought him close to Fairbairn's notion that the libido is object-seeking and not pleasure-seeking. Earlier, Matte-Blanco was used to delineate the cognitive elements of the problematic of belonging. We will now look at the emotional aspects of belonging, and begin with the self same question – why is there a need to belong?

Self evidently, the need to belong is a very powerful impulse. For example all are familiar with situations in which children or adults are arbitrarily divided into groups for the sake of some game or other. It does not take long before the attachments to these groupings become fierce and sometimes extreme.

One set of arguments, in line with Elias, explain the sudden loyalties by reference to the power structures. In a game situation, this would be the motivation to win. This explanation, via the pragmatics of the situation, makes 'loyalty' out to be a strategy that increases the chances for winning. Notwithstanding the fact that it is a strategy, it remains the case that many of the emotional and psychological elements of 'strategy' are always unconscious. Next to this, there are another set of experimental findings from social psychology that demonstrate that there is a strong tendency to invent and create belonging groups, even when there appears to be no particular gain.[7] If one puts a random group of people together they will invariably fragment into smaller groups. The question is: why should this occur? A partial answer can be given from the work of the social psychologists Cialdini *et al.* (1976). They showed that the development of self-esteem was dependent on the possibility for individuals to demonstrate in-group bias and favouritism. In other words, people needed to show in-group favouritism in order to feel good about themselves. In fact things can be taken even further. Rupert Brown describes the outcome of an experiment by Tajfel *et al.* (1971) which demonstrated two critical things. First that 'mere categorization was sufficient to elicit ingroup favouritism' (Brown 1988, p.223). And second that the in-group favouritism took place even when in overall terms the group ended up a little worse off as a result of the favouritism.

This is a very interesting finding, as it shows that in-group affinities are not just about power and resource, it is something more than that. So how is one to explain it? Well for one thing the findings of these social psychologists not only verify what Elias and Scotson called group charisma, they also extend it. Elias said that the possibility of attributing charisma to the 'we' group was intimately bound up with where the group was positioned in the power differential. What we are now in the position to say is that the mechanism of in-group favouritism is a part of idealization. The group is idealized so that one can bask in its reflected glory. Another way of putting it is this – the group is fed, this makes the group feel good, and this in turn feeds the self. Love and gifts are being constantly transacted back and forth, between individual and group, each basking and growing in the other's adoration. So the question, why is there a psychological need to create an 'us', is answered in part by the idea that one needs to create a belonging group, so that one can feed it, in order for it to feed the self. Additionally, the fact that the 'we' is already a part of the 'I'[8] means that when one is feeding the 'we' one is simultaneously feeding the 'I'.

These experimental findings happen also to further undermine the arguments of the kin selectionists whom, as we saw earlier, sought to give nepotism a biological foundation, saying that in-group favouritism occurred because of the genes that were shared. Instead of genes and kin, what we have found is that it is (a) function and (b) self esteem that drive the tendency towards in-group bias and favouritism. It is the fact that at times the kinship group happens to be identical to the functional group that allows the sociobiologists to make their insidious claims.

7   This discussion was first presented in Dalal (1993b).
8   The argument for this statement is developed later.

From here to infinity: further structures of thinking

Matte-Blanco says: '…Behind every individual or relationship…the self "sees" an infinite series…' (1975, p.170). When he says this he is referring to asymmetric logic. But to my mind this is true of both systems of logic, the asymmetric and the symmetric.

In the world of asymmetric logic, everything is connected, through some attribute to everything else. Take something like 'tree'. This belongs to an infinite number of sets – green objects, brown objects, red objects, vertical objects, growing objects, edible objects, useful objects, mortal objects, objects that change their appearance, objects that compete, stationary objects, objects that move and so on. By creating increasingly generalized sets with specific attributes in a kind of taxonomy, 'tree' can be connected to any other object in the universe. To be facile for a moment, tree and nostril both belong to the set of 'material objects'. The critical word in this logic is *connected*. Perhaps a better word would be *linked* – things are linked by the sharing of an attribute. Eventually everything is linked to everything else.

Next to this, in the world of symmetric logic, everything is the same as everything else. Note the collapse, from 'connected' to 'same'. In this world, the part comes to stand for the whole. A particular taxi driver comes to be equated with the class of taxi drivers. Thus one person's rash driving comes to sully all the members of the class of taxi drivers. The attribute 'taxi driver' is the channel that allows the brush to tar *all* the members of the class.

One can see then that in both logic systems, every object is part of an infinite regress. We can now see what Matte-Blanco means when he says that behind any one thing we see an infinite series. 'Things' that belong to *one* relationship potentially become a part of *all* relationships, purely because of the attribute 'relationship'. From 'relationship' one slides easily into the notion of 'relatedness'. Relatedness is intrinsic to existence itself, in the sense that any two objects are inevitably positioned relative to each other, if only in space and time. Thus 'the things' that began with one relationship end up belonging to everything.

This is a dizzying and terrifying vertigo: a cascade towards infinity. In order to exist one somehow has to disconnect from the infinite. To have some notion of 'I', or 'we' or 'it', or 'this' or 'that', one somehow has to interrupt this vertigo.

At its most basic, *the interruption is thought itself.*

However, one of the things that is being said is that the thoughts (ways of sorting information) and emotions (ways of positioning oneself relative to the information) are not free to take any shape, they are being driven in certain directions. But given that everything connects to everything else – how and why is it that things get linked and fixated in particular directions?

There must be a complex interplay between these two forces, the tendency to merge and the tendency to get fixed. We have been discussing the mechanisms of logic that drive towards merging. We now move on to looking at what drives the psychological mechanisms towards partitioning and then fixing.

Categorization

The question that we will take up now is that given the world of experience is partitioned, where and how are the lines drawn?

THE INSTINCTIVIST ANSWER

Freud and Klein would say that it is the instincts and their vicissitudes that drive the partitioning of the world and one's experience of it. They would say that the infant comes into the world with tools with which to organize experience – the tools being the life and death instincts. In this sort of theory, *it is emotionality (particularly anxiety born of fear and hatred) that drives categorization.*

FOULKES' ANSWER

Foulkes on the other hand says that the infant has a series of experiences which then *condense* and *polarize*. He suggests that the variety of experiences somehow coagulate into two globules of extremity. As we have already asked of Foulkes, why should experience be *collected* in this way? Why should the continuity of experience be fragmented and polarized? Why can't the experiences exist in a continuum? What drives the tendency to polarize?

Foulkes is mute on these points. He does not address the matter. However, it seems to me that he leaves open two possible interlinked avenues for us to pursue.

Dividing with language

The first concerns language. As many people have shown, the deep structure of language is a binary one – things are categorized as 'A' or 'not-A'. Using Matte-Blanco's terminology, the structure of language is bi-valent. If we now ask what might have given rise to language taking this particular form, there are two possible answers, one from the domain of emotion and the other cognition. Those who believe in the life and death instincts might say that it is the instincts, the ultimate in binary opposition, that have structured language in this way. In other words, the binary structure of language reflects the duality of the instincts. The cognitive answer would say that in order to be able to think at all, one has to partition and name parts of the continuity of experience. Intrinsic to the act of naming is the act of partitioning – 'A' – 'not-A'. Thus *naming is intrinsically a binarizing act.*

But whatever drives categorization, instinct or cognition, the fact remains that experience has to be categorized, partitioned somehow. Before it can be an experience at all, it has to be framed.[10] To use language to frame, is to automatically polarize and binarize: this is John, this is not; this is nice, this is not.

The hypothesis is that it is the structure of language, and therefore the structure of thought, that leads, at some level, to the inevitability of experience falling into one of two camps. To consider the nature of these two camps, and what this 'level' might be, we have to move to the second 'avenue'.

Creating extremes

The second avenue concerns primary process thinking or symmetric logic. Here, we enter a logical labyrinth that leads eventually to the realm of absolutes. The question we have to answer is this: how is it that the deepest unconscious is not a unity but bifurcated? It is hard to communicate the importance of this question, why is the unconscious not one place but *two* extremes? If, as Freud said, in this region all things are made similar and same, then all would become one, not two. Religions too tussle with this question, albeit in a different realm. Some faiths, such as Christianity and Islam, begin with the notion of one God; Hinduism gives the appearance of many Gods, but they are all eventually part of the One. Meanwhile, Zoroastrianism begins with Two – Good and Bad entwined in eternal battle.

The place of maximum symmetry is where everything is homogenized to such an extreme degree that there is no differentiation whatsoever, the universe is collapsed into a single point. Here, *no*thing exists, or everything exists. In the language of the mystic, 'All is One'. In the same sort of way that one cannot ask the question 'what was it like before the Big Bang?', one cannot ask anything of the state of maximum symmetry. This is because there is no space or time, no before or after – literally, no space for the question. In the language of information theory, maximum chaos means that no information is possible. It is not possible to say anything, because to say anything is to differentiate and thus *precipitate existence itself.*

Now, if we let the minimal amount of asymmetry enter the picture, then differentiation is at its most basic – 'two'. A thing and its name. Logically it would seem that 'existence' must begin with the notion of a 'two-ness' rather than one-ness. Even to say 'exist' implies its inverse 'not-exist' giving rise to 'two'. *The minimal number at which existence is possible, is two.* Nothing can exist without recourse to a minimal amount of asymmetry – differentiation.[11]

---

10   We cannot engage with the conundrum of whether language forces reality into binary oppositions, or whether language reflects the binary nature of reality. For our purposes, it is sufficient to note that the two appear to reflect each other, and leave issues of cause and effect well alone.

11   The sequence is very Biblical in its structure. In the beginning is the Void, i.e. no-thing. Then the Word that cleaves the unity into two, Day and Night. This is where existence begins. Then progressively more asymmetry (i.e. differentiation) is added over the next seven days of Creation. And

Thus at the deepest levels of the unconscious, where things *exist*, but are also as homogenized as possible, where symmetry is maximal and asymmetry is minimal, there must be a 'two-ness'. With just 'two' possible states within this region 'there are no degrees of certainty' (as Freud put it) only extremes and absolutes.

The absolutes and extremes that occur in this region are the outcome of the structure of existence itself – rather than having anything to do with the instincts. It is as though there are only two boxes in the deep unconscious, which through the processes of condensation and association accrue notions of good and bad, purity and dirt, safety and danger, love and hate and so forth. After all, experience has to be put somewhere, and in the deep unconscious the only places available are two absolutes.

This argument is a further undermining of individualism. The argument shows that Leibniz's monad is a logical impossibility. Existence begins with two, with difference – it cannot be otherwise. The notion of one, of the unity, is retrospectively constructed, after existence has begun. *This* is what Foulkes means when he says that the individual is an abstraction.

A gravitational metaphor

We can put these thoughts together in an analogy, that gives some veracity to Foulkes' notion that experience condenses and polarizes, *without* help of the instincts.

We begin with two random experiences, that will inevitably have differing emotional valences, however slight, because no two things are ever the same. This differentiation forms the basis of two nuclei. Through the mechanism of association, the nuclei draw to themselves things that resonate and are emotionally similar to them in some way. Much like two neonate suns gathering up interstellar gases in their vicinity, the 'gathering up' results in their gravitational pulls getting larger. The process continues, with them progressively pulling more and more to themselves, which results in their gravitational pull continuing to increase, to pull ever more remote things to themselves, until some future point when all

---

as to the question where did the Word come from, we are unable to ask it. We can say with Godel's incompleteness theorem, that the system has to take something outside and beyond it as a given – this given is the Word. This gives the appearance of One thing precipitating existence. The other part of Godel's theorem is that if a system aims to be complete then it will have an unresolvable contradiction within it, thus if the Word is included, then the impossibility we have to live with is that something comes from nothing. The same sequence is found in modern cosmology: of before the Big Bang we can say nothing, as there is no space, time or things. After the Big Bang there are two basic things, matter and energy. As the universe cools, these get progressively complex, differentiated and asymmetric. To computer buffs this is an impossibility that they deal with every time they get computers to turn themselves on. In their language it is called bootstrapping, literally lifting oneself by one's bootstraps, impossible but true!

intervening space is emptied. In the end there will be two large collections of polarized experience and nothing else in between.

Every experience will have an emotional valence, however faint. There is no such thing as a 'neutral' experience; there will always be some feeling, towards or away. Fundamentally, it is not possible to have experience devoid of affect. This ultimately must be the basis of the two coagulations. At its most basic, these two collections will have names like safe and dangerous or pleasant and unpleasant, or good and bad. Taking it further, through the various historical associations, it must be inevitable that their names also become white and black.

It is interesting to note that this end situation will have the same appearance as of splitting having taken place, but we have derived the same end result from very different mechanisms.

Of course an object can be pulled to either gravitational centre, because it will have attributes that resonate with both. So in one sense the 'choice' is fickle – things can easily flick from one centre to another. One moment someone is loved, the next hated, because of some triviality. In another sense, once the 'gravitational pull' gets strong enough, there are powerful constraints as to which centre things will get drawn towards. Thus there will be constraints on the ways things are able to be experienced. For example, the notion of blackness and whiteness. The thoughts of Elias and Scotson (1994) readily come back here, that structure has a history and history has a structure.

Between the extremes: Analogues and digits

So far we have delineated how the admixture of Foulkes' notion of condensation with that of symmetric logic might give rise to two extremes within the psyche. At this point one can raise the valid objection that the world and our everyday experience is not one of continual extremes. This is true. One can shed light on this anomaly by drawing a parallel from the world of quantum physics. On the scale of the atomic and sub-atomic, the world is found to be quantized, that is, of packets, of abrupt and sharp changes with no in-betweens. A thing can be (say) in a place A or place B. In the quantum world there is nothing between A and B, the space between simply does not exist. We cannot comprehend how a thing might go from A to B without going through something in between. It seems like magic. There is no gradation. At this level it is a digital universe. However, at the level at which we ordinarily experience the universe, we find it to be analogical; things are smoothed out, there are transitions, and in-betweens. To go from London to Edinburgh, one has to travel over intervening territory. In the quantum universe one somehow gets from London to Edinburgh without moving through intervening territory – because there is none.

Returning to the two interpenetrating logics, at one level we manage to say complex things. But at a deeper level behind the complexity, there exists a binary structure embedded within it. *Smooth sentences always contain 'sharp pieces'*; sentences relate globules of things like red shoes.

To summarize the points made in this section:

At the level of symmetric logic, things are homogenized, merged and collapsed. This is similar but not identical to Freud's primary processes.

At the level of 'everyday' asymmetric logic, things are never absolute. They are more or less similar, more or less true, and so on. Things are differentiated. This is similar but not identical to Freud's secondary processes.

As we have said, the two logics are always mixed, but to differing degrees. At its most extreme, there is only symmetry. Nothing can be said about this, because to say anything is to introduce asymmetry. When the smallest amount of asymmetry is introduced, then differentiation is at its most basic – that is 'two', either/or. This is a description of the state of the deep unconscious. As we add more asymmetry to the mixture, we progressively move towards everyday sentences like 'there are more brown shoes than black ones'; but in parts of the asymmetric sentence, we find elements that have been symmetrized.

It is tempting to equate asymmetric logic with the conscious mind and symmetric logic with the unconscious mind. However *all* thinking is a mixture of the two. Matte-Blanco calls it bi-logical thinking. What *is* true is that our conscious thoughts tend to have more asymmetry than symmetry, and our unconscious thoughts tend to have more symmetry than asymmetry. As we have already shown, it is not possible to make an asymmetric statement without using symmetric logic to homogenize the parts that are being talked about. And it is not possible to say anything, without naming something, that is bringing asymmetric logic to bear upon it.

In certain situations, symmetric logic breaks out of its allocated role, and symmetrizes parts of everyday experience to an extraordinary degree. If this experience is too overwhelming, then it is named psychosis. This model will be very helpful in allowing us to understand some of the mental mechanisms of racist thought, as and when we come to it.

Meanwhile, it is apparent that the 'states' and logics being described bear more than a passing resemblance to Melanie Klein's developmental stages of the paranoid-schizoid position and the depressive position. However, the similarity gives rise to many confusions. It will be helpful at this point to make another digression, to unpack the intricacies of this territory, which are caused by the proximity of the notion of splitting, to that of categorization.

Name calling and hair splitting: a critique of splitting

What is the relationship between categorization (naming) and splitting?

In discussions on racism or violences of any sort, in psychoanalytic forums, it does not take very long before the notion of splitting is introduced. It is almost as though once it has been said, it is thought that something has been explained. The formula, splitting–repression–projection, is at times used as a catch-all. The simplistic version of which is: hatred occurs because people split off the nasty parts of their psyche, repress the fact that they have done so, and then project it onto other groups. The thing that one hates in the other is something belonging to the self. Of course there is much to be said for this formulation, but things are (as always) much more complex.

Splitting is a defence against anxiety. Hinshelwood says that there are two elements to splitting, the thing that is split, and the way that it is split, the combination of which lead to four configurations. The two types are: '(i) There is a splitting of the object or of the ego; (ii) and the splitting may be coherent (as in good versus bad), or it may be fragmenting.' (1991, p.127) Splitting is the central defence employed early in the developmental process during the paranoid-schizoid phase, and also in adult life when thinking is conditioned by the paranoid-schizoid position; 'splitting became a term employed to describe the way in which objects came to be separated into their good aspects and their bad ones' (Hinshelwood 1991, p.434).

However, what is often forgotten is that for things to be separated, they need to be previously joined. So when it is said that an infant has split something, logic dictates that in order to be able to split the thing, the infant must previously have *known it* in some sort of an un-split state. In other words, *un-split events are ontologically prior to split events.*

The confusions are compounded by two different uses of the notion of part-objects. According to Kleinian developmental theory, the infant's perceptual faculties are such that it is not capable of experiencing the whole person, and so it only experiences parts of the person. But as Hinshelwood cautions: 'from the infant's point of view, the part is all there is to the object' (1991, p.379). Thus to say 'part-objects' in this sense, is to say that the infant's experience of reality is partial. This 'part-object' has nothing whatsoever to do with splitting, and alludes to the limited experiential capabilities of the infant. The infant experiences the tongue, the breast, a touch and so forth, and to the infant they remain discrete entities, unconnected to each other. Thus the breast is a part-object, but only to the observing adult and not the infant.

The other use of the term 'part-object' is for the resulting fractional parts of something previously connected, but now fractured. In other words the term part-object is now being used for a split-object. 'The breast' as experienced by the infant is a whole-object, but is perceived by the adult to be really a part-object. This part-object is then split by the infant into the good breast and bad breast. This splitting is a manifestation of the paranoid-schizoid defence. Thus strictly speaking, the good breast is a split-part-object.

The main point to be taken from the discussion so far, is that for something to be split, be it ego, object, or object-relationship, it has to be *known and experienced* before in some sort of an un-split state. It is difficult to know what to call this un-split state, and not to fall into the trap of thinking of the prior state as a 'whole' or as some sort of a unity. All one can actually say is that the un-split state is some sort of joined-upness, some sort of connectedness.

Let us keep this in mind as we take up the second type of splitting as described by Hinshelwood, 'the splitting may be coherent (as in good versus bad), or it may be fragmenting'. The first is a description of neurotic splitting and the second of psychotic splitting. Let us begin with the first of these – 'coherent splitting'.

This type of splitting looks very much like what we have called categorization. Is what Hinshelwood calls coherent splitting, really another way of describing categorization? To put it another way again, is this form of splitting the basis for 'naming' or vice versa? Let us recall that splitting is a function of emotionality, particularly anxiety, and categorization is a function of intellect.

Coherent splitting has two elements to it: first, collecting together things which are *thought* to have an attribute in common (like 'good' or 'brown') – this is the meaning of 'coherent'. This part of the activity is indeed the same as categorization, that is, naming. The second part of the activity is denying and forgetting the fact that these things have been collected *out of something*. The other name for this 'forgetting' is splitting. Once splitting has occurred, 'the part' looks and is experienced as 'a whole' – i.e. all links to anything outside it are annihilated, as if they were never there in the first place.

We can now formulate the following proposition:

The intellectual act of categorization differentiates and divides; the emotional act of splitting represses the fact that there ever was a connection between the divided.

I think that errors arise in sometimes equating splitting with the act of division.

One should add here a reminder that we have already problematized the act of categorization, revealing its contingent nature as well as its ephemeralness. This we have done through our deconstruction of belongingness. To restate the formulation: there are always many ways of dividing (categorizing) none more intrinsically valid than any other. Effectively, we have already undermined aspects of the notion of coherence. Thus we are forced to disagree with Hinshelwood's assumptions that the terms 'good' and 'bad' are not only coherent, but that they are also self evident categories. Coherence is an artifact, Foulkes would say that it is an abstraction. Coherence is constructed on the basis of repressing innumerable other differences. In the language we have been using – the internal differences have been homogenized by the application of symmetric logic. However, the illusion of coherence is of course a very necessary illusion, and is fundamental to the process of thought itself. Next, the notions of good and bad are typologies and not innate essentialisms. What is *felt* to be good or bad is informed *also* by that which is *thought* to be good and bad.[12] Although it might appear to be a truism, it is worth stating that emotions are not pure experiences, but have thoughts embedded in them, thoughts that mediate and structure the experience, in other words, *name it*. On the other side of the fence, as we have previously noted, categorization, the act of naming, is not a straightforward observational activity. Emotionality is critically implicated in the act of categorization, the decision as to where the line is drawn delineating this from that. Thus good and bad are contingent constructions informed by many things, and not innate in any Kantian sense. At this point it will be useful to look more closely at the notions of good and bad.

Looking for danger

One of the problems with the sole use of the traditional notion of splitting (in the strict Kleinian sense) to explain the animosities in the world, is that the animosities are derived exclusively as the outcome of the projection of the internal drama. The basis of 'good' and 'bad' is derived from the feelings of safety and danger, and they in turn are based on the location of the life and death instincts. Thus *what* one is led to separate from, is in part determined by *where* one projects the instincts. This is an extremely solipsistic picture.

However, it seems to me that the arguments that we have been deriving above lead to a problematizing of the strict Kleinian versions of 'good' and 'bad' by widening them to incorporate the external as well as the internal. And by external, we *do* mean also the social, and the power relations embedded there. Thus what is experienced as safe and dangerous, good and bad is also informed by the social, by history. This leads to the notion of splitting becoming much more complicated and less solipsistic. This allows us to retain the rich mechanism of splitting, with the proviso that what is considered to be the nature and cause of the 'dangerous' is vastly expanded.

There must be three distinct sources for the subjective experience of danger, and no doubt more than one are active at the same time. So, the thing that is thought to be dangerous might be (1) the outcome of a projection in the classical sense, or (2) it might be the outcome of a concrete external danger, and (3) it might be the outcome of something that one has learnt to think of as dangerous. The last of these is akin to the contents that Freud (1933, p.67) ascribed to the superego, 'the time resisting judgements of value... the traditions of the race' and so on. The fact that these 'judgements of value' begin life outside and before the

---

12   A banal example is that one may like to eat sweets all day because it *feels* a pleasurable experience, but one does not because one also *knows* that it is detrimental to the body.

advent of any particular psyche is critical. I would suggest that the domain that these 'judgements of value' exist in is what Elias has called Symbol; in other words in knowledge, thought and language. As I will show a little later, another name for this same territory is the Foulkesian social unconscious. This is the medium that the infant is born into and which it interiorizes with every psycho-cultural breath to construct itself.

Thus the felt danger might have a basis in external reality, or it might be imagined. If it is imagined, that is, if danger is wrongly imputed to some object or situation, then it has two bases, from the internal world: projection; and from the external world: the time-resisting judgements of value. The last of these have many names: stereotypes, prejudice, racism, ideology, and so on.

One can perhaps make this further distinction: the first is a splitting that has its basis in the id – the instincts. The second is a splitting that has its basis in the superego – the weight of history and tradition. Both splits are, by definition, unconscious. The importance of the argument lies in the fact that it has managed to give some aspect of the social a critical role in the mechanism of splitting, not only in *what* is split, but also *why* it is split.

To summarize the argument so far: categorization is not the same as splitting. Sometimes splitting follows out of categorization (forgetting that the divided were ever connected), but always categorization must follow splitting (the sides of the divides are inevitably named). Splitting is not just the separation of the good and the bad, but also the annihilation of all linkages between them. Splitting is an extreme application of asymmetry between the divides, and an extreme application of symmetry to the internal parts of the divided.

A reprise

One of the consequences of the arguments being developed has been the problematizing of the notion of splitting. It seems to me that in the back of Freud's mind (and hence Klein's), was the implicit belief that life and individual existence proceeded from a unity to a multiplicity. The 'one' is given ontological precedence over the 'many'. But although Freud's developmental trajectory began with a unitary individual wrapped up in autoerotocism, within the individual he inserted the *two* instincts. So Freud too begins with a multiplicity – two instincts. The fact that the two instincts are antithetical to each other is what gives the notion of splitting its *raison d'être*. The interplay between the two instincts, and the interplay between the instincts and the world, gives rise to the complexity of existence. We can put it another way, Freud thought that he needed to explain the presence of differentiation in the world and in the psyche, and he derived it through the presence of an *a priori* differentiation in the instincts.

Against this, what the arguments above have shown are that differentiation and multiplicity do not need to be explained, or derived – they are already present. What needs to be derived is the existence of the individual, an individual that is a precipitate of the group. With this last thought we find ourselves back with Foulkes, repeating him almost word for word. It can all be boiled down into a single aphorism: multiplicity has ontological priority over unity.

Another thread of the preceding argument has been the proposal that for order and structure to arise, it is not necessary to introduce the idea of splitting. Structure and form can arise purely out of mathematical inevitability – structure giving birth to itself. This is not to say that splitting in the psychological sense does not take place – of course it does, and of course it plays a critical role in all psychology. It is an idea of the *inevitability* of splitting that is being undermined. Splitting has also been undermined from a different direction, that of symmetrical logic. Because symmetrical logic allows contradiction, there is no necessity to split. Contradictory events can comfortably live together side by side. I would say that splitting really comes into its own, once development has proceeded sufficiently for asymmetric logic to be the primary organizing principle. This idea goes against the Kleinian proposition that allocates splitting a fundamental and *necessary* role at the very beginnings of development. Perhaps the first true act of splitting is that of the 'I' from the 'We', and being a true split, the connection between the 'I's is repressed and forgotten, so much so that now it appears a bizarre and counter-intuitive idea.

I should stress that the arguments were not begun with the intention of disputing the critical role given by psychoanalysis to splitting. Rather, it is the process of developing a group centred theory that has of itself led in this direction to arrive at these rather controversial propositions.

Whilst the preceding arguments have overturned the usual priority given to the individual, they have tried not to replace it with a simplistic priority of the group over the individual. The arguments have gone some way to destroying any complacent notion of 'we-ness' as though it were a self evident category. The certainty of a 'we' has been questioned from two main directions so far: first, through the mechanisms of cognition and categorization. These mechanisms in their own way lead towards a form of cognitive determinism, saying that we have to cut the continuum somewhere, anywhere. We have to divide, we have to categorize to exist. Second, a straightforward unitary notion of 'I' or 'we' is disrupted through post-structuralism, which has made the subject, be it individual or group, unstable and plural. However, a limitation of the cognitive arguments that have gone before are that they make the order or types of categorization almost arbitrary. Post-structuralism meanwhile makes the genesis of differences a kind of *fait accompli*, in that the divisions are said to have an *a priori* existence in discourse.[13] True, different discourses arrange differences according to their own

---

13   Which is another version of the *a priori* existence of the instincts in biology.

internal logic, but what discourse theory tends to leave out is sociology and socio-politics, in other words the power relations between people. And this is exactly where it will be profitable to bring Elias back into the picture, and particularly readings of Elias as developed by the social theorists Burkitt and Mennell. But before we do that there are a couple of gaps left to be filled.

Identity as unconsciousness

Earlier we had said two things about identity, that it was a name of a category, and that it was a sense of belonging to a name. We are now in a position to widen these two statements, and also to add a third statement. The widening consists of moving from the singular to the plural – which is to say that we have not one identity, but many, and so we belong to many places simultaneously. However, these two statements as they stand still pander to essentialist notions of identity, which somehow make an appeal to a true internal asocial nature. To explain: true, the addition of plurality has allowed the sociological notion of role to come into the picture – 'role' in the sense of a variety of hats that can be worn. However, that is also its limitation, the hat is in itself a surface phenomenon, because the head that wears the hats remains the same. This is why it is still an essentialist and individualistic model of identity.

Let me now propose a group analytic way of thinking about identity. Much like Elias' statement about power, we can say that identity is not a possession, but rather it is a phenomenon that is embedded in a network of social interactions and relations. This shows up the usual notion of identity for what it is – a reification, something that has been abstracted out of a living continuum of interchanges. This definition removes the notion of identity from inside the individual, and makes it a property of the interactional network. The social theorist Craig Calhoun says '…identity is always project, not settled accomplishment' (1994, p.27). So although we may grasp and cling to certain categories, we grasp them out of a flux of interaction, and then it becomes something to hang on to in a turbulent ever changing interactional network. Much earlier, we caught a glimpse of the paradox that the act of naming requires one, in a sense, to blind oneself to the thing being named. The explication of this will also give forth a novel way of representing the unconscious.

We saw earlier how every sentence contains globules of homogeneity, which are connected by heterogeneity. To put it another way, sentences are globules of similarity in a sea of difference, and to put it yet another way, sentences are globules of symmetry in a sea of asymmetry. The example of this used earlier was 'there are more brown shoes than black shoes'. Identity, the act of naming a belonging, is a similar process to this. To say 'we are group analysts', or 'we are vegetarians', is to impose a homogeneity onto the named category. The heterogeneity within the category is annihilated. It has to be so for the sentence to work.

And here is the thing: we could say that the heterogeneity is made *unconscious*. One is obliged to blind oneself to the internal complexity and heterogeneity of the thing being named. *Thus all thought could be said to consist of a weaving together of islands of unconsciousness.* We name the grouping 'brown shoes' and render all the differences contained therein unconscious. This picture, of thought as linked beads of unconscious, is in contrast to the usual diagram used to visualize the conscious and unconscious, a horizontal line separating two entire regions, the unconscious below the conscious.

Thus when one says I am British, or I feel English, or I am a Freudian, or I am a girl, one *cannot* actually look at these terms, or look within them. One cannot question them, one can only use them from a distance, as it were. For identity to work, the internal space *must not be tested*. Perhaps in much the same way that Winnicott said that for infant development to proceed, there were certain paradoxes that ought never to be challenged. These paradoxical spaces consist of illusions, one of which is that the infant thinks that it omnipotently creates something (say the breast), whereas in fact it is presented to the infant. I would suggest that another such paradoxical space is that of 'knowing who I am'. If it is tested then it is either replaced by another sort of 'I am' (say from brown shoe to leather goods), or it would lead to complete fragmentation and chaos, in other words madness. To exist one has to find a place to belong to, to stand on. It is the fact that this place is illusory, that is the fact that must not be known. It is so important not to know this fact that our minds are structured to make it literally – emotionally and mentally – incomprehensible. Thus at the centre of identity is something unconscious, a symmetrized space.

How different is this kind of unconscious from the orthodox description? Well for one thing, here is an unconscious which is not the outcome of repression *per se*, but seems to arise spontaneously out of the structure of communication, be it internal or external. It would appear then that for something to be said, something else has to be left unsaid. For something to be seen, something else has to be hidden. And the thing being hidden is at the centre of the thing being revealed. The fact that this unconscious is fragmentary rather than all encompassing makes it no less profound for that. This version of the unconscious makes it possible for us to link Foulkes' notion of the social unconscious with discourse theory.

Each discourse has its blind spots, its own way of organizing the world. Each discourse takes certain territories and categories to be 'natural' ones. I would like to suggest that it is precisely within these naturalized categories, within these blind areas, that varieties of social unconscious lie. Ideology decides what is to be homogenized, and what must be differentiated.

What is being spelt out here is an alternative model – a model which brings together the notion of social unconscious with that of discourse. By definition, the social unconscious must be embedded in invisible, that is unconscious, places. The suggestion is that these invisible places are to be found close at hand, within everyday sentences and everyday experiences. The structure of language, reflecting particular discourses, orders and forms the visible and the invisible, the differentiated and the differentiating, the conscious and the unconscious. If we remember now Elias' injunction that language, thought and knowledge are one and the same thing, as well as Lacan's injunction that the unconscious is like a language, we have a way of beginning to grasp how these symmetrized spaces are instituted within psyches to form their contingent and plural natures.

These thoughts have enormous consequences for identity politics. Identity, being an imposed homogeneity, is constantly threatened both from without by homogeneity, and from within by heterogeneity. Thus the boundaries and internals of identity have to be constantly policed to ensure its continuance. We have moved a considerable distance from an essentialist kind of identity spontaneously arising out of a true self. Identity is now problematized. Identity is made an expression of the linkages within the communicational and socio-political network; it is contingent, temporary and fragile. Additionally, some kind of police work is constantly having to be done, the work of continually patrolling the boundary between the us and the them to keep each in place. The notion of policing will eventually provide us with a link – a link back to power relations.

But in the meantime, we have to move elsewhere to fill out another forgotten gap, and this time it is a gap between the notions of identity and self.

Self and identity: ego and wego

In the foregoing, Identity and Self have been taken to refer to the same thing. But are they? There is a huge debate going on in social theory about the notion of self as counterposed to that of identity (Lemert 1994). The notion of Self found favour with the Romantics. It is said to be internal and innate, and is bound up with a notion of a true self. It is something that is universal in that every human has one, but unique in that each person's Self is unique to them. This version of Self is an essentialist category and is bound up with individualism. Meanwhile, the notion of identity has the meaning of literally 'identity' as in identity card, and it also has the meaning of an 'identification' with something. Thus identity is something that has its basis in a relationship to the external. This version of identity is a contingent category and bound up with the group.

Thus one could say that Self is located in the province of the individual and has the name 'I', whilst Identity is located in the province of the group and has the name 'us' or 'we'. We could then use Foulkes' figure–ground conceptualization to say that sometimes it is the 'I' part of personality that is in the forefront and at other times it is the 'we' part of the personality that is prevalent. Well perhaps, but if we followed this course then we would be following orthodox Foulkes, by giving succour to an asocial version of Self. In fact by going back to Freud, we will find that he himself had a much more complicated picture than the one proposed just here.

Let us begin with the previous description and see where it leads. In this way of thinking, the Self is said to encapsulate the true essence of the individual, whilst Identity is thought of as a description of the *identifications* that this Self makes with aspects of external reality. Some people have suggested that because the aspect of the personality that has its basis in the individual is what is called 'ego' or 'I', so the aspects of the personality that have their basis in the group should be called the 'we-go'. So far so good – or so it would appear. But in fact the battle has already been lost. This is because the formulation *begins* with the notion of an asocial individual Self, which is *then* used to build the social aspects of the psyche. Our task, meantime, has been to try to build a theoretical frame that does *not* begin with the individual.[14]

If we now look to psychoanalysis and Freud in particular, what do we find? In Freud we find the ego or I (*ich* in German). What we do not find is a theorization of Self. In their dictionary of Freudian psychoanalysis, Laplanche and Pontalis (1973) have no section for Self. This is a striking omission which is clearly not born of neglect, so what does it mean? As we saw in the first chapter, the Freudian ego was given two trajectories. The first one is as an organ of adaptation that is precipitated out of the id, and is the means by which the psyche engaged with the external world. The second trajectory consisted of the idea of ego as graveyard. Here, Freud described the ego as consisting of a set of *identifications* with lost objects. We can see then that in Freud, the territory of the 'I' is already infused with the 'we'. The ego is already a we-go. If the ego is not available to be linked with Self, then what else can we find? An alternative is to equate the Self with the id as this is the domain of innate instincts, but this was never Freud's intention (he called the id the it). However, in some circles this is often the implicit equation, of id and Self. We have seen that this is exactly what Rousseau and the Romantics had in mind, saying that being true to oneself was the same as being true to one's feelings. Implicit in this are the now familiar equations of feelings with instincts,

---

14   Someone might still argue for the notion of the individual Self by saying that because there are *a priori* elements to the psyche, these must constitute the basis of the individual Self – as these elements already exist at birth, they must therefore be asocial. The answer to this is that the fact that something is innate, does not necessarily make it asocial. We saw in the chapter on biology that what is innate are mechanisms for socialization – our biology is social. The mistake is added to by the assumption that that which is biological is fixed and universal and so more 'true' than anything which might follow. The metaphor that is being alluded to is that of seed and tree, or gene and organism. The idea behind it is that the true essence is that which is innate and coded into the seed in the following manner. The seed will grow into any number of shapes depending on context, but because the thing that remains the same is what is in the seed, it is called its true nature. One might with equal validity call a particular environment the seed's true nurture. The point is that both are needed and the weight of value and meaning given to seed over environment is not necessarily correct or inevitable.

with true nature and so forth. The philosophy of humanistic psychology, which seeks to elevate feeling over thought, does so on the basis of this self same fallacy.

We find that we have argued ourselves round in a circle. We began with the unthinking conflation of Self and Identity, then differentiated them, and then found that the distinction Self and Identity is, in a sense, a false distinction. Because as Freud has said, the 'I' consists in itself of identifications. Freud makes no reference to a notion of Self because he has no use for it, it is redundant. There is no necessity for inventing the notion of the we-go, as all its work is already done by the ego.

It is possible to interpret Freud's schema as validating the Romantic vision, saying that the true self is the same as an asocial id; the id in turn, in its attempts to engage with the external, gives forth the ego, to the 'we' part of the psyche. To my mind this is too simplistic a rendering of the complexities and elegance of the Freudian schema, because a human being that was only id would not be human at all. Some humanistic counsellors and psychotherapists actually think that this is what the therapeutic process is – getting rid of all the internalized 'messages' from external sources, to leave the true individual self free to be itself.

The attempts to build theories and explanations on the basis of there being two aspects to the psyche, one personal and one social, are in error. The division of the personal from the communal is mistaken and based on a slippage in logic. The argument starts with the true statement that there is something unique about each individual. It continues, if it is unique then it is not shared. If it is not shared then it is *not* communal. Not communal equals outside the social. QED.

Against this what we have to say is not that uniqueness and autonomy do not exist, but that the uniqueness of each individual is constructed out of common material. This common material is what Elias has called symbol, the nature and basis of which is social. The fact that individuals have some autonomy does not make that autonomy asocial. These conflations arise out of the false, but by now familiar, linkages of autonomy with individual, and constraint with group. The question that is to be put to all these theories is this, from whence comes the purely personal? These theories cannot derive the basis of the purely personal from biology, because as the previous chapter has argued, our biology is *designed* to be social. We have left the personal no territory that is outside the social. To paraphrase the popular saying, 'the personal is political and the political is personal', from the 1970s – the personal is social.

There is a Sufi saying, 'we are in this world, but not of it'. The thesis of the book is the polar opposite of that – it is saying we are completely of this world, from our molecules, to our thoughts, to our feelings, to our aspirations. To counter the Sufi saying, let me indulge in inventing an elliptic epigram: The I is We.

Conflict

Nitsun (1996) was driven to evolve the thesis of the anti-group because Foulkes had given little attention to the destructive forces in groups. However, Nitsun derived the anti-group forces out of orthodox psychoanalytic mechanisms; in other words they had the individual as their basis, and used the familiar mechanisms of splitting, projection and so forth. The challenge now is to derive violences and hostilities without recourse to the instincts. Foulkes is no help in this matter, for as we have seen when he does discuss destructive forces in groups, he derives them from the mother–infant paradigm. Instead, we will find some assistance in this project from the work of Elias, Fairbairn and Winnicott.

From inter-group to intra-psychic conflict

For all his emphasis on the external, Fairbairn's theory is asocial. He strikes out against the instinctivists, and instead of instincts he talks about 'forces'. He builds his theory of groups on the basis of an analogy drawn from cosmology. In fact it is not clear whether he sees it as an analogy at all, or whether he thinks there is a direct equivalence between the two domains, or whether he thinks that it constitutes an explanation in itself. On concluding a short discussion of the changing paradigms in physics, he says: 'The major forces at work [in the universe] are attraction and repulsion (cf. libido and aggression)' (Fairbairn 1944, p.127–128). This brief sentence carries two enormous burdens. First it is the sole basis of a rather large intellectual jump from cosmology to psychology. There is no further elaboration. Second, the instincts of libido and aggression are now called 'forces'. This is Fairbairn's basic idea, that groups cohere through libido and fragment through aggression, and that there is a constant struggle between the two. For all his innovative and dramatic reformulations of psychoanalytic theory, and his many criticisms of Freudian instinct theory, in this arena Fairbairn ends up repeating Freud.

In Fairbairn's theory the most fundamental object is the individual. The most fundamental of groups is 'the family'. 'The family is the original social group' (Fairbairn 1935, p.235). But to understand the family, Fairbairn would say one has to look at the different components within it – the individuals and their psychopathology: '...since group psychology ultimately reduces itself to the psychology of the individual in a group, it follows that the fruits of psycho-analytical research on the unconscious motivation of the individual must be relevant to the explanation of group phenomena' (Fairbairn 1935, p.246).

Stability in the family is achieved by libido (now no longer an instinct, but a force) being bound up inside the group, and aggression (ditto) being put outside it. Aggression, in Fairbairn's schema, makes its first appearance within an individual as a consequence of frustration. This aggression is then used to fragment the psyche and repress parts of it. According to Fairbairn's theory, the externalization of this internal aggression within the context of the family gives rise to the appearance of the Oedipal conflict. Now the aggression, having emerged from Pandora's box, exists within the family circle where its tendency will be to fragment and destroy it. Thus to preserve itself, the family places the aggression outside it: the aggression is displaced and so enters the larger social context.

The stability of the family group is also threatened by libido, which according to its tendency, seeks to attach with objects outside the family, thus diluting it. Thus the family as a structure is faced with two dangers, fragmentation from within, and absorption from without. He argues that the tendency of libido is to expand and draw more and more to itself, ultimately, connecting up with everything: '...the general tendency characterizing this evolutionary process, viz. the tendency for the individual's libido to become increasingly expansive, and for the group to become correspondingly more comprehensive' (Fairbairn 1935, p.238). At each level, the aggression from within the structure is projected out onto an external equivalent structure. Aggression is a kind of hot potato, that is passed increasingly upwards and outwards, continually projected beyond the realm of the territory that has been connected up by libido.

To reiterate the Fairbairnian chain of events regarding aggression. The first impulse comes from libido which seeks to relate to external objects. The difficulties inherent in object relating give rise to frustration. A consequence of this frustration is aggression. The aggression is now projected out into the family where it gives the *appearance* of Oedipal conflict. In order to manage the threat of this aggression, the family project the aggression outwards into other territories.

According to Fairbairn, the evolutionary ladder of group development begins with the family, then the clan, then the tribe, and finally the nation. There are many arguments to be had with this idea, reminiscent as it is of individuals joining up to form societies, but these will not be pursued here. To continue, Fairbairn says that there is always competition between the different organizational levels for the libido, which threatens the life of each level of grouping. For example he says about the clan: '...the social cohesion of the clan is threatened by...too much libido being bound up within the family...and the danger of the individual's libido finding attachment outside the clan' (Fairbairn 1935, p.237).

Fairbairn thinks of communism, a supra-national movement, as the next inevitable step which will lead to nation states falling away, with libido attached to all of humankind. He argues that communism attacks the family as a social structure as an '...attempt to deal with the Oedipus conflict by abolishing the Oedipus situation, out of which the conflict arises' (Fairbairn 1935, p.242). However if one stays with the internal logic of Fairbairn's theory, which he himself doesn't, this attempt is bound to fail, in the sense that one will still be left with the problem of the aggression in the various individual's psyches. His hope for humankind is encapsulated in this passage:...

> the emergence of a world state... If this goal is attained, the individual's libido, which was originally bound within the family, and which later became extended by successive stages to the clan, the tribe and the nation, will eventually be weaned from its national loyalty and become invested in a world state embracing humanity at large. (Fairbairn 1935, p.239)

But this hope is constantly undermined by aggression located in the individual (which made its first appearance after inevitable frustration): 'The source of social disintegration in all groups is to be found in aggression. It is to the aggression of the individual that we must look for the source of the disruptive forces found in all societies' (Fairbairn 1935, p.235). We can see then that Fairbairn more or less remains with a version of the model that has conflict between the individual and the group. Whilst the details of the conflict itself are quite different from the Freudian and Kleinian version, the overall structure remains, something emanating from the individual tends to disrupt the social. The key thing is that this disruption emanates from within the individual and so is not group specific.

Despite the anomalies and contradictions in Fairbairn's theory, there is much of interest here. His descriptions of the levels of grouping and the problematic this gives rise to, is a familiar echo of some of the ideas developed earlier. Specifically, in the discussions on the structure of thinking. There we saw how existence was a constant tension between a pull towards merging, and a pull towards fragmentation. In the language developed earlier, existence manifests in the tension between homogeneity and heterogeneity.

I will use the notion of racism to develop Fairbairn's ideas on aggression, in ways that will complement the project of taking the group seriously.

For the moment if we broadly think of racism as hatred of one group for another, then we can invent an aphorism that would encapsulate the spirit of Fairbairnian theory:

'Racism begins where libido ends.'

This is a restatement of his idea that aggression *has* to be projected out of the group that is bound together by libido, in order to stop the group fragmenting. As Fairbairn puts it, aggression is placed outside and beyond the territory in which libido rules. This formulation of his goes a considerable way to addressing the anomaly in Freud's idea of the 'narcissism of minor differences' which became the 'narcissism of major differences'.

We saw earlier that Freud developed two theories of aggression, one where difference was said to cause hatred, and the other where difference was activated in order to get rid of endogenous aggression. Fairbairn follows the second of these, with two caveats that describe the difference between his version of aggression and Freud's: (1) Fairbairn's aggression is a force and not an instinct, and (2) it is secondarily present as a consequence of frustration.

In the Fairbairnian frame, the aggression has initially to be removed from the family circle. And so it is put outside it into another equivalent structure, other families. Here the differences between the groups will indeed be minor – as between two neighbouring families. As the groups become more inclusive, the differences between them do become greater – between tribes, clans and finally nations. So the 'amount of difference' is irrelevant in itself. What is central is the level that the group is operating at – family, tribe, clan or nation – and it is this level that will determine the type and amount of difference that will be *made* relevant. To use Fairbairnian language, difference is a *technique* and not a cause.

This idea, of the 'activation of difference' being a technique rather than an end, can be taken even further to address the other component of racism – the management and appropriation of material resources. If this is taken as the other organizing principle of racism (the first one being the evacuation of aggression), then we can see that which particular difference will be relevant will be determined by the *function* it is to serve – which resources are to be appropriated by which groups, who is to be excluded and so on. In saying this we have gone much further than Fairbairn would have – because for him (like Foulkes) the structures of family, tribe, clan and nation are 'natural' structures inevitably occurring along an evolutionary scale. Whereas we are saying that the structures are not at all natural or inevitable, but are a function of the current material conditions – and the politics arising from them. This is a Machiavellian idea, that alliances and groupings will be driven by the pragmatics of a situation, rather than because of any inherent significances in the differences themselves.

What is being suggested here is that the *name* given to the difference that is activated is a rationalization that covers over and renders invisible the 'real' reasons. *The naming of the difference has essentialized it.* So depending on the context, family, religion, colour, gender, nation or any other difference might be activated or *invented* at different points, to rationalize particular sets of actions. As we will see, this last idea finds common ground with certain ideas in Winnicott.

Before going on to them, I would like to draw on some of the thoughts of the sociologists Calhoun and Mennell as they have a contribution to make to the subject of conflict by extending the Fairbairnian idea of nested groups and loyalties, but this time in the language of sociology and discourse.

Calhoun (1994) takes the now familiar idea of simultaneous multiple identities to explain internal conflict. Each of us is implicated in innumerable simultaneous discourses. Each discourse imposes a particular kind of homogeneity on the subject, indeed it uses that homogeneity to define the type of subject one is. These subject positions can be given very ordinary names such as mother, miner, clever, drunkard, surly. The demands of these plural identities are often in conflict with each other. Calhoun says that the variety of desires can be mutually exclusive and so set up internal tensions: 'Thus acting on certain identities must frustrate others'. This constitutes a redefinition of internal conflict. It has now been described as a battle between conflicting discourses, each seeking to structure the Self in its own image. The interesting thing about this battle is that it is interminable and victories are always only partial and temporary, constantly being undone.

In contrast to Calhoun who has sliced identity horizontally by laying bare other contemporary claims on the subject, Mennell (1994) slices identity vertically to expose a historical structure embedded in it. Mennell makes reference to Elias' notion of *habitus*. Habitus, Elias tells us, is like second nature. In other words these are habits born out of the places we inhabit, and become so deeply ingrained, they become part of our nature, and make us who we are. Whilst I agree with this up to a point, I think that the main arguments of the book allow us to take this idea much further and dispense altogether with 'first' nature. The arguments to be used are similar to those used earlier to show that the 'I' is always a 'we'. We have been continually arguing that there is no human existence outside the social. Thus this so-called first nature is nothing more than the attempt to retrospectively abstract something asocial out of the web of human existence, and allocate to it an ontological priority. The ideas of first or second nature are quite redundant. There is only one nature and it is intrinsically social.

In any case Mennell says: 'habitus and identification, being related to group membership, are always – in the modern world...multi-layered'(1994, p.177). He continues: 'It is possible that in the very early stages of human social development, when all people lived in small...bands, social habitus and identification had only a single layer...in more complex societies there are always many layers'. Once again, whilst in broad agreement with the proposition that the more complex society becomes the more layers there are, the point I would take issue with is the fantasy that there was ever a time of singularity. As we saw in the chapter on biology, the division of labour, and the multiple roles that imposes on one, is as old as existence itself.

Mennell now delivers the punchline: 'it can be seen that various layers of habitus simultaneously present in people today may be of many different *vintages*. Strong identification with kinship groups and local communities historically preceded that with state-societies... Earlier and later layers of identity may conflict with one another' (1994, p.178; emphasis added). At first glance, this proposition appears to have a problem in that it appears to be a version of recapitulation theory, which says that the development of the individual repeats the evolutionary history of the species. But on closer examination this is not what is being said; instead it is verifying another one of Elias' propositions, that structure has history. If we take any contemporary conflict – the horrors of the old

Yugoslavia, Algeria, Ireland – we will find allegiances of different *vintages*. Thus despite the reservations voiced, to my mind this is a very interesting proposition, and has much to commend it. Among other things it finds affinity with the speculations of evolutionists.

In conclusion we can see that Fairbairn was on the right track, but over-simplified the situation by allowing just one conflict. The sociologists meanwhile have developed the ideas, and made the conflicts multiple and historical.

Name calling and dividing

According to Winnicott, the infant's first moments of feeling I AM, mean that there is an experience of Me and Not-Me. This is experienced as a dangerous moment, first because of the fragility of the state, and second because of the fear that that which has been excluded from the Me will attack because of it; '...the paranoid state is inherent in the newly integrated state' (Winnicott 1965, p.149). Interestingly, the first moments of integration come about because of impingement. When there is an impingement, the infant gathers itself together to face it. This 'gathering together' constitutes the first moments of integration. However, in this state, the infant is a potential paranoiac. The mother's care helps neutralize this state. However, if the mother fails at this point 'to make it better', then the individual starts off with paranoiac potential. For the sake of com-pleteness we should add here the other source of paranoia given by Winnicott, traumatic birth: '...a severe birth trauma can cause a condition which I will call congenital, but not inherited, paranoia.' (Winnicott 1949, p.185) Returning to the fragile and dangerous moment of integration: this moment can be managed by the infant because the mother 'covers' the infant with her own ego, and so protects it until it can understand and manage these feelings itself.

The construction of the individual is repeated in the construction of the group.

With his theory of groups, Winnicott allows aggression a new route into existence. This time it is not to do with the instincts, but with topology.[15] The critical event takes place at the moment of creation of a group, that is something with a boundary, an inside and an outside.

The formation of groups, Winnicott says, brings about paranoia. Paranoia is about imagined attack. It is never really clear in Winnicott's writings whether the attacks are imagined or real. In the following quote there is no mention of paranoia, and so this would imply that the attack is real:

---

15   This is a metaphoric use of a technical term. Topology is the mathematical discipline of the study of shapes and structures. For example, circles, ellipses and rectangles are topologically equivalent: they each have one boundary, one inside and one outside. Similarly the letter 'S' and the letter 'L' are also equivalent, as are the number '8' and the letter 'B'.

A group is an I AM achievement, and it is a dangerous achievement, [because] the repudiated external world comes back at the new phenomenon and attacks from all quarters and in every conceivable way' (Winnicott 1965, p.149)

In any case, the subjective experience is of being attacked, be this real or imagined. The next question we have to ask is what attributes are included within the I AM, 'the group'? What are the bits included in the 'I', or to be more accurate, the 'We'?

Whatever the attributes (X) designated to be part of the 'Us', Winnicott would say that the group will inevitably fear attack from those designated Not-X. Thus if 'white' is a significant designator of the 'Us', then the group will fear attack from those designated as Not-White, and perhaps attack in turn, or even, instead.

We are led then to a deeper question: why make 'psychoanalyst' or 'vegetarian' or 'white' a designator of the 'Us'? As we have seen from our previous discussion, they are clearly not 'natural' groupings. The groupings are contingent, which means that they are informed by context, the socio-historical context. I would say that the groupings are pragmatic, and are then rationalized as natural and biological. To understand the contextualization we have to enter the domain of history, which we have done to some degree in our exploration of Elias, and will return to again.

What we can say using Winnicott's theory is that the name taken on by a group to define itself will inform the name of what the group fears, and perhaps what the group attacks. This is in line with the material we have already developed – naming a group essentializes it.

We can add weight to this idea by referring to three elements of Winnicott's discussion of transitional phenomena.

First, transitional phenomena are the basis of cultural life: 'There is a direct development from transitional phenomena to playing, and from playing to shared playing, and from this to cultural experiences' (Winnicott 1980, p.60).

Second, transitional phenomena are necessary but illusory. They occur in a paradoxical space that allows the illusion of a connection between the inside and the outside. Winnicott says that the transitional space is a mad space, and that we return to it through cultural modalities like art and religion. '…We allow the infant this madness… We adults use the arts and religion for the off-moments which we all need in the course of…reality acceptance' (Winnicott 1952b, p.224).

Third, and most importantly, this illusory experience is the kernel around which groups form:

We can share a respect for illusory experience, and if we wish we may collect together and form a group on the basis of the similarity of our illusory experiences. This is a natural root of grouping among human beings. Yet it is a hallmark of madness when an adult puts too powerful a claim on the credulity of others, forcing them to acknowledge a sharing of illusion that is not their own. (Winnicott 1951, p.231)

The fact that group identity is always based on an illusion means that all it has in a sense to hold it together is its name. To change the language, group identity is always a reification. This reading of Winnicott brings him very close to the post-structuralists. The consequence of his formulation led him into exactly the same territory as the discourse theorists. Winnicott's formulation too makes identity precarious, and so sheds some light on why it is defended so ferociously. The defence is a kind of reaction formation. If group identity is so precarious, then one will have to try to anchor it in some aspect of external or internal reality. These anchors might be of various types: diplomas, attitudes, beliefs, habits, religious affiliations, geographical locations, and of course skin colour. The anchor, in part, always contains elements of rationalization, and so the boundary needs to be bolstered continually, and particularly when there is danger of collapse of the boundary. For instance, Jews and Arabs are both Semites, pork is taboo to both groups, and both groups practice circumcision. The danger that they will merge is countered by a reinforcing of the boundary between the two in various ways, but ultimately by emphasizing the differences between them.

Through a circumlocutory route we have arrived back at an idea of the 'Narcissism of Minor Differences' – but not quite in the Freudian sense. Earlier we had critiqued Freud's notion of the Narcissism of Minor Differences for containing within it the slippage from minor differences to that of major differences. As we saw, this slippage was possible in part because it was derived out of the theory of instincts. However, it seems to me that now we can re-instate the theory of Minor Differences, but this time re-couching it in terms of identity rather than instinct. The difference is more than one of semantics. We can agree with Freud that indeed there is a focus on minor differences,[16] but not because the self preservative instinct is provoked, but because identity, the sense of self, is threatened. To be more precise, it is felt to be threatened; 'felt' because it was never there in the first place. With this thought, Winnicott is joined up with Fairbairn.

This leads us then to a bigger question: why do we have this need to belong? This is another way of asking, why do we have a need to be named? What we saw in the discussion of Matte-Blanco was that naming drew a boundary around a finite aspect of the infinite, because to be part of the infinite would lead to a catastrophic kind of vertigo, a madness (or enlightenment as some would call it). Naming creates an illusory region of safety. This is Me, this is Not-Me. This is Us, this is Not-Us. This is part of the answer. Another pertinent part of the answer is linked to power relations. Naming and being named is a way of creating a

---

16   Remember the Lilliputians with their division according to which end the egg was broken.

uniform, a uniform which signals to all and sundry who is and is not allowed access to particular resources.

To reiterate the point: the logic of the argument leads us to say that all group formations are ultimately based on reifications, arbitrary lines drawn in the cosmos. To change the language again, we can say that group identity is ultimately a fantasy, an illusion.[17] It is a very necessary illusion, necessary for the sense of existence itself, but an illusion none the less.

Let us look further at the illusion. Once something is named as Us, then the world is divided into two regions: one safe 'Us', and one dangerous 'Not-Us'.[18] In other words the moment of becoming brings with it anxiety; *existence triggers anxiety.*

It is in this sense then that I use the word 'topological'. Existence itself is a topological event in the sense that two regions are precipitated, a Me and a Not-Me. As Winnicott says, existence is an I AM moment and a dangerous one at that. Thus safety and danger are inevitably born out of the formation of the sense of existence, one could even say structured into existence itself.

By stepping back we can see now that we have allowed anxiety and hatred into the picture, without needing to postulate the presence of instincts. We have found that hostility (driven by fear) will be an inevitable outcome of any group formation. The formula that has been developed is:

> One cannot exist without the divisions. To exist is to divide. To divide is to fear.

Let me summarize the arguments developed from this reading of Fairbairn and Winnicott. First, the *name* taken on by a group to define itself, will inform the *name* of what the group fears, and perhaps what the group attacks. Second, the particular name that will be relevant will vary and depend on the current material conditions. Third, aggression is purely an outcome of the structure of existence. And fourth, these ideas bring Fairbairn and Winnicott in close proximity to the models developed in discourse theory.

Power relations in action

Elias' contribution to this debate is twofold. First, he has emphasized that power relations are central to all human relations. One of the consequences of this conception is a disruption of comforting definitions of identity which are based *exclusively* on notions of similarity. Thus explanation for the 'us' is often put in these terms: it is said that 'we' are naturally drawn together, because we are similar to each other in our habits, customs, beliefs and so forth. So when someone different comes along, it is equally 'natural' that they are shunned because they are

---

17   Interestingly, one is very close to Buddhist philosophy here.
18   We should keep in mind that both are ultimately illusory.

not one of us. This is also a version of Freud's narcissism of minor differences. This is the manifest reason for exclusion, and is a partial truth, but really it is a mythology.

We have already engaged considerably with the structure of this mythology with discourse theory, Matte-Blanco, Winnicott and Fairbairn. It has been demonstrated that there are fallacies hidden in the mythology which are expressions of the social unconscious. The main fallacy is the fallacy of similarity and homogeneity. The use of the label 'British' (or 'psychoanalyst') gives the illusion of homogeneity. The constituent elements of each of these labels, the actual people, are found to be diverse in every possible way: politically, spiritually, culturally and so forth. They have different aspirations; some are murderers and some altruists; some football hooligans and others opera singers. The list of diversity would be tediously long, and perhaps as long as the number of people living in Britain. Faced with this diversity, the essentialist trump card is played. This card says that below this surface diversity, there is a commonality, a British essence, which is deep within each one. That is one solution, but not a very convincing one in my opinion. With Elias, I would give another answer, which is that the illusion of similarity is there for a reason. The reason is to hide something, and the thing being hidden is material, physical, psychological power.

This is an example of the social unconscious at work; the manifest level says something innocent, and in the process hides something latent and more problematic. A contemporary and more parochial example closer to home is the struggle going on in the psychotherapy movement in Britain to form an umbrella body. The attempt was made to form an all-inclusive body, the UKCP. Then some of the schools that held the 'high' ground in terms of status and power, the psychoanalytic psychotherapies, found that their identity was threatened, so they split off to form a new body, the BCP. To be sure the 'rational' manifest reason is couched in terms of standards (and there is a large element of truth in this), and the notion of identity. The hidden latent reason is to be found in the pragmatics of the situation, by which is meant the power relations. If you hold the high ground, then you have more access to the resources – bluntly, patients – and from that follows money.

Now, this is a very distasteful thought, and so like all uncomfortable thoughts there is an enormous resistance to knowing about it, and it is denied. One could say that the paragraph above is an *interpretation of the contents of the social unconscious*, and being social it is an interpretation made to a group, and not an individual.

The psychoanalytic theory of identity has been extended by a group analytic theory in which power relations have now been instituted as a component of identity. Thus people do not just gather or form because of similarity; they group around vortices of power, but use their similarity to hide the vortices from view and deny their existence. The pertinent thing is that all concerned are unaware of the entire process, and this is an expression of the social unconscious. At the risk of over-repeating the point, these identities are not to be thought of as surface phenomena, as the essentialists would have it. The proposition here goes much further than that, and is describing how socio-political power relations might be instituted within the psyche, to become a fundamental part of the deep structure and organization of the Self.

The structure of gossip

From here we can move to the second of Elias' contributions, which consists of the mechanisms that are used to bolster and reinforce identity structures. These mechanisms we have already met in Elias and Scotson's (1994) description of the use of gossip mills and gossip streams as very effective policing strategies, policing the territory between the 'us' and the 'them'. Gossip was also used to monitor and control members of the 'us' to keep them in line, to ensure that they upheld the unspoken rules of the 'us'.

We can now use the theory of thinking developed from Matte-Blanco to explain the structure of gossip. Elias and Scotson said that it was the 'minority of the worst' that was used to tarnish the outsiders, and that it was the 'minority of the best' that was used to aggrandize the established. This mechanism works by exploiting symmetrical logic, where the part is identical to the whole. Thus one bad apple means that the whole barrel is bad. The heterogeneity of each group is rendered invisible by the application of symmetrical logic. In Freudian language, it is an aspect of primary process thinking.

This cognitive mechanism is not sufficient to explain everything. For example, it is equally feasible, in terms of pure logic that is, for the established to be known by the minority of their worst, rather than their best. And vice versa for the outsiders. So why does this does not happen? Here we are bound to invoke the notions of ideology and discourse. These naturalize social orders by disguising their contingent and pragmatic aspects. The gossip structure does not take place the other way, because of the confluence of power and charisma.

Gossip is the dissemination of ideology through the institutions of polarizations. Thus that which does not fit into the ideology, say, the existence of a corrupt member of the local council, is ignored by the gossip mills, *because they are blind to it*. Gossip puts forward the notion of identity based on similarity and difference, and renders invisible to all participants of the social structure the aspects of identity that are built around the power differentials.

But like the Freudian unconscious, the social unconscious constantly threatens to reveal itself. In particular because there is not just one monolithic ideology, one discourse, but many. And as Foucault (1972) has shown, they are not all organized around material realms, some are centred around patriarchy, some around a religious belief, some around a public bar, some around a football team. It is the fact of the presence of the multiplicity of discourses that constantly works to exposing the mythologies behind the naturalized orders. And it is for this reason that gossip's work is never done. It has to be continually reapplied at the boundaries, monitoring and repairing the day-to-day damage caused by rude and recalcitrant facts that will not cooperate with the instituted mythologies.

The shrill voice from the margins

What the foregoing discussion has done is to problematize any straightforward view of identity. This applies as much to the 'I', the so-called personal part, as it does to the 'we', the so-called social part. In fact, what has been demonstrated is that the 'I' is a set of identifications, and so the 'I' is a 'we'. The problem of course is that there are no essentialist foundations to be found for the 'we' either. Similarities and differences are constantly set against each other to manufacture identities (Dalal 1993a, b). Put another way, identities are constructed out of the tension between the two logics – symmetrical and asymmetrical. Either way the identity is tenuous.

Racism, like splitting, consists of an extreme application of symmetry to the interior of groups, and an extreme application of asymmetry to the region between the groups. In fact it is the application of symmetry that has constructed the groups in the first place. We are *all* like this, and they are *all* like that, and never the twain shall meet.

What, if any, is the difference between, say, a white racist group using these mechanisms, and a black group, or a women's group, or a gay group, or a group of psychotherapists? In the realms of pure logic – there is no difference. But as there never was anything so pure as pure logic, we are forced to dirty our hands and engage with the material world. On the one hand any of these 'new' identities can be seen as last-ditch fundamentalist attempts to preserve and assert something that begins to slip away. And there is some truth in that. On the other hand, as we have also seen, these identities are grouped around vortices of status and power. So the biggest difference between the groupings is where they are located in relation to the vortices of power. In Eliasian language, the difference is expressed in the power differential between the two groups, and this gives a different meaning to the acts of the two groups.

As Elias has shown, the attempt of the outsiders to stigmatize the established is not effective as they do not have the power with which to drive the stigma in. What the marginalized groups are then forced to do, *as a strategic necessity*, is to use the same weapon, and assert a new essentialism at the margins, effectively trying to create a new centre at the margins. These groups insist that there is something essentialist about being black, or being a woman, or working class, or Freudian, or whatever, and use it to cohere around this identity. Elias has demonstrated that cohesion is a necessary prerequisite for the formation of political strength. The name, the identity, is the ensign around which resistance is organized. The margins of this identity are patrolled as ferociously as any other. Thus there emerges what looks to the eye to be new fundamentalisms, be they Christian or feminist or Islamic or black. Lal (1986) called this phenomenon 'the ethnicity paradox'. So it is true that they are indeed new essentialisms, but they are formed as a reaction, they assert their difference to the dominant group – in order to cohere themselves and so challenge the dominant order, in order, eventually, to participate at the centre. The paradox is that they form in order to eventually dissolve. It is important that the knowledge of this eventual fact is kept hidden, that is, unconscious.

The point about being at the margins is that the centre finds it hard to hear, partly because of psychological distance, and partly because what is being said is inconvenient. And so the marginalized are forced to shout until hoarse, and can end up sounding shrill. This of course is clearly heard and is easy enough to mock. For instance, consider the number of 'jokes' around that suggest that it is the disabled lesbian black person that has the hegemony of power. This 'joke' is Eliasian gossip in action.

The notion of constraint is helpful in unravelling some of this. Once 'whiteness' exists and is used to organize the social order, then blackness is forced into existence. The shape and meaning that this notion of blackness can take is constrained by what has been allocated to whiteness. The power of ideology is such that the 'whiteness' as organizing principle is unconscious. In other words the white ensign at the centre is invisible, and it is only the black ensign at the margins that is able to be seen. Thus those at the centre feel themselves to be innocent, unfairly assaulted from without. A similar analysis can be made of the situation in Northern Ireland and other colonial situations.

The mechanism of psychologization that Elias put forward asserted that although these categories, black, white and so on, might be logical fictions, once they exist and inform social practice, they become part of the deep identity structures of the participants. The paradox being that something that is actually an abstraction ends up having a deep and profound psychological reality.

Additionally, this more group specific way of thinking about racism does not explain it in terms of instinctual discharge, and it avoids the easy gloss of essentialism, which says that we love those that are similar and hate those that are different. This discussion has problematized similarity as much as it has problematized difference, by asking: where does similarity end and difference begin? We are left with but one anchor, and it is Eliasian – the power structures and power relations in the world.

The racialized psyche

Let us remind ourselves of Foulkes' belief that, 'The group, the community, is the ultimate primary unit of consideration, and the so-called inner processes in the individual are internalizations of the forces operating in the group to which he belongs' (1971, p.212). If this is to be accepted, then it must follow that the racist structures and dynamics within the larger social group will become internalized and part of the psychological world of each and every individual within that group. In other words, *the psyche and its mechanisms will have been racialized*. Another way of putting it is to say that things in the mind – conscious and unconscious – have been blackened and whitened (Dalal 1997a).

As we have already noted in the chapter on Foulkes, a simplistic reading of the developmental model, of the external world mapped onto the internal world, leads us into problematic waters.

> When you take this individual fragment out of its context, it is shaped and formed, or deformed, according to the place it had and the experiences it received in this group. The first group is normally the family. This family, willy-nilly, reflects the culture to which it belongs and in turn transmits the cultural norms and values. (Foulkes 1974, p.275)

To apply this idea baldly, that the psyche is formed by the internalization of the external, with no other elaboration, then leads inevitably to the conclusion that different outsides must make for different insides. In other words, different cultures create different psyches and therefore different psychologies. We find ourselves giving a justification for apartheid. We find ourselves in this *cul-de-sac* because we have taken a wrong turn somewhere, and the wrong turn is a simplistic version of the notion of 'culture'.

This model of culture is that it is a sort of brand, a stamp. And different cultures have different stamps, that leave different imprints on the psyche. This idea presupposes that one can neatly draw lines between cultural groups – that they are mutually exclusive, each a self-contained set of beliefs, ways of living and so on. To use the ideas developed earlier: cultures, as much as groups, are abstractions carved out from a greater whole. And harking back to Figures 6.6 and 6.7, we saw that whether shape 'A' belongs to the 'cultural' group of triangles or coloured shapes is to some degree a matter of viewpoint.

We have problematized the idea of a cultural group; thus we have problematized the nature of the 'imprint' that the outside might make on the inside. To put it another way, as there are no neat divides between cultures, it follows that there are no neat divides between psyches. To my mind even to say something like: cultures overlap, and interpenetrate, is to perpetrate a logical fallacy, because one has begun at the wrong end. The correct end to begin with is the continuum of social existence, the mass from which a set of 'cultures' is abstracted, culture A, culture B, and so on (Donald and Rattansi 1992). It then *looks* like these self consistent entities overlap with each other. To spell out the difficulty further, it will be helpful to repeat an analogy I have used elsewhere.

'[E]very time two individuals meet it is a transcultural event in that they each have unique histories. So what is different when Mr Singh and Mr Jones meet, from when Mr Smith and Mr Jones meet?' (Dalal 1997a). Why is the first meeting, and not the second, called a transcultural event when all might have been born and bred in the same place? At the risk of pedantically repeating myself, the difference is partly a matter of definition, a chosen way of viewing the situations. But the choice is determined by the discourses that are active, discourses that decree that the second meeting is monocultural. Discourses that say – they will never be one of us. To my mind it is the socio-political signifiers of blackness and whiteness that are the ones used, sometimes consciously, sometimes unconsciously, to brand and differentiate. The argument is not that there are no differences, rather which differences are given meaning. As Cronin says 'there is nothing unique about being unique' (quoted by Ridley 1996, p.156).

The social unconscious

Much of the work concerning the development of the theory of the social unconscious has already been done in the preceding pages. Let me summarize them here.

1. We have used the notions of symmetry and asymmetry to define the mechanisms of the social unconscious.

2. We have seen how the structure of language is made for the purpose of carrying and disguising the relationship between the visible and the invisible, the conscious and the unconscious.

3. We have seen that the act of naming is itself an expression of the social unconscious.

4. We have noted that the social unconscious is not unlike the old-fashioned notion of ideology, functioning as it does to naturalize the social order.

5. We have also noted that the social unconscious is not unlike the more modern notion of discourses, making it a conflicted and turbulent territory, that is constantly in a state of flux.

6. The social unconscious contains, among other things, several deceits. One of these deceits is the disguising of power relations.

7. The social unconscious is a representation of the institutionalization of social power relations in the structure of the psyche itself. In this sense

it is a bridge between the social and the psychological. The material of this bridge is language, or as Elias put it: symbol.

8. When power relations are instituted in the psyche, they are given names such as self esteem and constrain the formation of internal structures such as ego ideals.

It should be said clearly that the social unconscious is not the same as the Jungian notion of the collective unconscious. The collective unconscious is another Platonic manifestation, filled this time with the Jungian version of Ideal Types, called archetypes. It is a biologistic notion, and an essentialist one. It harks back to recapitulation theory, and Jung used it to subjugate the black under the white. I have described these and other pernicious aspects of the collective unconscious elsewhere (Dalal 1988). To my mind Foulkes was mistaken when he suggested that the social unconscious was similar to the collective unconscious and called them both primordial. To be more accurate, when Foulkes said this, it was orthodox Foulkes speaking.

We have yet to distinguish the notion of the 'social unconscious' from the notion of the 'unconscious life of groups'. These are two quite different territories. Bion as we saw does give much attention to the unconscious life of groups, but this was an asocial unconscious. Similarly, the 1997 Foulkes lecture by Earl Hopper was entitled 'Traumatic experience in the *unconscious life of groups*' (emphasis added). The emphasis here was on how the social impacts on the unconscious life of groups. Perhaps it can be said that Hopper's work (which I have much sympathy with) concerns itself with the social *in* the individual unconscious, and group unconscious. Thus he describes many clinical events in which the social infiltrates the psyche: 'People are affected profoundly by social and cultural facts and forces, and such constraints are largely unconscious at all phases of "life trajectories"' (Hopper 1996, p.15). He demonstrates that the 'complete interpretation' should include not only the familiar trio of analyst, past, and internal objects, but also the social context in which the dramas are taking place. All this is in line with the general tenor of the book – but only up to a point. And the point is that the social and the individual still appear to be divided, with the social *entering* the individual. This is true – the social does enter the individual, but the language unfortunately implies that the individual begins outside the social, which I am sure is not what Hopper means. Despite the affinities and linkages in Hopper's work to the social, it seems to me that Hopper is operating primarily from an individual psychoanalytic frame, which he has extended to include the social.

It seems to me that on the whole when group analysts give attention to the social it is in the sense of *the social in the unconscious*. Against this, many psychotherapists, psychoanalysts and group analysts proceed as though the structure of the psyche is universal, and there is no place whatsoever for considering the social in their work. Indeed some say that reference to the social is displacement from the 'real' internal work. Returning to the point, what is meant by the social *in* the unconscious, is that attention is given to how someone is affected by their particular cultural system. This will inform what is thought to be good and what is thought to be bad by a particular person, it will inform some of the contents of the repressed unconscious, and so on. And this in itself is an extremely important project. For example, Hopper gives an example of how 'class' in the English context, affected the formation and the possibilities of expression of aggression in women: 'social and cultural facts must be taken into account in attempts to understand the nature of aggressive feelings and of aggression' (Hopper 1996).

Now, there is a 'strong' and a 'weak' version of how the notion of the social *in* the unconscious is understood. The weak version belongs to Orthodox Foulkes and, although it pays attention to the social, is still firmly individualistic. In this version, the individual exists first, and the social enters secondarily. This model is that of nature as container which is filled with social content, the social poured into the individual. The strong version belonging to Radical Foulkes goes much further, and can be encapsulated in the phrase: the social *as* unconscious. In other words the idea being mooted is that of the unconscious structured *by* the social.[19] Although it has been said before, it needs to be said here again, that this is not a simple unidirectional deterministic model. Elias' view should be remembered here, that the individual is formed by, and simultaneously informs, the social.

There is precedence for this radical idea in Freud, but in a limited way. The two great Freudian schemas are the trinities of conscious/preconscious/unconscious, and superego/ego/id. There id is wholly unconscious, its contents are the innate biological instincts. As we have seen, he additionally allows phylogenetic *experience* to be converted over time into biological instincts too, and so also reside in the id.

The social is instituted by Freud in the superego. Thus the unconscious parts of the superego can quite legitimately also be called the *unconscious social*. The particular rules encoded here will then act on the instinctive forces, and acculturate the forms that the instincts take in their discharge. Useful as it is, this is still a model of the social *in* the individual, the social *in* the unconscious. It is still a model of the social against the biological. It is not a model of the social individual *per se*.

Although the social unconscious contains all of these elements, it is much more than this collection. To my mind the most critical of components in the social unconscious is the figuration of social power, and how that organizes our

---

19   Although Lacan, and his thought that the unconscious was structured like language, cries out to be brought in here, this has to be left to another day.

thoughts and feelings, and our interactions with each other. The social unconscious, as I use the term, describes the structured network of human existence itself.
The network itself, the web, consists of two elements: one is what Elias calls the
figuration of interdependencies, and the other is what he calls symbol, language,
knowledge and experience.

This sort of idea finds sympathy with what Burkitt, from a sociological
perspective, calls the structural unconscious. Burkitt takes Elias' thoughts and
joins them up with Mead, Vygotsky, Litchman and others to create a helpful
synthesis. He begins with Mead, saying that the Self and the inner psychological
terrain emerge out of social interaction. In the structural unconscious there reside
the 'structural aspects of social life [which] are hidden from symbolically
constructed consciousness. We think in ways that are determined by the symbolic
and linguistic dialogues of our culture' (Burkitt 1991, p.198). The twist comes
with this: behind the linguistic dialogues lie the figuration of power balances, and
it is these that are unconscious. To paraphrase the proposition: what is invisible to
us are the rules and constraints, and the socio-cultural power figurations in which
they are embedded, all of which *structure* our being, and it is this that I take the
structural or social unconscious to be.

The infinite and the absolute

The social unconscious includes, but is bigger than, what might be called the
cultural unconscious. The cultural unconscious can be described as consisting of
the norms, habits, and ways of seeing of a *particular* culture, that are so deeply
embedded in each of us that they are indeed unconscious. This notion is the same
as that of discourse. But we have already said that we are subject to more than one
discourse at a time – none of us is monocultural. The social unconscious, as I think
of it, includes the power relationships *between* discourses. The social unconscious
is a discourse which hierarchically orders other discourses. This ordering is also
unconscious. This gives the social unconscious the appearance of an absolute,
which it is not, it is still a discourse. This appearance of an absolute is the outcome
of a limitation of thought, which is that we are unable to comprehend or process
the notion of infinity.

We saw earlier that the infinite is part and parcel of everyday existence in a
variety of ways. There, it was suggested that the infinite was made manageable by
interrupting it with thought, thus dealing with it finite piece by finite piece at a
time. Another way of dealing with the paradoxes that the infinite throws up is to
insert an imaginary absolute somewhere in the proceedings, once again rendering
the infinite finite. This we are always obliged to do, and it is another way of saying
that we have to begin somewhere.

Returning to the discourse of discourses, this is a place to stand from which to
view other discourses. However, it is always a temporary place, it is a temporary

state-of-things, which is mutable. With the infinite there is never any end in sight, it is always possible to add one more layer, one more thing. The discourse of discourses can always in turn be viewed from other vantage points, thus making it one of a kind with other discourses. This is a rather worrying thought, that something so powerful is also potentially so transient.

Cultural transmission and cohesion

Richard Dawkins has suggested that social behaviours, belief systems and so forth, evolve and change according to the Darwinian rules of natural selection. In other words things that work to promote the survival and expansion of a group, get incorporated and woven into the cultural tapestry. Elias too thinks something like this, saying that this would push in the direction of neighbouring groups differentiating from each other, each evolving their own traits benefiting them in their contexts. Dawkins has coined the term 'memes' to denote capsules of cultural information. He suggests that these memes are transmitted linguistically, in much the same way that genes are transmitted biologically. Memes are understood by Dawkins as memories of some sort. Plotkin has described, from a biologist's perspective, many inconsistencies and difficulties with the notion of memes as put forward by Dawkins. For example, Plotkin points out that culture is also transmitted through social structures, that have lives and momentums bigger and longer than any single individual. Plotkin concludes that 'our ignorance of the psychological and neural mechanisms involved in imitation makes all judgements as to what is being replicated hazardous, to say the least' (1997, p.255). At first glance it appears that the notion of memes might have something to it – if only at the level of metaphor. But before one gives it any weight whatsoever, several cautionary things need to be said about it.

First, the notion of a meme is a reification of an ongoing process. It is trying to encapsulate something fluid, fluctuating and alive, and put it into an inert form. The notion of the anti-group has the same problem. Although Nitsun has said that the anti-group is not to be taken as an entity, that is how people use the term, as though the anti-group were a thing in itself. The anti-group is the reification of 'destructive' group processes. This need not be an insuperable problem in itself either for the meme or the anti-group. After all, every psychoanalytic term is a reification. There is no such entity as the ego, or the superego and so on. These are inventions, terms that draw together certain attributes (real or imagined is another question again) and give them a name. We group particular bits of the continuum of personality, give them names and then say it is *as though* there were an entity called the ego, whose properties are such and such, and it is *as though* it was behaving in a certain way.

The second criticism of the meme is that by encapsulating an element of culture, it has been isolated. And this is an impossibility. Culture, by definition, has an existence only with people and in their network of relations. To encapsulate culture, is paradoxically to make it asocial.

The third criticism of the meme is more telling. The way the term 'culture' is being used is global. So even if we allow the existence of a self contained cultural group (of which there are none), it is never homogenous. It will have its own internal power and social structures, the cultural group will be found to be internally differentiated. At the very least there will be a division of labour. It follows then that this culture cannot have a global meme, or set of memes, because within this culture there are subcultures, and so on. So the question is: which group of behaviours or beliefs are to be encapsulated in memes?

Taking this idea further, cultural memes would favour those in power, or to put it another way, successful memes would put their carriers in positions of power. Fine, but then we have to ask, what sorts of memes have those with less power? A cultural meme might be: the King deserves better than the serf. One can see how this meme will benefit the King, and why royalty would want to transmit this belief, but why should the serf perpetuate it, when it is against their interest?

One can continue to test the meme for what it is supposed to do, and one will continue to find it wanting. There is something appealing about the meme, perhaps because it simplifies things; unfortunately the meme as a method of cultural transmission plainly does not work. We have already met other more successful agents of cultural transmission – these have been variously called the social unconscious, symbol (in the Eliasian sense), ideology and discourse. These concepts do the job much better of engaging with the messiness of culture and cultural transmission, and also of allowing for the multiplicity of culture itself.

In praise of imitation

Imitation, like influence and conformism, has a bad press generally, and a bad press in the world of psychotherapy particularly. Imitation is redolent with many negative connotations, for example if something is an imitation then it is not genuine but artificial. 'Artificial' comes from 'artifact', and artifact means manufactured by people – and so not-natural (*sic*). Thus as we deconstruct the term 'imitation' we find the familiar dichotomy embedded within it, genuine (true) nature over artificial (manufactured) nurture. The idea of imitation is not that far from mimicry, and mimicry is close to monkeys. Thus there is an idea of 'true' learning (deeper) which is distinguished from imitative learning (shallower).

Another reason why imitation is looked down upon is that inherent in the idea of imitation is a reference to the external world, i.e. something is taken in from the outside. We find that we are back with Plato, Socrates and Aristotle again. Socrates and Plato say that true knowledge is internal and is gained through introspection and reasoning. Thus according to them, any knowledge gleaned by reference to the external world is not as profound as this internal knowledge. We can see here the evolution of a new dichotomy, pure reason versus emulation. This ideology is the basis of *some* psychoanalytic systems, systems that look down on emulation and the external. This then leads to the suggestion that 'insight' based psychoanalytic knowledge is deeper than knowledge that is 'learnt'. These same trajectories lead some psychoanalytic discourses to denigrate the notion of a 'corrective emotional experience'.

Against this Platonic ideology the work of the previous sections has argued for an Aristotelian ideology, saying that there is never any knowledge that is not learnt, in other words knowledge that is 'taken in' in some way. Support for this has come from several arenas. First and foremost is Elias' Symbol Theory. Second, also from Elias, is the function he allocated to conformism and the impact this has on cohesion. Third, from game theory, which says that for a successful and sophisticated system to evolve, all that is necessary is for each to blindly copy the strategy of someone else who has done better.

The problem that we are continually faced with is the assumption that if something is learnt in part through imitation, then it cannot be deep, profound and unconscious. In fact, *the process of imitation itself is often deeply unconscious.* As we saw, the biologists have argued that we are genetically programmed to imitate. In other words imitation is of itself a natural (*sic*) process and not at all artificial.

It will be helpful here to describe a series of experiments conducted by social psychologists that demonstrate both unconscious imitation, and cultural transmission in action.[20] The social psychologist Muzafer Sherif (1936) based his experiment on a phenomenon known as the autokinetic effect. This consists of an illusion, in which a stationary point of light in a dark room appears to move. When subjects are individually asked to estimate the distance moved, there are a wide range of answers. But if a group of subjects are put in the darkened room and asked the same question in the presence of each other, their answers tend to group around a 'norm'. Sherif argued that there is a fundamental drive to form norms in all aspects of social life, from beliefs to tastes. Of particular interest to group analysts is the extension of the experiment by Jacobs and Campbell (1961). They set up a kind of 'slow open group'.[21] They began with one 'innocent' subject and the rest were primed to give similar answers. As one might expect, the innocent's answer was in the vicinity of the primed answers. Over time, the primed members were replaced, one by one, with innocent members, until the group membership contained none of the original group and all were 'innocent' of the original deceit. It was found that the culture artificially established at the start of the group

---

20   These experiments are described in Plotkin's volume.

21   This is a structure for psychotherapy groups, in which the group has a slowly changing membership, with new members joining when a vacancy occurs. Thus the group is 'open' in that people leave and join, but the turnover is 'slow'.

continued to have a life despite the changing membership. The fashion industry is a clear example of this process in action. I only have to contrast my current genuine feelings about flared trousers with those from 25 years ago, to deflate any idea that *I* decide what I like and dislike all by myself in conjunction with my 'true' tastes.

This is an uncomfortable realization, that to some extent we are behavioural and cultural sheep. Elias has this view as do the evolutionary theorists, and both use the same armchair logic. They say that it is too expensive, in terms of time and energy, for each new individual to arrive at the same or similar solutions from first principles each time. Much cheaper is a programmed-in tendency to copy what has gone before, or to copy what appears to be working in the current environment. This is not at all a foolproof strategy, but it must work enough of the time for the processes of natural selection to have preserved it. However, the tendency to conform is not to be taken to mean that our thoughts and feelings are completely determined, rather, they are constrained. And as we have seen before, autonomy is always a part of constraint.

There is another reason why there is a tendency to conform, and whilst the reason is socio-political, it is profoundly unconscious for all that. By conforming, through dress, beliefs, attitudes and so on, one is putting on a uniform. Uniforms serve two functions. One, they add to the illusion and *feeling* of similarity, belonging and cohesion. Symmetric thinking plays its part in this, where some similarities are used to construct the fantasy of homogeneity. Two, uniforms are signals and signifiers of belonging, in other words they serve a cognitive function and determine who is one of us and who is one of them. But at the centre of groups of belonging are always vortices of power and resources, be they material, or cultural, or whatever. The uniform thus signals who is and who is not allowed to partake of the cake, and how one feels towards those that try to partake of the cake.

Plotkin says that social conformism is the same as group cohesion, but I would put it another way and say: the normalizing processes serve the function of cohering the group. This is of benefit to the group, because cohesive groups do better than those less cohesive. This is exactly what Elias and Scotson described in the relations between the established and the outsiders.

Loops and mirrors

Pines' (1982, 1985) notion of mirroring is in effect a description of the critical role that imitation plays in the developmental process. Pines builds on Winnicott's comment that 'psychoanalysis has neglected the face in favour of the breast'. With this idea Pines seeks to steer group analysis away from the Freudian preoccupation with the internal and instinct, and towards the external and relatedness. In doing this Pines allies himself with the ideas of radical Foulkes.

Drawing on the baby observation studies of Stern and others, Pines demonstrates that the developmental process is not a unidirectional one from seed to flower, unfolding with no regard to environment. Instead, Pines shows that the developmental process is a corrective feedback loop. We have already come across the notion of feedback in the chapter on Foulkes. Here, Pines is using the term in relation to what takes place between the carer and infant. This includes not only the exchanges of gestures and actions, the 'play', which Pines calls imitative mirroring, it also includes the matching of emotion and atmosphere which Stern calls state-sharing. Importantly, the very beginnings of dialogue between parent and infant are predicated on repeated imitation of the infant's gestures by the parent.[22] The parent imitates the baby's random gestures, which are in effect a simulation of dialogue. This imitation is the starter motor needed by the infant to move towards true dialogue. With these ideas Pines has driven another wedge between the orthodox and the radical Foulkes. The flowering or unfolding model of development is biologistic and belongs to classical psychoanalysis and orthodox Foulkes, whilst the corrective feedback loop belongs with group analysis and radical Foulkes. This cybernetic notion is of enormous importance as it cuts through, quite literally, all possibility of solipsism. It denotes a circle of development, that cuts through the internal and the external, each forming and transforming the other, each modifying and correcting the other. But what does 'correcting' mean in this context? Many will balk at the use of the term, precisely because it goes against a notion of natural or innate or true correctness. The meaning of 'correcting' here is that of fit, of adjustment, of imprint, of bridge. In essence what is felt to be correct on the inside will depend on what is on the outside, and what is felt to be correct on the outside will depend on the inside. The elements of this 'correctness' are manifold, from emotion and mood, to language and cultural norm.

The importance of mirroring and the corrective feedback loop lies in the fact that they link the structure and content of the psyche with the structure and content of the environment in which it is situated. This allows Pines to align himself with Lichenstein's (1977) idea that 'the primary identity is always based on a mirroring experience'. In other words, identity is always formed in relation to the Other. So although the language being used by Pines is different to that of the post-structuralists and also that of Elias, it seems to me that he is in broad agreement with each of them, and also the general thesis of this book. It is clear that the mirror and the corrective feedback loop are not unlike Elias' Symbol Theory, as all mediate the engagement of the inside and the outside. Perhaps one could say that the feedback loop is one of the mechanisms through which the

---

22   Pines uses Pawlby (1977) as his authority here.

Eliasian symbol and the structure of human beings are mutually evolved and devolved in an endless cycle of transformation.

Having shown that the process of infant development is not one of 'unfolding', it is tempting to say that the development is a dialectic or an iterative process. Whilst these terms are indeed a better description of the complexity of the developmental process, they too fall short of what is required here. This is because each of these processes begins with an idea of separateness – such as thesis and antithesis, inside and outside – which *then* engage with each other to form something else. However, despite their limitations, it seems to me that for the moment at least, the notions of iteration and dialectic are important ones to hang on to.

In summary, there are four main reasons why we think and behave in broadly similar ways. The first is biological and says that we are genetically programmed to conform with the environs to some degree, because it is advantageous to the project of survival and replication. The second reason is in the realm of group dynamics; a cohesive group functions better than an incohesive group. Third, conformism adds to the *emotional* sense of belonging. Fourth, we think and behave in broadly similar ways because we share the same structures of thought processes. Elias has called these structures 'symbol', the political radicals have called them 'ideology', the structuralists have called them 'langue', the post-structuralists have called them 'discourse', and I am suggesting that group analysts call them the 'social unconscious'. And finally, Pines has described the mechanisms of this 'grouping' process through the idea of mirroring and the corrective feedback loop.

The therapy group

Whilst the translation of these themes into the consulting room is enormously difficult, one simple but powerful thing can be said straightaway. This thing is a riposte to those who imagine that a therapy group is a contradiction in terms. They cannot imagine where the therapeutic element comes from when a collection of people with a variety of difficulties are put together. What we have seen from many different sources is that order arises spontaneously out of chaos, in other words the group will tend *of itself* to work together and set up a productivity. To be sure the 'working together' is not inevitable or straightforward, it will be continually disrupted from any number of directions. And sometimes the order instituted is a malign one. What we can say to the sceptic is that the therapeutic element in a group relies on a 'natural' impetus within all human beings, the deep need to belong, and in order to do this one has to find a way to work together. The point to be made is that the process of arriving at the point of working together, of arrival at a place of belonging, *is in itself* the therapy.

A consequence of taking the group seriously, in the sense of involving the social in the construction of individuals, is that the clinical arena has to expand to engage in new territories. This includes taking the social into account when considering the psyche in the clinical setting. This task is the same as looking for the social *in* the unconscious. Critically important here is Hopper's notion of the full interpretation, which weaves the social context into the interpretation. Difficult enough as this is, this is the easier part of what lies before us. Here at least there is something to get a hold of, slippery and tenuous as it is. We at least know that some words exist that will be helpful in this project, words like class, or history, or oppression, or gender, or race and so on. On the other hand many therapists might feel bemused at these suggestions. Some will take the suggestion of attention to the social as a flight from internal, and so think it irrelevant or therapeutically unhelpful. One group analyst said at a conference that the fact that she knew of some 'coloured' people who did well in the current British social system meant that there was nothing to be looked at in the system. Therefore, she argued, when other 'coloureds' did not do so well, it was because of disturbances in their personality, which they mistakenly attributed to society.

I have argued elsewhere (Dalal 1997a) that the difficulty some practitioners have in incorporating the social into their clinical work is a transference resistance, and that it is a resistance to knowing about particular ideological structures that favour their socio-cultural-economic positions. There is a resistance to knowing about privilege because to know about the privilege is also to feel guilt. The guilt is avoided partly because of pain, and partly because of anxiety in that it might set off a dangerous chain of events called reparation. The feeling of reparation is felt to be dangerous because it would undermine the structures of privilege.

Next to this difficulty of ignoring the social, there is also the contrary problem of being fixated by the social in a deterministic way. The fact that it is possible to name certain things can lead some to simplify and essentialize at a different level. These simplifications are exemplified in some so-called cross-cultural texts, and in some so-called intercultural psychotherapy or counselling trainings. Cultures are essentialized, and placed in an antagonistic either/or relation to each other. These attitudes then lead to formulaic suggestions and 'rules' that have to be followed dogmatically. Some so-called 'race' trainings are of this ilk.

Another graspable consequence of the social unconscious, in the way that it has been defined here, is that the notion of transference is inevitably extended. Transference in the broadest sense consists of the movement of things from one context to another. In the main the contents of the transferred are said to be past events, unconscious and difficult feelings, and internal object relations. The contents of the transferred are intimately personal. A consequence of taking the group seriously is to say that the personal includes the *impersonal personalized*. What is meant by the impersonal in this context are the structuring forces of ideology and discourse as they are instituted in the social unconscious. Among other things discourses delineate good from bad, safe from dangerous and so on. In Derrida's (1976) language discourses create violent hierarchies, that is polarizations in which one pole is subjugated by the other. 'Good' subjugates 'bad', 'nature' is put over 'nurture', 'black' over 'white', 'man' over 'woman' and so on. These impersonal structures are instituted in language and social structures. As language is taken in, one inevitably and uncomprehendingly swallows the structures within it, what Harland called 'an undigested piece of society'. It seems inevitable to me that these elements of the personalized impersonal must also get activated in transferences – thus we can have feelings and reactions to things outside our experiences. A 'white' in deepest Cumbria might never have met a 'black', but each has been well prepared for the meeting as and when it might happen.

The attempt to naturalize these reactions by biologizing them or imputing them to instinctual forces, is to my mind a kind of resistance. Perhaps in line with the new terminology one could call it a structural resistance, in that it is a resistance to knowing about the structures of thought, emotion, power and existence itself. The group analyst mentioned earlier is an example of this. Another example is the explanation some offer for ambivalent feelings towards blacks. The hostility and fear is naturalized and made acceptable by saying that it is natural to fear the dark and this fear is transferred to the black. This proposition can be taken to task in three ways. The first experience that each of us has of profound safety and perhaps harmony, takes place in the womb where darkness reigns. Thus one might as easily equate darkness with bliss. Second, black and dark are not at all the same thing. One is a colour of sorts, and the other is an intensity of light; they are two quite different types of things. Third, it has been strongly argued in several sections of the book that it is too simplistic to equate difference with fear and hostility. It has been argued that it is only some differences that act as triggers for these feelings, and that these are the differences that are used to organize the social order. In other words the linkage between darkness and fear, and darkness and blackness are not at all inevitable.

Unfortunately some use these sorts of cogitations to close things down rather than open things up. This leads to simplistic formulae, such as all whites are racist, and so they can never work with blacks, similarly for gender, sexual orientation, and so on. This is a retreat into a binarization and does not allow for subtleties, degrees and variation. It is another application of symmetric logic. The point about it being a social unconscious is that it structures all the participants in the social order, be they men, women, blacks, whites, therapist, patient or whatever. No one is immune. If there are negative connotations with femininity or blackness or a particular accent, then all are impregnated with these connotations, albeit not in identical ways. Remember constraint allows for degrees of autonomy. Another mistake that some might make is that of thinking that because something is *social*, it must be *conscious*. For example, some counselling organizations ask their prospective clients whether they would like to, or whether they 'mind' working with a particular category of counsellor/therapist, man/woman etc. To take the answers given at face value is to take an answer exclusively from the conscious and so avoid engaging with the unconscious. Whether these questions should or should not be put to clients is not the issue here – what is at issue is how the answers are handled, and whether the assessor would then dare probe and question the answer, in other words delve into the unconscious. After all, the point about the social unconscious is that it is unconscious!

The harder part of taking the group seriously, at least for me, is finding a new way to think, a new way to visualize group processes. As Foulkes has implied, rather than particles, fields and networks are more accurate metaphors for group processes. The problem is that it is much easier to visualize a unitary particle, and nigh on impossible to visualize a field. A particle, an individual, is bounded and looks finite to the eye. We grasp it with our eye (we imagine) in its entirety, we see its beginning and its end. This makes it easier for us to formulate thoughts about it, relate it to other things, think about what might be going on inside it, and so on. In contrast a field is so much more amorphous, it is fluctuating continuum with no end in sight. It is the nature of fields that they are infinite and fluid. Even Fairbairn's attempt to institute the notion of forces in place of instincts is impoverished in comparison to the field. As I suggested earlier in the chapter on Foulkes, the level of the group is beyond the structure of our linear language. Language was not built to describe multiplicities and simultaneous pluralities. Evolution, being parsimonious, selects the lowest level of complexity to do a certain task. One can speculate that our minds, and in tandem with that, language, were built to comprehend linearities, and finitude. Minds evolved to cope with just one cause and effect at a time, because that was all that was necessary to engage with a three-dimensional existence. As Elias has said, because thought, speech and knowledge are one and the same, all of them fail to reflect the true multiplicity of existence. Thus the territory that one needs to get to, is forever out of reach of the vehicles we have.

But all is not lost. There is the possibility of doing something partial. In much the same way that we can infer something about a three-dimensional object by looking at its two-dimensional shadow, we can infer things about the field from the behaviour of the particle. As one might expect, the possibilities of mistaken inferences are endless. How would one ever get to postulate the curved surface of a sphere from the flat two-dimensional shadow? Perhaps if one takes many shadows, pictures of the same object, then one would have a better chance of getting closer to what it might be. Of course we will never arrive at the complexity itself. This perhaps is what the discourse theoreticians have meant, when they say that all one can do is move from discourse to discourse, from shadow to shadow. In a sense the collection of individual experiences in the group can perhaps be construed as the collection of shadows.

To my mind, these difficulties and impossibilities are an expression of the nature of the social unconscious. It must be so, it is the thing that structures us; we are its manifestation, it makes us and so it is forever beyond us. An individual is inevitably completely blind to his or her unconscious. The only way that they get glimpses of it are through the eye of another. If there were no other, then one might still get glimpses of it through slips or dreams and so on. But as a revelatory project, it is seriously restricted. Next, move this idea up a level to that of the social, the group. Now all are unconscious of the structuring forces. As no one is privileged to be outside the social, we are all blind to the structure. It is beyond our ken. Nevertheless, through painstaking analysis, by one discourse testing another, one can catch glimpses of something, only shadows to be sure, but shadows of *something*.

Analogy and metaphor can be thought of as kinds of two-dimensional shadows. Paradoxically, shadows which can be used to shed light on the active processes. Analogy and metaphor are bound to be partial and reductive to some degree. Within these constraints, it seems to me that the ocean as an analogy for 'field' gives up some interesting information. Consider: a wave moves through the ocean horizontally, as does the energy that is being conveyed. However, if one looks at a particle of sea water, or more realistically a cork (as particles of sea water are curiously difficult to spot), one is surprised to find that its movement is not horizontal but a vertical oscillation. The lesson to be taken from this is that the parts of the whole can do things that appear to have no bearing on what is happening at the level of the field. The movement of the cork seems anomalous and bizarre in relation to the wave. Imagine the difficulty if one were to try to infer the presence of the ocean, and the presence of the horizontal movements of its waves and energy, if all one had access to were the vertical motions of a few floating corks. Well, as group analysts we are in a not dissimilar position, attempting to understand how the field is moving the individual, and how the individual is affecting the field.

But what exactly is this 'field'? Orthodox Foulkes named the field the matrix, and radical Foulkes called it a communicational network. This latter notion subsumes all group phenomena, because as Foulkes says, everything that happens is a communication. The strength of the notion of communication is its all-encompassing stature. It takes under its wing many terms derived from the individual psychoanalytic situation – transference, counter-transference, projection, introjection, projective identification and the like. These are all aspects of communication. Foulkes described psychopathology as a blockage in the communicative network. In this arena Foulkes cannot be faulted, and this part of his theory must take a central place in any post-Foulkesian presumptions.

Now, let us ask a deeper question, what is it that is being communicated? At its most basic, the thing that is being communicated is information. Not information in a passive sense of 'description', but information in a more active sense of precipitating change. Information is another name for what Elias has called knowledge, and in his Symbol Theory this is the same as language and thought. Elias' insight was that the state of knowledge is inextricably entwined with the state of the psyche. When this is joined up with Foulkes' notion of communication, we can see how and why speech is potentially a transformational and therapeutic act.

To speak is one thing, to listen is another. To listen is potentially a very frightening process, because to hear the words of another is literally to let their words and meanings into the self – it is to let a stranger into the home. And once they have entered, who knows where they may go, what havoc they may wreak, or what changes they may precipitate? This fear is the basis of one of the central defences used in groups, where participants deny the interdependencies, and retreat into a monad-like state by blowing up all bridges between the inside and outside. The flight into individuality is a defence mechanism that seeks to build fortifications against the therapeutic processes which, if allowed to enter, will inevitably transform.

As well as the communicational field Foulkes offered us the notion of matrix, but then promptly undid its complexity, by collapsing back into the nature–nurture dichotomy and the orthodox frame. To my mind the only way that the notion of the matrix can be rescued is by identifying it with the social unconscious, with discourse and with ideology.

One last point needs to be made. Taking the group seriously means to acknowledge that some of the things that take place in our groups do so not because of past history, or because of the social unconscious, but because of the structure and nature of groups. For example, Elias and Scotson (1994) demonstrate that the ranking process is endemic to the structure of groups, it is part and parcel of the mechanics of group formation.[23] Thus not all rivalries and jealousies in groups are to be derived from siblings and early family life, nor are they all to be derived from internal object relations. Some of the rivalrous structures will come about purely because of the structure of the group situation itself.

Greenberg and Mitchell (1993) say that from the mess of data, one of the things paradigms dictate is which of the many elements are to be taken as primary

---

23   An analogy would be the way a gas would organize itself in a chamber, with the hotter particles near the top and the colder particles near the bottom.

and which are derivative; to this we can add that paradigms also dictate which elements are noise and so not pertinent. In short, paradigms are ways of seeing. Thomas Kuhn (1962) suggested that science did not evolve gradually, bit by bit. Instead, he said, science operated within a particular paradigm, until such time as when there is a sudden shift into a new way of seeing – a new paradigm. The new paradigm might incorporate the previous one, or it may refute it. For example the geocentric model of the universe was one paradigm, and all data was interpreted in this model. Later it was supplanted with a solar-centric paradigm. This gave a new way of reading old data, and was able to see data in places that were blind to the previous paradigm.

Paradigms are not unlike the discourses we have already met, because both impose a particular type of order on chaos. The mother–infant psychoanalytic paradigm has taken the individual as primary and the group as secondary. This book has been an attempt to shift that. Although we are still a considerable distance from the possibility of a fully operational group analytic paradigm that can be used in the clinical situation, certain things have been put in place. One could say that the arguments presented here have begun a process of deconstruction on the mother–infant paradigm, but a new group analytic paradigm, however partial, is yet to come into focus.

There are certain elements which a group analytic paradigm is bound to have – elements which are not to be found in orthodox psychoanalysis. First is a constitutive primacy given to Elias' symbol, or social unconscious, instead of to instinct. Second is a philosophical primacy given to multiplicity over and above the unity. Third is problematization of identity as a secure, stable space. Fourth are mechanisms through which the illusion of an individual centre are instated. Fifth is the centrality of power relations and their constitutive repercussions. Sixth is the notion of a communicational field. Seventh is the notion that order can spontaneously arise out of chaos. Eighth is importance given to figurations of interdependence. Ninth are realizations that some structures such as mind, thought and superego, that were thought to be internal and private in the old paradigm, are now thought of as the property of the group. Tenth is a new way of visualizing the unconscious. Eleventh is the power of naming. Twelfth is the realization that the 'I' is always a 'we'. Thirteenth is a reluctance to denigrate the external. Fourteenth is the thought that first and last we are always inside the social. Fifteenth, that hierarchical social *relations* inform the structuring of the psyche. And finally, that there are no universals or absolutes.

Constraint and order: a summary

We have travelled through many diverse territories, from psychoanalysis to group analysis, from sociology to biology. We have touched on chaos theory, economics, game theory and discourse theory. We have spent considerable time in the realms of formal logic, politics, philosophy and metapsychology. We have met characters as diverse as Mrs Thatcher and Socrates. In this long process many traditional elements of individual psychoanalysis and group analysis have been tested and questioned. Perhaps the most profound realization to emerge from these explorations is that mind and thought are not private properties of the individual, but properties of the group. We have noted how affects are not just internal reservoirs of instinct or whatever, but social processes arising out of interactions. (For example Rose *et al.* (1984) say that aggression is a verb that has been redefined as a noun.) We have seen that individual conscience is not a reflection of a celestial ethic, but more prosaically the internalization of the norms of the group.

Despite the variety of territories covered, in each of them one term has recurred over and above all else, and this has been 'constraint'. Constraint is a fact of life, it is an inevitable outcome of interdependence. Those who seek to flee from constraint to the fantasy of a Rousseauian island of limitless individual freedom unrestricted by Mind or the Other, do so because they have misunderstood the nature of constraint. One may as well say that one is constrained by one's skin or one's boundary. One may as well say that a circle is constrained by its circumference. The point is that without the circumference, there would be no circle. Remove constraint and you remove existence. Chomsky (1980) makes the same point when he says 'the very same factors that permit these achievements [i.e. the possibilities of thought] also impose severe limits on the states that can be attained; to put it differently, there is an inseparable connection between the scope and limits of human knowledge' (quoted in Plotkin 1997, p.244).

In considering the social basis of human existence, we have witnessed the 'natural birth' of order from apparent chaos, with constraint acting as midwife, and a midwife moreover, who has had no necessity of using force or injunction to help with the birth. The order thus born is not an order of infinite harmony and bliss, but a problematic order, an order that is continually disordered. Order is always ruptured at its boundaries; regions of order are separated by disorder. But when we look within any region of order we find within it difference and differentiation, sub-orders and sub-sub-orders in infinite regress. Additionally, the areas of order are not tidy and mutually exclusive, but overlap, push, shove and contest each other. Thus one could say that ultimately order is temporary at best, and illusory at worst.

> …human groups are largely mythical. People do undoubtedly think in terms of groups: tribes, clans, societies, nations. But they do not really live in isolated groups. They mingle continuously with those from other groups… Human groups are fluid and impermanent. People do not live in groups…they merely perceive the world in terms of groups, ruthlessly categorizing people as us or them. Yet this is a double edged discovery. That we see the world in terms of

groups – however falsely – still tells us something about the human mindset, and it is inside the skull that evolution leaves many of its social marks. (Ridley 1996, p.188)

This is one of the enduring ironies, that the project of taking the group seriously has led to the acknowledgement that groups do not exist as natural fixed entities, but are always constructs. Foulkes was well aware of this point and realized that the notion of group was an abstraction. He was also conscious of the fact that the individual too was an abstraction. However, he said these things in different places and at different times. What he never did was to join them up. If he had, he would have realized how modern his thinking was. To bring them together is to reveal the radical within Foulkes, showing that, potentially, he was not only a post-modernist but also a post-structuralist. Consider, if the *parts* are abstractions and the *whole* is an abstraction, then where are we left to stand? Where are we to find any stability or centre? This is the frightening and exciting proposition we have to engage with in post-Foulkesian theory. As we saw earlier, Foulkes allowed a partial and temporary rescue from this earthquake land when he said that: 'In order to see something whole, we have to...step outside of that which we want to see' (Foulkes 1973a, p.230). The thing that we step outside and into, is context. But the rescue is temporary, because to get a perspective on that context, we would have to step outside that too, into another context, and so on *ad infinitum*. The post-Foulkesian dilemma is the double realization that not only do we have to stand somewhere, but also that the thing we stand on is but a precarious abstraction likely to give way at any moment.

The project has almost dissolved the object of its study – almost, but not quite. We are rescued from infinite regresses and cognitive and discursive solipsisms by remembering the power structures in the world, and this shows us that the constructions of varieties of 'us' and 'them' are not arbitrary. It might be helpful to represent the argument in a schematic and pseudo-mathematical formula (see Figure 6.8).

The territories between regions of order, territories between the us and the them, are injected with acrimony, in order to maintain a sense of identity by seeking to differentiate the us from the them, the I from the we. The task is made difficult in part because of the number of possible varieties of us and them, and in part because of the number of levels of us and them, from the singular 'I' to the many varieties of 'us'. These competing plural allegiances continually problematize the hostility and acrimony, shuffling it from here to there, from there to here, and with each shuffle different varieties of 'I', 'us' and 'them' are thrown to the fore.

Similarities constantly disrupt differences and differences constantly disrupt similarities – there is no place of rest, only the state of tension. Even as difference divides, it also joins. To take the group seriously is to come face to face with nested Chinese boxes within boxes, each filled with paradox. One of the many paradoxes is that the act of differentiation is simultaneously the act of creation. In the very act of differentiating the 'us' from the 'them', the 'us' and the 'them' are created. Another paradox then follows, which is that the 'us' and the 'them' need to be differentiated before they can work together. This was the insight of Durkheim and Levi Strauss who saw that differentiation had to take place before exchange was possible. This was also Elias' insight who described it in terms of inter-dependencies and figurations of power. Adam Smith came to the same conclusion and described it as the necessity of the division of labour. Numerous biologists echoed these findings in their descriptions of organisms.

Matte-Blanco's bi-logical theory can be directly mapped onto each of these insights to show that the structure of each of them is the same. His theory can be used like a sophisticated optical instrument that is both a microscope and a telescope. This instrument allows us to examine the structure of the figurations at different levels of magnification. The Matte-Blanco tele-micro-scope is adjusted by varying the amount of symmetry to asymmetry. When the knob is turned in the direction of more symmetry, then the microscope becomes a telescope giving us a view from a distance – seeing the wood rather than the trees. As asymmetry is increased, the magnification is increased, which allows new differentiations to progressively come into view. It is this facility to act as variable optical instrument that gives Matte-Blanco's theory of thinking its importance to the study of

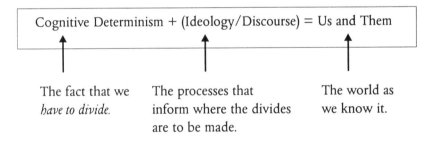

Figure 6.8

groups. In comparison to the Matte-Blanco tele-micro-scope, the familiar conceptual tool of figure–ground is crude. Not only does the figure–ground model allow just two states to come into view, it also lends each of them a comforting illusion of stability and permanency.

As we moved from Foulkesian territory, we moved from the 'I' to the 'we', and then found that the 'we' was not a stable object at all, but a frozen moment cut out from a field of fluctuating interdependencies. Although Foulkes said that the individual–group dichotomy was a false one, he had no way of conceptualizing the linkages between the two and the overall picture. This meant that he often fell on one or either side of the dichotomy. The Matte-Blanco tele-micro-scope, our new conceptual tool, allows us to see fluid unity where before there was dichotomy, and with these new possibilities we discover that we have arrived in a post-Foulkesian land. And now it is truly possible to understand what Elias meant when he said that the individual is a level of group.

Bibliography

Adler, A., (1938) *Social Interest: A Challenge to Mankind.* London: Faber and Faber.

Althusser, L. (1969) *For Marx* [trans. Ben Brewster]. London: New Left Books.

Bion, W.R. (1961) *Experiences in Groups.* London: Tavistock/Routledge.

Brown, D. (1994) 'Self development through subjective interaction: a fresh look at "ego training in action".' In D. Brown and L. Zinkin (eds) (1994) *The Psyche and the Social World.* London: Routledge.

Brown, R. (1988) *Group Processes.* Oxford: Blackwell.

Burkitt, I. (1991) *Social Selves.* London: Sage.

Calhoun, C. (1994) 'Social theory and the politics of identity.' In C. Calhoun (ed) *Social Theory and the Politics of Identity.* Oxford: Blackwell.

Campbell, J. (1982) *Grammatical Man.* Harmondsworth: Penguin.

Chomsky, N. (1980) 'Rules and representations.' *The Behavioural and Brain Sciences 3.*

Cialdini, R.B., Borden, R.J., Thorne, A., Walker, M.R., Freeman, S. and Sloan, L.R. (1976) 'Basking in reflected glory: three (football) field studies.' *Journal of Personality and Social Psychology 34,* 366–374.

Dalal, F. (1988) 'The racism of Jung.' *Race and Class 19,* 3, pp.1–22. Republished as 'Jung a racist.' *British Journal of Psychotherapy 1988,* 4, 3, pp.263–279.

Dalal, F. (1993a) '"Race" and racism – an attempt to organize difference.' *Group Analysis 26,* 3, pp.277–293.

Dalal, F. (1993b) 'The meaning of boundaries and barriers in the development of cultural identity.' In W. Knauss and U. Keller (eds) *Ninth European Symposium in Group Analysis 'Boundaries and Barriers'.* Heidelberg: Mattes Verlag.

Dalal, F. (1997a) 'A transcultural perspective on psychodynamic psychotherapy.' *Group Analysis 30,* 2, pp.203–215.

Dalal, F. (1997b) 'The colour question in psychoanalysis.' *Journal of Social Work Practice 11,* 2.

Dawkins, R. (1976) *The Selfish Gene.* Oxford: Oxford University Press.

Dawkins, R. (1988) *The Blind Watchmaker.* London: Penguin.

Dawkins, R. (1996) *River out of Eden.* London: Phoenix.

Derrida, J. (1976) *Of Grammatology* [trans. G.C. Spivak]. Baltimore: Johns Hopkins University Press.

Dollard, J., Doob, L.W., Miller, N.E., Mowrer, O.H. and Sears, R.R. (1939) *Frustration and Aggression.* New Haven: Yale University Press.

Donald, J. and Rattansi, A. (eds) (1992) *Race, Culture and Difference.* London: Sage, Open University Press.

Douglas, M. (1991) [1966] *Purity and Danger.* London: Routledge.

Eagleton, T. (1983) *Literary Theory: An Introduction.* Minneapolis: University of Minnesota Press.

Elias, N. (1976) 'Introduction.' In N. Elias and J. Scotson (1994) *The Established and the Outsiders.* London: Sage.

Elias, N. (1978) *What is Sociology?* New York: Columbia University Press.

Elias, N. (1991) *The Symbol Theory.* London: Sage. First published in *Theory, Culture, Society* in three parts in 1989.

Elias, N. (1994) *The Civilizing Process.* Oxford: Blackwell. First published in German in 1939. First English editions: Volume 1, *The History of Manners.* (1978) Oxford: Blackwell. Volume 2, *State Formation and Civilization.* (1982) Oxford: Blackwell.

Elias, N. and Scotson, J. (1994) *The Established and the Outsiders.* London: Sage. First published in 1965 by Frank Cass & Co.

Fairbairn, R. (1935) 'The social significance of communism considered in the light of psychoanalysis.' In R. Fairbairn (1994) *Psychoanalytic Studies of the Personality.* London: Routledge.

Fairbairn, R. (1943) 'The repression and the return of bad objects.' In R. Fairbairn (1994) *Psychoanalytic Studies of the Personality.* London: Routledge.

Fairbairn, R. (1944) 'Endopsychic structure considered in terms of object-relationships.' In R. Fairbairn. (1994) *Psychoanalytic Studies of the Personality.* London: Routledge.

Fanon, F., (1982) [1952] *Black Skins, White Mask.* New York: Grove Press.

Fanon, F., (1983) [1961] *The Wretched of the Earth*. London: Pelican.

Foucault, M. (1972) *The Archaeology of Knowledge*. [trans. A.M. Sheridan Smith]. New York: Pantheon.

Foulkes, S.H. (1941) 'On Helen Keller's "The World I Live In".' In (1990) *Selected Papers*. 83–87. London: Karnac. First published in *Psychoanalytic Review 28*, (1941) 512–519.

Foulkes, S.H. (1944) 'Psychoanalysis and crime.' In (1990) *Selected Papers*. 119–124. London: Karnac.

Foulkes, S.H. (1948) *Introduction to Group Analytic Psychotherapy*. William Heinemann Medical Books. Reprinted (1983) London: Karnac.

Foulkes, S.H. (1957) 'Psychoanalytic concepts and object relations theory: comments on a paper by Fairbairn.' In (1990) *Selected Papers*. 107–117. London: Karnac. First published in *British Journal of the Philosophy of Science* (1957) 7, 324–329.

Foulkes, S.H. (1964) *Therapeutic Group Analysis*. London: George Allen & Unwin.

Foulkes, S.H. (1966) 'Some basic concepts in group psychotherapy.' In (1990) *Selected Papers*. 151–158. London: Karnac. First published in J.L. Moreno (ed) *The International Handbook of Group Psychotherapy*. (1966) 167–172. New York: Philosophical Library.

Foulkes, S.H. (1971) 'Access to unconscious processes in the group-analytic group.' In (1990) *Selected Papers*. 209–221. London: Karnac. First published in *Group Analysis 4* (1971) 4–14.

Foulkes, S.H. (1973a) 'The group as matrix of the individual's mental life.' In (1990) *Selected Papers*. 223–233. London: Karnac. First published in L.R. Wolberg and E.K. Schwartz (eds) *Group Therapy 1973 – An Overview*. New York: Intercontinental Medical Books.

Foulkes, S.H. (1973b) 'Oedipus conflict and regression.' In (1990) *Selected Papers*. 235–247. London: Karnac. First published in *International Journal of Group Psychotherapy* (1972) 22, 3–15.

Foulkes, S.H. (1974) 'My philosophy in psychotherapy.' In (1990) *Selected Papers*. 271–280. London: Karnac. First published in L.C. Kreeger (ed) *The Large Group* (1975) 33–56. London: Constable.

Foulkes, S.H. (1975a) 'Problems of the large group.' In (1990) *Selected Papers*. 249–269. London: Karnac. First published in L.C. Kreeger (ed) *The Large Group* (1975) 33–56. London: Constable.

Foulkes, S.H. (1975b) 'Notes on the concept of resonance.' In (1990) *Selected Papers*. 297–305. London: Karnac. First published in L.R. Wolberg and M.L. Aronson (eds) *Group Therapy 1977: An Overview*. (1977) 52–58. New York: Stratton Intercontinental Book Corp.

Foulkes, S.H. (1975c) 'The leader in the group.' In (1990) *Selected Papers*. 285–296. London: Karnac.

Foulkes, S.H. (1990) *Selected Papers*. [Edited by Elizabeth Foulkes]. London: Karnac.

Foulkes, S.H. and Anthony, E.J. (1957) *Group Psychotherapy – The Psychoanalytic Approach*. Reprinted (1984) London: Karnac.

Freud, A., (1936) *The Ego and the Mechanisms of Defence*. London: Hogarth Press.

Freud, S. (1895) 'Project for a scientific psychology.' *SE I*. 281–397. London: Hogarth Press.

Freud, S. (1905) 'Three essays on sexuality.' *SE VII*. 125–245. London: Hogarth Press.

Freud, S. (1910) 'Five lectures on psychoanalysis.' *SE XI*. 3–58. London: Hogarth Press.

Freud, S. (1911) 'Psycho-analytic notes on an autobiographical account of a case of paranoia.' *SE XII*. 1–82. London: Hogarth Press.

Freud, S. (1914) 'On narcissism.' *SE XIV*. 67–102. London: Hogarth Press.

Freud, S. (1915a) 'Instincts and their vicissitudes.' *SE XIV*. 117–140. London: Hogarth Press.

Freud, S. (1915b) 'The unconscious.' *SE XIV*. 161–215. London: Hogarth Press.

Freud, S. (1917) 'Mourning and melancholia.' *SE XIV*. 239–260. London: Hogarth Press.

Freud, S. (1921) 'Group psychology and the analysis of the ego.' *SE XVIII*. 67–144. London: Hogarth Press.

Freud, S. (1923) 'The ego and the id.' *SE XIX*. 3–68. London: Hogarth Press.

Freud, S. (1924) 'The dissolution of the Oedipus complex.' *SE XIX*. 172–179. London: Hogarth Press.

Freud, S. (1926) 'Inhibitions, symptoms, anxiety.' *SE XX*. 75–175. London: Hogarth Press.

Freud, S. (1930) 'Civilization and its discontents.' *SE XXI*. 59–145. London: Hogarth Press.

Freud, S. (1933) 'New introductory lectures on psychoanalysis.' *SE XXII*. 5–184. London: Hogarth Press.

Friere, P. (1972) *Pedagogy of the Oppressed*. London: Penguin.

Frosh, S., (1991) *Identity Crisis*. London: Macmillan

Golding, W. (1954) *Lord of the Flies*. London: Faber and Faber.

Gödel, K. (1962) *On Formally Undecidable Propositions*. New York: Basic Books; (1931) 'Uber Formal Unentscheidbare Sätze der Principia Mathematica und Verwandter Systeme, I' *Monatshefte für Mathematik und Physik 38*, 173–198.

Gould, S.J. (1984) *The Mismeasure of Man*. London: Pelican.

Gould, S.J. (1989) *Wonderful Life*. London: Penguin.

Greenberg, J. (1991) *Oedipus and Beyond*. London: Harvard University Press.

Greenberg, J.R. and Mitchell, S.A. (1983) *Object Relations in Psychoanalytic Theory*. London: Harvard University Press.

Guntrip, H. (1961) *Personality Structure and Human Interaction: the Developing Synthesis of Psychodynamic Theory*. New York: International Universities Press.

Hardin, G. (1968) 'The tragedy of the commons.' *Science 162*, 1243–1248.

Harland, R. (1987) *Superstructuralism*. London: Methuen.

Hinshelwood, R. D. (1991) *A Dictionary of Kleinian Thought*. London: Free Association Books.

Hobbes, T. (1981) [1651] *Leviathan*. London: Penguin.

Hopper, E. (1996) 'The social unconscious in clinical work.' *Group 20*, 1, 7–42.

Hopper, E. (1997) 'Traumatic experience in the unconscious life of groups.' *Group Analysis 30*, 4, 439–470.

Hume, D. (1956) [1738] *A Treatise of Human Nature*. London: Everyman's Library.

Hunt, M. (1993) *The Story of Psychology*. London: Doubleday.

Jacobs, R. and Campbell, D. (1961) 'The perpetuation of an arbitrary tradition through several generations of a laboratory microculture.' *Journal of Abnormal and Social Psychology 62*, 649–658.

Jakobson, R. (1962) *Selected Writings Vol.1 (Phonological Studies)*. Gravenhage: Mouton.

Jones, S. (1996) *In the Blood*. London: Harper Collins.

Kahl, R. (ed) (1971) *Selected writings of Herman Von Helmholtz*. Middletown, Connecticut.

Kant, I. (1990) *Critique of Pure Reason*. New York: Colonial Press.

Klein, M. (1928) 'Early stages of the Oedipus conflict.' In M.Klein (1988) *Love, Guilt and Reparation*. London: Virago Press.

Klein, M. (1953) 'The early development of conscience in the child.' In M.Klein (1988) *Love, Guilt and Reparation*. London: Virago Press.

Klein, M. (1959) 'Our adult world and its roots in infancy.' In M. Klein (1988) *Envy and Gratitude*. London: Virago Press.

Klein, M. (1988a) *Envy and Gratitude and Other Works 1946–1963*. London: Virago Press.

Klein, M. (1988b) *Love Guilt and Reparation*. London: Virago Press.

Kuhn, T. (1962) *The Structure of Scientific Revolutions*. Chicago: Chicago University Press.

Lacan, J. (1977) *Ecritis: A Selection*. trans. Alan Sheridan. London: Tavistock.

Lal, B.B. (1986) 'The "Chicago School" of American Sociology, symbolic interactionism, and race relations theory.' In J. Rex and D. Mason (eds) *Theories of Race and Ethnic Relations*. Cambridge: Cambridge University Press.

Laplanche and Pontalis (1973) *The Language of Psychoanalysis*. London: Karnac Books.

le Bon, G. (1896) *The Crowd*. London: Unwin

Lemert, C. (1994) 'Dark thoughts about the self.' In C. Calhoun (ed) *Social Theory and the Politics of Identity*. Oxford: Blackwell.

Lichenstein, H. (1977) 'Narcissism and primary identity.' In H. Lichenstein *The Dilemma of Human Identity*. New York: Jason Aronson.

Litchman, R. (1982) *The Production of Desire: The Integration of Psychoanalysis into Marxist Theory*. New York: Free Press.

Mahler, M., (1952) 'On child psychosis and schizophrenia: autistic and symbiotic infantile psychoses.' *Psychoanalytic Studies of the Child 7*, 286–305.

Matte-Blanco, I. (1975) *The Unconscious as Infinite Sets: An Essay in Bi-Logic*. London: Duckworth.

Matte-Blanco, I. (1988) *Thinking, Feeling and Being*. London: Routledge.

Mead, G.H. (1964) *Selected Writings: George Herbert Mead*. Andrew J.Reck (ed) Chicago: Chicago University Press.

Memmi, A., (1974) [1965] *The Colonizer and the Colonized*. London: Souvenir Press.

Mennell, S. (1994) 'The formation of we-images: a process theory.' In C. Calhoun (ed) *Social Theory and the Politics of Identity*. Oxford: Blackwell.

Nitsun, M. (1996) *The Anti-Group*. London and New York: Routledge.

Pawlby, S.J. (1977) 'Imitative interaction.' In H.R. Schaffer (ed) *Studies in Mother–Infant Interaction*. London: Academic Press.

Pines, M. (1982) 'Reflections on mirroring.' *Group Analysis 15*, supplement. Also published in *Circular Reflections* (1998) London: Jessica Kingsley Publishers.

Pines, M. (1985) 'Mirroring and child development.' *Psychoanalytic Inquiry 5*, 2, pp.211–231. Also published in *Circular Reflections* (1998) London: Jessica Kingsley Publishers.

Pines, M. (1998) *Circular Reflections.* London: Jessica Kingsley Publishers.

Pinker, S. (1994) *The Language Instinct.* New York: William Morrow and Company.

Plotkin, H. (1997) *Evolution in Mind.* London: Allen Lane, Penguin Press.

Rayner, E., and Tuckett, D., (1988) 'An introduction to Matte-Blanco's reformulation of the Freudian unconscious and his conceptulization of the internal world.' In I. Matte-Blanco (1988) *Thinking, Feeling and Being.* London: Routledge.

Ridley, M. (1996) *The Origins of Virtue.* Great Britain: Viking.

Rogers, C. (1967) *On Becoming a Person.* London: Constable.

Rose, S. (1997) *Lifelines.* London: Allen Lane, Penguin Press.

Rose, S., Lewontin, R. C., and Kamin, L. S. (1984) *Not in Our Genes.* London: Pelican.

Rousseau, J.J. (1913) *The Social Contract and Discourses.* New York: E. P. Dutton & Co.

de Saussure, F. (1959) *Course in General Linguistics.* Edited by C. Bally and A. Sechehaye. New York: The Philosophical Library.

Selden, R. (1989) *A Reader's Guide to Contemporary Literary Theory.* London: Harvester Wheatsheaf.

Sherif, M. (1936) *The Psychology of Social Norms.* New York: Harper and Row.

Spitz, R. (1958) 'On the genesis of superego components' *The Psychoanalytic Study of the Child 13*, pp 375-404.

Stern, D. (1985) *The Interpersonal World of the Infant.* New York: Basic Books.

Tajfel, H., Flament, C., Billig, M.G. and Bundy, R.P. (1971) 'Social categorization and intergroup behaviour.' *European Journal of Social Psychology 1*, 149–178.

Thatcher, M. (1987) 'Interview.' *Woman's Own.* 31 October.

Turner, J.C. and Giles, H. (eds) (1981) *Intergroup Behaviour.* Oxford: Blackwell.

Vygotsky, L. S. (1978) *Mind in Society.* London: Harvard University Press.

Wilson, E.O. (1992) *The Diversity of Life.* Cambridge: Harvard University Press.

Winnicott, D.W. (1951) 'Transitional objects and transitional phenomena.' In D.W. Winnicott (1982) *Through Paediatrics to Psycho-analysis.* London: Hogarth Press.

Winnicott, D.W. (1952) 'Psychoses and child care.' In D.W. Winnicott (1982) *Through Paediatrics to Psycho-analysis.* London: Hogarth Press.

Winnicott, D.W. (1958) 'Psycho-analysis and the sense of guilt.' In D.W. Winnicott (1982) *The Maturational Processes and the Facilitating Environment.* London: Hogarth Press.

Winnicott, D.W. (1980) *Playing and Reality.* London: Penguin Press.

Winnicott, D.W. (1949) 'Birth memories, birth trauma, and anxiety.' In D.W. Winnicott. *Through Paediatrics to Psychoanalysis* (1987) 174–193. London: Hogarth Press.

Winnicott, D.W. (1965) *The Family and Individual Development.* London: Tavistock Publications.

Winnicott, D.W. (1982) *The Maturational Processes and the Facilitating Environment.* London: Hogarth Press.

Wynne-Edwards, V.C. (1962) *Animal Dispersion in Relation to Social Behaviour.* London: Oliver and Boyd.

Subject Index

Author Index

Adler, A. 120
Althusser, L. 84
Bion, W.R. 166, 167, 168, 169
Brown, D. 157
Brown, R. 178
Burkitt, I. 94, 105, 212

Calhoun, C. 190, 199
Chomsky, N. 225
Cialdini, R.B., Borden, R.J.,
    Thorne, A., Walker, M.R.,
    Freeman, S. and Sloan, L.R.
    177

Dalal, F. 29, 31, 177, 206, 208,
    209, 210, 219
Dawkins, R. 129, 130, 132, 133,
    138, 152, 153
Derrida, J. 220
Dollard, J., Doob, L.W., Miller,
    N.E., Mowrer, O.H. and Sears,
    R.R. 71
Donald, J. and Rattansi, A. 209
Douglas, M. 119

Eagleton, T. 19, 80, 83, 84, 116
Elias, N. 88–93, 95–109, 111,
    114, 115, 118, 120,
    121, 123, 124, 139, 143,
    158
Elias, N. and Scotson, J. 110, 116,
    119, 122, 123, 183, 205,
    223–224

Fairbairn, R. 79, 158, 195, 196,
    197
Fanon, F. 119
Foucault, M. 206
Foulkes, S.H. 34–59, 62–64,
    66–70, 160, 208, 226
Foulkes, S.H. and Anthony, E.J.
    12, 34, 36, 40–42, 44,
    53–59, 62, 63, 67–69, 71,
    73–75, 159
Freud, A. 120
Freud, S. 19–32, 121, 123, 158,
    163, 187–188
Friere, P. 115
Frosh, S. 173
Gödel, K. 27
Golding, W. 127
Gould, S.J. 73, 132, 143, 144
Greenberg, J. 21
Greenberg, J.R. and Mitchell, S.A.
    26, 224
Guntrip, H. 145

Hardin, G. 142
Harland, R. 80, 81, 82, 98, 141
Hinshelwood, R.D. 185
Hobbes, T. 127
Hopper, E. 210, 211
Hume, D. 92
Humphrey, N.K. 147
Hunt, M. 12, 18

Jacobs, R. and Campbell, D. 215
Jacobson, R. 82
Jones, S. 153

Kahl, R. 12
Kant, I. 50
Klein, M. 45, 78, 108, 158
Kuhn, T.S. 224

Lacan, J. 49
Lal, B.B. 207
Laplanche, J. and Pontalis, J.B. 19,
    22, 23, 24, 193
le Bon, G. 30
Lemert, C. 192
Lichenstein, H. 217
Litchman, R. 212

Mahler, M. 145
Matte-Blanco, I. 15, 178
Mead, G.H. 78
Memmi, A. 119
Mennell, S. 199, 200

Nitsun, M. 69, 156, 195

Pawlby, S.J. 217
Pines, M. 9, 217
Pinker, S. 148
Plotkin, H. 17, 128, 130, 134,
    142, 148, 149, 213

Rayner, E. and Tuckett, D. 162
Ridley, M. 132, 133, 136, 137,
    138–139, 140, 141, 143,
    155, 156, 209, 226
Rogers, C. 81
Rose, S. 134, 143, 150, 155
Rose, Lewomtin and Kamin 116,
    150–151, 152
Rousseau, J.J. 127

Saussure, de, F. 81
Selden 80, 176
Sherif, M. 215
Spitz, R. 45
Stern, D. 145

Tajfel, H., Flament, C., Billig, M.G.
    and Bundy, R.P. 178
Thatcher, M. 38
Turner, J.C. and Giles, H. 30

Vygotsky, L.S. 78

Wilson, E.O. 135

Winnicott, D.W. 79, 158, 200,
    201, 202
Wynne-Edwards, V.C. 135

239